Waterfalls of Colorado

WATERFALLS

OF COLORADO

BY
MARC CONLY

PHOTOGRAPHS BY
NANCY MISCIA CONLY

PRUETT PUBLISHING COMPANY
BOULDER, COLORADO

Printed in the United States
10 9 8 7 6 5 4 3 2 1

Library of Congress Cataloging-in-Publication Data

Conly, Marc, 1946-
    The waterfalls of Colorado / Marc Conly ; photographs by Nancy
Miscia Conly.
        p.   cm.
    Includes bibliographical references (p.) and index.
    ISBN 0-87108-823-1 (alk. paper)
    1. Hiking—Colorado—Guidebooks. 2. Waterfalls—Colorado—
Guidebooks. 3. Natural history—Colorado—Guidebooks.
    4. Colorado—Guidebooks.   I. Title.
GV199.42.C6C66   1993
917.88—dc20   92-42496
                                                   CIP

Cover design by Kathy McAffrey
Book design by Cover to Cover Design

Contents

Preface

Nancy and I were inspired to produce this book in 1988, when we returned home from a visit to Basaseachic Falls in the Sierra Madre in Mexico. This trip was quite an adventure for us because it involved renting a car in Chihuahua and driving into the Mexican mountains to see a waterfall. Basaseachic used to require several days' travel to visit. We rented a car in Chihuahua and drove a couple hundred miles to get to the falls. It took us over twenty-four hours to get there from Denver.

Every time we return to Colorado from anywhere else, we marvel at the beauty of our home state. It occurred to us that we shouldn't have to travel twenty-four hours just to see a waterfall. When we tried to find out where the exceptional falls in the state were, we discovered to our surprise that there was no comprehensive list, map, or guide to Colorado's falls.

It's ironic that the time, travel, research, and cost of writing and photographing for this guide have far exceeded—several times over—any commitment to simply go see a Mexican waterfall. Our quest has left us with no regrets, however. We've traveled our favorite state from corner to the four corners and poked our noses into places we never even knew existed before starting this project.

The richness of Colorado's natural beauty has never failed to move and refresh us. Every time we drove home, a bit haggard from the trail, we were already talking about where our next trip would take us. We drove one faithful "fallsmobile" into the ground, jeopardized the lives of every friend who was persuaded to accompany us, proved conclusively that every town in Colorado has the same restaurant, the same waitress, the same restroom, the same convenience store, and the same motel next door. We put our heads in the line of fire in October and froze in November. The net result is the information and images gathered in this book, and four years of wonderful memories. We hope it helps you create a few of your own.

Acknowledgments

During the research for this book, we were helped in our quest especially by the staff at the Pagosa Springs ranger station; the staff of Rocky Mountain National Park, including Dave Stevens, biologist; the librarians of the Denver Botanic Gardens; and various friends and acquaintances who passed on to us information about their own favorite waterfalls. Thanks also to David Van der Laan for editing assistance, and to the landowner who granted us permission to see a falls and taste the wild raspberry.

I am especially grateful to Nancy for her sensitive eye and her tolerance for, and participation in, what has sometimes seemed to others only a frivolous obsession.

Boulder Falls

Introduction

Waterfalls create wonderful places to visit. Sunlight and air mix with the water, the sound is soothing or exciting, the surrounding plants and trees are constantly refreshed. So waterfalls are almost always a good destination for a trip or picnic spot in every season but winter. Even then, falls can provide recreation for the skier, snowshoe hiker, or ice climber.

The rugged, high-altitude, heavily glaciated Colorado mountains contain several hundreds of falls. In this guide, we include over 265 separate waterfalls in over 250 entries. The count cannot be exact without splitting hairs about whether one falls with two leaps and a cascade is one, two, or three waterfalls. And in any case, we don't kid ourselves that we could possibly have listed all the falls in the state. We know we haven't, and we hope you'll pass along any information you have about what we missed.

The great majority of falls in this book are on public land, mostly in the state's national forests. The residents of Colorado enjoy the benefit of living where nearly half their state, and arguably the prettiest half, is publicly owned and available to enjoy, responsibly, by every citizen.

We certainly have had our qualms about exposing some of these places to more visitors. The political reality, however, is this: Control, use, and exploitation of public lands are up for grabs. Government policy will dictate what happens to pristine places in the years to come: whether their water will be appropriated, whether the forests will be sold off, whether a hundred years from now there is any place left in the state worth visiting. Money talks. Where is the money? In the cities. The only way Colorado's precious natural lands, its wildernesses, its wetlands, will be preserved is if the people in the places where the money is care enough to pay to preserve them. Our fervent hope is that if more people know about these hideaways, more people will care about, and protect, them.

How to Use This Guide

This book is organized around the state's natural geographic divisions—its river drainages. The Continental Divide splits the state in two. Rain falling on the Western Slope drains into the Colorado River drainage system. The Colorado drainage, in turn, is contributed to by the smaller Colorado basins of the Gunnison, San Juan, and Green rivers, and of the upper Colorado River itself.

Moisture that falls on the Eastern Slope drains ultimately to the Gulf of Mexico, from either the Platte River basin, the Arkansas basin, or the Rio Grande basin.

Information about the waterfalls we've located in the state is organized into eight chapters, seven of them corresponding to the major river basins. Chapter 1 is composed of waterfalls from two basins—the Colorado and the South Platte—which are located within Rocky Mountain National Park.

At the beginning of each chapter there is a detailed map of its drainage area. Each of the numbered squares on these maps locates a group of waterfalls that share a common access road or trail. The numerals inside the squares identify the waterfall groups listed in the text.

Falls listings and descriptions are usually given in the order of approach: that is, from the falls nearest the foot of a drainage to the falls at the head or farthest from a trailhead.

Each listing begins with a seven-point summary, of access, rating, type, USGS topographic quad map, trail miles, altitude, and elevation change.

Access

Falls are categorized by how difficult or easy they are to see according to one or more of the following criteria:

Roadside: Visible from a vehicle on a designated roadway

Wheelchair: Accessible by wheelchair on a designated path

Four-wheel-drive: Accessible on a four-wheel-drive roadway

Walk in: Within .25-mile on a well-developed trail

Hike: Requiring a day hike on an established trail of more than .25-mile but less than 5 miles

Overnight: Accessible by an established trail, but at a distance from a trailhead, requiring an overnight stay in the mountains

Bushwhack: Requiring hiking or climbing without a trail

Rating

Ratings are made according to a subjective four-star system, based on a consideration of, first, how pleasant is the approach to the falls? Is the scenery boring, overgrown with tin shacks, or what? Two, how great is the flow, height, or breadth of the falls? Three, how much traffic does the area around the falls see? Are the mosses beaten to a pulp, is there trash, broken glass, more trails than vegetation, or human bodies jiggling to rap music? Four, how striking is the setting for the falls, what kind of mood does it create?

This system compares waterfalls within the state: One star is the lowest rating, four the highest.

Type

There are eight basic categories of waterfalls applied in this book. They've been adopted, with modifications, from Gregory A. Plumb's *A Waterfall Lover's Guide to the Pacific Northwest* (Seattle: The Mountaineers Books).

Plunge: Water is free-falling for most of its height without coming into contact with the underlying rock.

Horsetail: Water descends rapidly down a nearly vertical wall, maintaining some contact with the underlying rock.

Fan: Stays in contact with the underlying rock, like a horsetail, but gets wider as it approaches the foot of its descent. Waterfalls often combine aspects of the fan, horsetail, and plunge; our descriptions refer to the predominant feature.

Segmented: Falling water is divided into two or more streams, the divisions usually increasing as the water approaches the foot of the falls. The segments may themselves be classified separately.

Punchbowl: Falling water enters a pool, particularly a plunge pool, instead of being immediately scattered by falling onto piled rocks.

Tiered: The length of the water's drop is broken into distinct falls, one succeeding another down the drainage, and both or all visible from a single vantage point. An upper limb of a tiered falls may be one type, the lower limb another.

Serial: Where the limbs of a tiered falls are not visible from one vantage point, where limbs are separated from one another by a good run of stream, or where there are many limbs.

Cascade: Water flows at an angle over a series of rocks or down a broad rock face with too many small leaps or segments to count. A cascade is often the result of a waterfall either eroding upstream or breaking down into smaller components through water action.

USGS Topographic Quad

This is the 7½ minute 1:24,000 quadrangle map compiled and printed by the United States Geologic Survey. The number following the quad name is the map's index number in the *Colorado Index to Topographic and Other Map Coverage,* published and distributed free by the USGS. This index, and its companion *Catalog of Topographic Names and Other Published Maps,* are extremely useful tools for trip planning and map purchase.

Trail Miles

Where available, mileages from trail signs or maps are used. In all other cases, mileages are a best estimate based on experience on the trail and measurements made on the quadrangle maps. Keep in mind that map miles on a flat surface or level trail are not the same as miles on trails that constantly go up and down, twist to the right, or switchback to the left, especially if you're carrying a fifty-pound pack.

Altitude

This is the elevation of the mark made across the stream on the map to indicate the top of the falls. This measurement is taken from the topographic contours on the quad, plus or minus 20 feet.

Elevation Change

This is a particular falls' elevation minus its trailhead elevation. In more complicated cases, as for instance if a trail climbs a 600-foot hill from a trailhead at 10,000 feet and then drops into a valley at 9,000 feet before climbing to a falls at 10,000 feet, the elevation change indication would read: From 10,000 feet to 10,600 feet, +600 feet; to 9,000 feet, -1,600 feet; to 10,000 feet, +1,000 feet. When more than one waterfall is described in a listing, a separate altitude is noted for each falls in order of access. Elevation gain or loss information is then stated in the same order, from trailhead to first falls, from first falls to second falls, and so on. For example, if the trailhead is at 9,000 feet and there are waterfalls at 10,000 feet and 11,000 feet, the altitude and elevation change indications would read:

Altitude: 10,000 feet, 11,000 feet
Elevation Change: From 9,000 feet to first falls, +1,000 feet; to second falls, +1,000 feet

What Are Falls?

What criteria have been used for inclusion in this guide? How high does a waterfall have to be, how much water has to flow?

The search for the waterfalls of Colorado began not by trying to define what a falls is, but by locating them. Because there is no comprehensive list in publication, I started by asking the USGS to run a computer printout of all the falls in its data base. The USGS computer searched for the word "falls" and came up with a list of seventy-four. But that was only the falls named on maps, and not all of them, as I was to discover.

Once I had an idea of what parts of the state had the most mapped waterfalls, I began looking at adjacent quadrangle maps, and then at quads covering the mountain ranges in general. Eventually I was forced to concede that only a systematic search of all the quads covering the state would locate all the falls marked on the maps. That took several months of cozying up to topos in the Denver Public Library. Even so, I later discovered falls identified only by local signage, or that are noted on national forest maps but not on the USGS quadrangles.

You would think that after looking at all those maps and visiting all those falls, I would have some idea of what constitutes a "falls." I even asked the field surveyors at the USGS what their criteria were for deciding some stretch of white water is worthy of being called a waterfall. Their field handbook states simply that if a waterfall has *landmark* significance, the top of the fall should be marked by a blue line across the river at that point on the map. In other words, if you're in a mountain valley and a falls is usable as a landmark, it's indicated on the map. What matters is whether it stands out in relation to the rest of the streamcourse.

Perhaps the best definition I've heard is one Phil Van der Laan made when we were discussing this issue in Glacier Gorge one balmy June day. She said, "If it looks like a falls, sounds like a falls, and feels like a falls, then it must be a falls."

Where a falls is unnamed on a map, it is designated here according to the name of the stream it is on. If the stream itself is unnamed, the waterfall is designated by the water the stream is tributary to, or it is identified with a prominent local feature such as a nearby lake. An asterisk next to a waterfall's name in the individual ratings indicates that the waterfall is officially unnamed and has been assigned a name according to this system. The number of asterisks indicates the number of separate falls.

Each listing gives an indication of the particular falls' most prominent features, including an estimate of its height. Some heights were taken from signs or published literature. I estimated wherever possible by a rough use of trigonometry, measuring a baseline and using a compass to gauge the angle of elevation to the top of the falls. In many cases, because of sloping ground or interfering foliage, my estimate is strictly a best guess.

How good is this information? In four years, we traveled to over 200 of the more than 250 waterfalls listed here. In some instances, we saw a waterfall at a less-than-optimal time of day or season, or on the run as we headed up the trail (one week, we recorded and photographed twenty-one falls). I wish we'd had the leisure to make a more comprehensive survey, but I think you'll find the inspiration for many an adventure—and even a dream or two—in these pages.

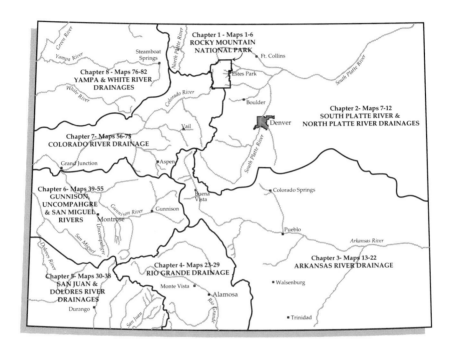

Chapter 1 - Maps 1-6
ROCKY MOUNTAIN
NATIONAL PARK

Chapter 8 - Maps 76-82
YAMPA & WHITE RIVER
DRAINAGES

Chapter 7- Maps 56-75
COLORADO RIVER DRAINAGE

Chapter 2- Maps 7-12
SOUTH PLATTE RIVER &
NORTH PLATTE RIVER DRAINAGES

Chapter 6- Maps 39-55
GUNNISON,
UNCOMPAHGRE
& SAN MIGUEL
RIVERS

Chapter 4- Maps 23-29
RIO GRANDE DRAINAGE

Chapter 3- Maps 13-22
ARKANSAS RIVER DRAINAGE

Chapter 5- Maps 30-38
SAN JUAN &
DOLORES RIVER
DRAINAGES

Green River
Yampa River
White River
Colorado River
North Platte River
South Platte River
South Platte River
Gunnison River
Uncompahgre
San Miguel
Dolores River
San Juan
Rio Grande
Arkansas River

Steamboat
Springs
Ft. Collins
Estes Park
Boulder
Denver
Vail
Grand Junction
Aspen
Colorado Springs
Gunnison
Montrose
Pueblo
Buena
Vista
Walsenburg
Monte Vista
Alamosa
Durango
Trinidad

River Drainages of Colorado

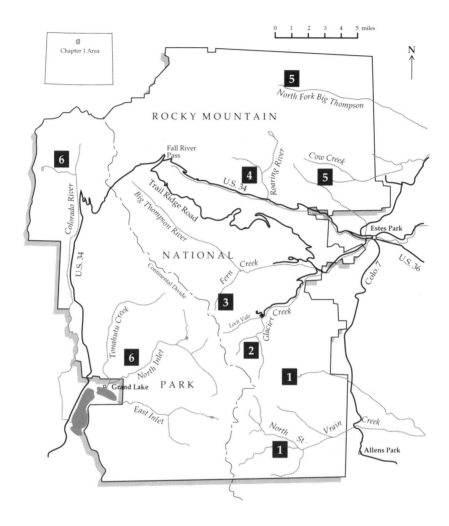

Rocky Mountain National Park Drainage Map

1: Wild Basin Waterfall Group
2: Glacier Creek and Loch Vale Trail Waterfall Group
3: Fern Lake Trail Waterfall Group
4: Fall River Road and Roaring River Waterfall Group
5: North Boundary Trail Waterfall Group
6: Rocky Mountain National Park Western Slope
     Waterfall Group

1

Rocky Mountain National Park

In its 412 square miles, Rocky Mountain National Park contains some of the most spectacularly beautiful scenery in the state of Colorado. It contains over seventy-one peaks above 12,000 feet and ranges from the open meadows and lakes of Estes Park to the talus-topped summit of Longs Peak. Straddling the Continental Divide, it has thirty-four waterfalls, most of them demonstrating the combined brute strength of ice and water in the carving, grinding, and transportation of granite.

Established in 1915, the park now attracts nearly three million sightseers every year, sometimes as much as thirty thousand a day. The National Park Service works very hard to provide convenient access to its visitors and to control their activities to protect the park's habitat. This has resulted in a system of well-established, well-maintained, and well-marked trails, and a long list of necessary rules and regulations.

Despite the sheer volume of humanity streaming into the park's four entrances, it is still possible to visit many of its waterfalls in pristine solitude. Others can be seen from a car or from a wheelchair.

Although there are exceptions, most of the waterfalls in Rocky Mountain National Park are the end result of its glacial episodes. Waterfalls in Rocky Mountain National Park act as markers for many of the features that result from glaciation. (A discussion of how glaciers create waterfalls is included in Chapter 9; all I'll attempt here is to identify a few of the park's waterfalls with the glacial features that created them.)

Paternoster Lakes, so called because of their resemblance to prayer beads, are in Glacier Gorge. They are Black Lake, Jewell Lake, and Mills Lake, and the waterfalls "strung" between these "beads" are Glacier, Ribbon, and Black Lake falls.

There are also more paternoster lakes in Loch Vale (Timberline Falls), on the East Inlet (East Inlet Falls), and on Ouzel Creek (Ouzel Falls).

A prominent glacial feature in the park is the "hanging valley," created when a large glacier cut more deeply than its smaller tributaries. Examples in the park are up the North Inlet at Bench Lake (War Dance Falls), on the Roaring River (the now-defunct Horseshoe Falls), and on Fern Creek (Fern Falls).

Horseshoe Falls is an example of another kind of destructive force entirely. In 1982, the dam above Horseshoe Falls failed, resulting in the Lawn Lake flood, one death, and the fascinating alteration of terrain at the head of Horseshoe Park. The park service has done an admirable job of converting this disaster into a geologic exhibit. But anyone who now hikes up the Roaring River into the Mummy Range cannot help being impressed by the incredible raw swath the water cut down the length of the river. Horseshoe Falls, whatever its ability to inspire, was destroyed forever by the flood—perhaps a reminder of the need for greater human vigilance if we hope to enjoy nature's finishing touches rather than obliterate them permanently.

Wild Basin

Wild Basin is the glacial basin carved along the drainage of North St. Vrain Creek in the southeastern corner of Rocky Mountain National Park. It is bordered on the west by the Continental Divide, which climbs past Ouzel Peak (12,716 feet), Tanima Peak (12,420 feet), Mount Alice (13,310 feet), and Chiefshead Peak (13,579 feet) to meet the ridge coming east from Longs Peak (14,256 feet), which encircles the basin from the north. The only remnant of the Wild Basin glacier is up the Eagle Fork of the St. Vrain, above Frigid Lake, although six separate glaciers (the St. Vrain glaciers) still exist just outside the park's southern boundary.

North St. Vrain Creek originates in the glacial lakes below Chiefshead Peak and Mount Alice. Before it leaves the park, it is joined by Ouzel Creek, Hutcheson Cony Creek, and Hunters Creek. The paternoster lakes and hanging valleys created by the Wild Basin glacier now host seven separate waterfalls.

There are two different trailheads for hikes to waterfalls in this basin, which is one of the lesser-visited areas of the park, as well as one of the wildest.

There is no fee to enter Wild Basin, but overnight camping requires a backcountry permit. Permits must be obtained from the backcountry office at park headquarters east of Estes Park, or by mail in advance.

The Wild Basin entrance to the park is 2 miles north of Allens Park, on Highway 7. Look for a sign directing you to the Wild Basin ranger station and Copeland Lake.

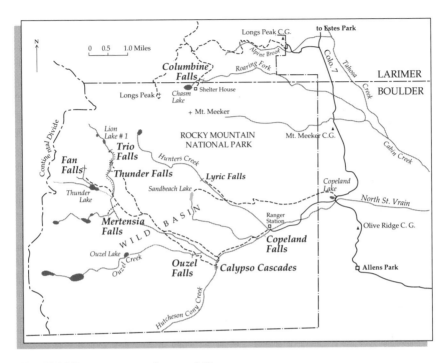

The Wild Basin group of waterfalls

(**#1** on Rocky Mountain National Park drainage map, page 8):

Copeland Falls
Calypso Cascades
Ouzel Falls
Trio Falls
Thunder Falls
Fan Falls
Mertensia Falls
Lyric Falls
Columbine Falls

Turn left off the highway at the sign. You can drive .1-mile to the Sand-beach Lake trailhead, east of Copeland Lake, to get to Lyric Falls. Or, drive 2 miles to the parking lot at the end of the road for the trail to Thunder Lake, Lion Lake, and the seven falls up the North St. Vrain.

Copeland Falls
(See Wild Basin group map, page 11.)

Access: Hike
Rating: ★ ★
Type: Block
USGS Topographic Quad: Allens Park
Trail Miles: .4-mile
Altitude: 8,560 feet
Elevation Change: +80 feet

Copeland Falls is a steep cascade down a granite shelf less than 10 feet high stretching the full width of the creek. It is the only falls actually on the North St. Vrain. Plenty of water flows over the falls, it's wonderfully noisy, and there are plenty of places for kids to explore safely. It's a pleasant spot for a rest in the shade or a picnic.

Copeland Falls is an easy .4-mile from the Wild Basin ranger station parking lot. The ease of the hike, the beauty of the valley, and the cheerful sound of the water ensure its popularity. Expect to be accompanied on your stroll by many happy people, some of whom may also walk with you to the next falls, 1.4 miles farther along the trail, Calypso Cascades.

Calypso Cascades
(See Wild Basin group map, page 11.)

Access: Hike
Rating: ★ ★
Type: Cascade
USGS Topographic Quad: Allens Park
Trail Miles: 1.8
Altitude: 9,200 feet
Elevation Change: +120 feet

Calypso Cascades is almost 600 feet long, by rough calculation, in a vertical drop of about 200 feet, and spans the width of Hutcheson Cony Creek as it spreads down the rocks. Bridges cross at the base.

The falls is 1.8 miles from the Wild Basin ranger station: A nice jaunt for visiting relatives, and there's a display about the 1978 forest fire that lit up the area, including Ouzel Falls, another 1.4 miles up the trail.

Ouzel Falls
(See Wild Basin group map, page 11.)

Access: Hike
Rating: ★ ★ ★ ★
Type: Plunge
USGS Topographic Quad: Allens Park
Trail Miles: 3.2
Altitude: 9,440 feet
Elevation Change: +960 feet

Perched high on a slope that is a mix of burned standing timber and new growth, Ouzel Falls is justifiably included in a list of Colorado's most impressive falls.

It's over 40 feet high and has several wonderful viewing points, including above the falls and downstream from the bridge at the trail. Tons of water come over a deep cut in the rock and shoot over the edge in a straight leap into a beautiful plunge pool. Lively cascades stretch under a bridge below the falls.

A big log crosses right through the mist above the main pool, offering a tempting, perilous perch for the would-be aerialist. Even using a safer approach, one can either bathe in the mist or stand right at the edge of the main leap.

There is a faint trail leading to the top of the falls by way of skirting the rock wall to the left of the falls. The climb is worth it for the view of the area burned by the 1978 fire.

Back on the main trail, there's a viewpoint just off the trail about an eighth of a mile beyond the Ouzel Falls bridge that looks out over the valley, with Longs Peak looming to the north.

The nearest campsites to Ouzel Falls are the North St. Vrain sites, nearly 2 miles away.

Ouzel Falls

Trio Falls
(See Wild Basin group map, page 11.)

Access: Overnight
Rating: ★ ★
Type: Segmented triplet
USGS Topographic Quad: Isolation Peak
Trail Miles: 7
Altitude: 11,200 feet
Elevation Change: +2,270 feet

Trio Falls is three falls, as the name implies: one a fulsome twisted leap, one a narrow braid, and one a set of trickling veils. The main leap is not more than 20 feet, but it's possible to step up and shower in it if you're inclined. The falls are high in the tundra, and there are many beautiful flowers in late July.

To get to Trio Falls, follow the trail to Lion Lakes. Take the right fork in the trail at about 1.4 miles, bypassing Ouzel Falls. This fork goes past the five sets of campsites in the valley nearest the trailhead. At 3.7 miles it joins the trail from Ouzel Falls.

The trail forks again at about 4.7 miles from the trailhead. The left fork would take you to Thunder Lake. Take the right fork steeply uphill toward Lion Lakes and Trio Falls. Lion Lake #1 has terrific views of Alice Peak and is a relatively sheltered place for a rest or picnic.

Above Lion Lake #1 about .5-mile, a faint trail climbs up through beautiful tundra and marshy ground near timberline over easily managed rock slopes to the falls.

It's possible to follow the 11,200-foot contour the .66-mile west to Fan Falls, but watch for inclement weather. Rain is one thing, but when lightning begins to come over the ridge of the Continental Divide, it's time to head below timberline.

Thunder Falls
(See Wild Basin group map, page 11.)

Access: Overnight
Rating: ★ ★
Type: 2 leaps and cascades
USGS Topographic Quad: Isolation Peak
Trail Miles: 7
Altitude: 10,880 feet
Elevation Change: +2,600 feet, -200 feet

Thunder Falls

Thunder Falls is in the woods below Lion Lake #1 (see directions above to Trio Falls). The trail to Lion Lakes comes up the east side of the lake. Go around the lake, skirt the marshes on the west side, and follow the streamcourse downhill. The stream soon begins to drop and leads inevitably (with the power of gravity) to the falls. This little trek is quite steep and plunges into the forest with lush, wet vegetation underfoot and plenty of fallen wood to trip you up (or down, rather). Do not take wayward children on this route.

The main leap off Thunder Falls is about 200 feet below the level of Lion Lake #1. It's about 22 feet high, with a long, beautiful cascade below it on the thirty-degree slope. The woods and fallen logs are thick, but passage down the watercourse is not too difficult and rewards the hiker with two more leaps and uncounted cascades for the .75-mile or so. Then the ground levels out and the stream meanders through a marsh and meadow, when it starts down the rocks again.

Stick to the water on the right bank and you will eventually run into the trail to Thunder Lake and Fan Falls or back toward the trailhead at the ranger station. If you are not experienced in route-finding through the woods, climb back up the drainage to Lion Lake #1 and return by the same trail you used to reach the lake.

Mertensia Falls can be seen across the North St. Vrain valley from the Thunder Lake trail on the way back down toward either Ouzel Falls or to the campsites on the north slope of the North St. Vrain.

Fan Falls
(See Wild Basin group map, page 11.)

Access: Overnight
Rating: ★ ★ ★
Type: Tiered plunges and cascades
USGS Topographic Quad: Isolation Peak
Trail Miles: 7
Altitude: 11,200 feet
Elevation Change: +2,720 feet

Fan Falls originates from the lip of a granite cliff wall that separates cleanly the montane and the tundra between Alice Peak and Longs Peak. The falls consists of two main leaps of 25 and 10 feet, one fast on the heels of the other, then a long fan or horsetail cascade hundreds of feet down the rocks through lush bluebells.

To get to Fan Falls, take the Thunder Lake trail from the Wild Basin ranger station. Take the right fork in the main trail at about 1.4 miles. This fork goes past the five sets of campsites in the valley nearest the trailhead. At 3.7 miles, this trail joins the trail from Ouzel Falls. (You can cut a half-mile off the distance to Fan Falls and Thunder Lake by bypassing Ouzel Falls.)

The trail forks again at about 4.7 miles from the trailhead. The left fork takes you to Thunder Lake at 6.8 miles.

There are beautiful meadows along the stream between the lake and the falls, and a good trail around the east side of the lake. Then the trail is intermittent as you approach the base of the falls, which can be seen as soon as you leave the woods.

The climb up the slope to the main leaps is several hundred feet and takes you to the lip of the tundra.

Rather than lose elevation where the trail dips down to Thunder Lake, I bushwhacked to this rocky ridge, so I came up east of the falls and saw it from a quarter-mile or so away. I crossed to the top of the falls, lingered for a while in the tundra for the great views of the surrounding mountain, and then slowly and very carefully made my way down to the lake. This is certainly not the easiest route!

In my opinion, Fan Falls ranks very high: steep slopes, noisy waters, few people, fabulous views.

Mertensia Falls
(See Wild Basin group map, page 11.)

Access: Overnight
Rating: ★ ★
Type: Cascade with several small tiered plunges
USGS Topographic Quad: Isolation Peak
Trail Miles: 4.5 + .5-mile bushwhack
Altitude: 10,400 feet
Elevation Change: + 1,920 feet

Mertensia Falls is on a tributary of the North St. Vrain from Eagle Lake, south of Tanima Peak. Visible from the Thunder Lake trail, the falls is mostly a long, steep cascade, although it appears to be almost vertical from across the valley. The lower part of Mertensia Falls contains a short 10-foot leap, then twists and spreads around a boulder into a plunge pool—sort of a twisted punchbowl falls. The noise of the hundreds of feet of white water is wonderful. And standing at Mertensia Falls, the view across the valley to Longs Peak is sublime.

To get to Mertensia requires 4.5 miles of hiking on the Thunder Lake trail, and then a .5-mile bushwhack down into the valley of the North St. Vrain.

I got to the falls by following the contour from the footbridge on the trail to Thunder Lake, but after reaching the falls returned to the trail by directly crossing the St. Vrain and climbing up the slope. This route is actually easier and more direct, though it requires a ford of the creek. There are delightful small leaps along the St. Vrain not visible from 20 feet away, much less from the trail.

If you hate bushwhacking, crossing fallen timber, and scrambling up steep slopes, be content to admire the falls from across the valley with a 200-millimeter lens.

Lyric Falls
(See Wild Basin group map, page 11.)

Access: Hike
Rating: ★
Type: Cascade with several small plunges
USGS Topographic Quad: Isolation Peak
Trail Miles: 3.3 + .7-mile bushwhack
Altitude: 10,160 feet
Elevation Change: + 1,680 feet

Lyric Falls consists of a long series of cascades with three short leaps many yards apart, none even 10 feet high—charming, but not what I would call true waterfalls. Where the plunges occur, the creek narrows to less than 3 feet wide. The sound of air bubbling up in the plunge pools is more impressive than the actual falls of water.

Although these falls are unremarkable, Hunters Creek, from which they form, flows through lush green woods, and the hike up the stream is intimate and mostly off-trail.

To reach Lyric Falls, take the Sandbeach Lake trail for 3.3 miles, obtaining nice views of the St. Vrain drainage. Shortly after you pass the Hunters Creek campsite, there's a footbridge that crosses the creek. The trail continues to Sandbeach Lake in another mile. But to get to Lyric Falls, turn to the right before crossing the footbridge and go upstream. There is a faint intermittent trail along the creek, but you will be essentially bushwhacking.

Continue .7-mile up the creek until you encounter Lyric Falls. Though not spectacular as waterfalls go, Lyric Falls does, however, offer solitude in a gorgeous forest setting.

Columbine Falls

(See Wild Basin group map, page 11.)

Access: Hike
Rating: ★ ★
Type: Plunge
USGS Topographic Quad: Longs Peak
Trail Miles: 3.25
Altitude: 11,600 feet
Elevation Change: From 9,400 feet, +2,200 feet

Like its floral namesake, Columbine Falls is a small jewel in a setting that surpasses and enfolds it.

As the trail to the Chasm Lake arcs like the flight of a bird to cross the Roaring Fork, flowing from Chasm Lake into the valley, it is easy to overlook Columbine Falls—a streak of white, a whispering accent, in the silence at the foot of Longs Peak.

Below the crossing, Columbine Falls shoots at an angle across the glacially smoothed rock, lifts into the air, and falls 30 feet, recollecting itself in the rocks for the cascade to Peacock Pool, nestled below in the tundra.

Talus creates a series of steps to enable a closer view of the falls, a shady place for a picnic, and occasional blasts of mist blown from the falls.

The naked roll of rock surrounding the head of the falls is very smooth, and dangerous when wet.

A short .5-mile hike beyond the falls the trail climbs up bare granite hills to the lip of Chasm Lake and the sudden silence imposed by the sheer mass of the east face of Longs Peak.

To reach the trailhead to Columbine Falls (and for the separate climb to the top of Longs Peak), take Highway 7 about 8 miles south from Estes Park or 15 miles west from Lyons to the turnoff to the Longs Peak ranger station.

The East Longs Peak trail is heavily used and begins at the large, often crowded, parking lot. From 9,500 feet at this trailhead, the trail climbs steeply through lodgepole forest, occasionally opening out across flowing streams. Winding up into the tundra, about half a mile past timberline the trail forks. The trail to the right goes on to the top of Longs Peak; the trail to the left continues to Chasm Lake. In another .7-mile the Chasm Lake trail passes a lonely outhouse provided with great views of the Tahosa Creek valley, Cabin Creek, and the St. Vrain valley.

The trail follows the land's contour 11,500 feet above the valley of the Roaring Fork into the gigantic bowl created by the connected ridges of Mount Lady

Washington Peak (13,281 feet) to the north, Longs Peak (14,256 feet) in the center, and Mount Meeker (13,911 feet) to the south. At the bottom of this bowl is the Peacock Pool. Above the pool you can see and hear Columbine Falls like a small diamond pendant at the throat of the Longs Peak massif.

The East Longs Peak trail is very popular, but most of the pilgrims here are headed for the Boulder Field and an attempt to scale Longs Peak. The place is big enough to accommodate all its visitors, but you will experience solitude in this area only if you've obtained a permit to camp in the park, which will allow you to stay behind when all the day-hikers have departed.

There are several campsites along the trail, but these require permits in advance from the backcountry office at park headquarters. Reservations are required to stay in the campground near the ranger station. There is a Roosevelt National Forest campground north of Meeker Park.

Glacier Creek and Loch Vale Trail

This group contains all the falls reached from the Glacier Gorge Junction trailhead, half a mile below the Bear Lake parking lot. This is a very popular area, and Bear Lake is one of the most photographed sites in the park. In this area, one can feel especially grateful to the national park's system of permits for camping. Only in this way could the area be preserved in anything resembling a wild state, for the pressure of tourists and day-hikers is enormous.

For this reason, however, the area will disappoint those who wish to camp in the gorge on the spur of the moment. There is only one campsite up the entire length of Glacier Gorge, and one in the valley of Loch Vale. Both of these must be reserved months in advance of the hiking and camping season.

Drawing tourists like a magnet, Glacier Basin is a direct line to the heart of the park. Gathered in this 20-square-mile area is some of the most awe-inspiring mountain-wilderness beauty in the Colorado Rockies, and a road takes you directly from Estes Park past the park headquarters to one of nature's most appealing glacial workshops.

From the Beaver Meadows Entrance (3 miles from Estes Park on Highway 262), take the first left turn for the road up Glacier Creek toward Bear Lake.

Five miles farther, drive along the edge of Moraine Park, the longest glacial basin in the park, with its fabulous open views of the Continental Divide. The road winds around the end of moraines left by the Big Thompson and Glacier Gorge glaciers, then turns southwest to follow Glacier Creek upstream, past the Glacier Basin campground entrance and up the switchbacks to Bear Lake.

There is a small parking area 1.1 miles below Bear Lake at Glacier Gorge Junction. Right across the road is the trailhead for Glacier Gorge and Loch Vale. If you cannot find parking here, you can park at Bear Lake (which is worth a look, despite the crowds) and walk the .5-mile trail down to the Glacier Gorge trailhead.

Looking directly south from this parking area, you face a moraine left by the readvancing glaciers of eight thousand to eleven thousand years ago. The site of Alberta Falls is hidden here by the groves of lodgepole pine and aspen. The trail climbs the face of this boulder-strewn moraine to a sort of glacial second floor, where the trail forks .5-mile above Alberta Falls.

The left fork is the North Longs Peak trail; the right fork continues up the gorge and in another .5-mile forks again. The right fork at this 1.5-mile mark goes up past Loch Vale along Icy Brook to either Andrews Glacier—the only active glacier in the park—or to Timberline Falls, Icy Lake, and Taylor Glacier.

The left fork at the 1.5-mile mark heads south, climbing past Glacier Falls into Glacier Gorge, Longs Peak's awesome backyard, containing Mills Lake, Black Lake, Frozen Lake, Jewell Lake, Ribbon Falls, Black Lake Falls, and several other unnamed falls described below.

The two available campsites here must be reserved very early in the year, especially for the weekends. But both gorges are good day hikes.

Alberta Falls

(See Glacier Creek and Loch Vale Trail group map, page 23.)

Access: Hike
Rating: ★ ★ ★
Type: Punchbowl
USGS Topographic Quad: McHenry's Peak (40105 C6)
Trail Miles: .4-mile
Altitude: 9,400 feet
Elevation Change: From 9,200 feet, + 200 feet

Alberta Falls is a single 25-foot leap with a long cascade below it. The cascades are turbulent and run through pleasant aspen groves. The trail climbs easily up the moraine .5-mile from Glacier Gorge Junction, providing wonderful views of Prospect Canyon, back down Glacier Creek. This is the place where people go if they only want to spend an hour in the park, and the atmosphere is very festive, replete with small children.

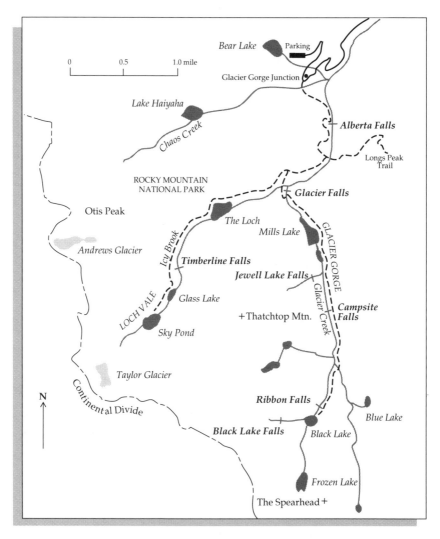

The Glacier Creek and Loch Vale Trail group of waterfalls
(**#2** on Rocky Mountain National Park drainage map, page 8):

Alberta Falls
Glacier Falls
Jewell Lake Falls
Campsite Falls
Ribbon Falls
Black Lake Falls
Timberline Falls

Glacier Falls

(See Glacier Creek and Loch Vale Trail group map, page 23.)

Access: Hike
Rating: ★ ★
Type: Segmented
USGS Topographic Quad: McHenry's Peak (40105 C6)
Trail Miles: 1.5
Altitude: 9,800 feet
Elevation Change: From 9,200 feet, + 1,400 feet

Glacier Falls is about 1.25 miles above Alberta Falls on the way to Mills Lake in Glacier Gorge. Its main leap is about 20 feet, tumbling out of a narrow defile to the lower cascades and a series of beautiful mossy rock platforms—a good place to watch ouzels dipping.

The falls is not visible from the main trail but is audible beyond a rocky slope just above the trail to the left. A number of cairns across bare rock show the trail, and they also identify the place where you step off the trail to the north to see the falls. This is just before you cross the bridge and head steeply up the trail on wooden stairs toward the head of Mills Lake. A flat rock cliff immediately north of the trail provides a view above the falls; a steep trail north and down to the left from the main trail leads to the bottom of the falls.

Even the park maps show Glacier Falls in the wrong place: It's *below* the bridge, not above it. There is a series of steep cascades down a deep cut right below Mills Lake, which is where maps show the falls, but this is not the most significant drop.

Jewell Lake Falls *

(See Glacier Creek and Loch Vale Trail group map, page 23.)

Access: Hike or overnight, bushwhack
Rating: ★
Type: Twin horsetails
USGS Topographic Quad: McHenry's Peak (40105 C6)
Trail Miles: 3.25 + .2-mile bushwhack
Altitude: 10,000 feet
Elevation Change: From 9,200 feet, + 800 feet

Continuing up Glacier Gorge, the trail skirts Mills Lake and then smaller Jewell Lake. You can see the white streak of Jewell Lake Falls from the trail at the north end of Jewell Lake. Look across the water to the cliffs west of the lake and above the trees in the valley bottom.

The easiest access to the falls is probably through the woods downstream from the Glacier Gorge campsite, requiring a hike of about fifteen minutes. But you need to know where it is first, and we approached through the woods by working around the marsh at the north end of the lake, then through the woods by dead reckoning. A compass heading would be useful once you are in among the trees.

Jewell Lake Falls consists of two 30-foot horsetails separated by a few yards of rock and surrounded by dense woods and fallen timber. This waterfall is isolated, somewhat difficult to get to, and not on the USGS quad or the park map.

Campsite Falls *
(See Glacier Creek and Loch Vale Trail group map, page 23.)

Access: Hike or overnight
Rating: ★
Type: Block
USGS Topographic Quad: McHenry's Peak (40105 C6)
Trail Miles: 3.5
Altitude: 10,000 feet
Elevation Change: From 9,200 feet, +800 feet

Campsite Falls is a 7- to 10-foot leap over a wide block of granite in Glacier Creek, visible immediately west of the main trail and located downstream from the trail to the Glacier Gorge campsite. It's not indicated on the quad. The best head-on view is from the other side of the stream. Cross Glacier Creek on the bridge to the campsite, go downstream 20 to 30 yards, and climb down to the watercourse.

Ribbon Falls
(See Glacier Creek and Loch Vale Trail group map, page 23.)

Access: Hike
Rating: ★ ★ ★
Type: Punchbowl
USGS Topographic Quad: McHenry's Peak (40105 C6)
Trail Miles: 4
Altitude: 10,600 feet
Elevation Change: From 9,200 feet, +1,400 feet

Ribbon Falls

The route up Glacier Creek is popular. It goes past Ribbon Falls and all the way to Black Lake. The crowd thins out a couple of miles beyond Mills Lake. Before you get to Ribbon Falls, which is not visible from the trail, you will see several "decoy" falls—one where the stream from Shelf Lake comes down, another at the southwest end of Mills Lake.

At 4.5 miles from the Glacier Gorge trailhead (a mile beyond the Glacier Gorge campsite) the trail climbs steeply through some woods. Ribbon Falls is 100 yards west of the trail at this point, out of the woods and into the valley.

Ribbon Falls is distinct from every other falls we've seen. It's 140 feet long and 20 feet wide, a ribbon of thin white water dancing very fast down a twenty-three-degree slope into a rock basin. It runs down a monolith of water-polished granite a hundred feet or more wide, which can be safely walked on where dry.

Black Lake Falls*

(See Glacier Creek and Loch Vale Trail group map, page 23.)

Access: Hike or overnight
Rating: ★ ★
Type: Fan
USGS Topographic Quad: McHenry's Peak (40105 C6)
Trail Miles: 5
Altitude: 11,300 feet
Elevation Change: From 9,200 feet, + 2,100 feet

When you reach Black Lake 5 miles from the Glacier Gorge trailhead, the waterfall streaming in the sun over the cliff 300 feet above the west side of the lake is of small consequence in the grandeur of the cirque, somewhat like a decorative piece of lace draped over furniture in Longs Peak's sitting room. Black Lake Falls starts very high on the cliff, sheeting and then leaping down to a pile of rock above the lake on the west side.

The cairn-marked trail continues around the east side of the lake, and glacier-climbing hikers pass this way in good numbers to the glaciers above Frozen and Green lakes.

I hiked around the north end of Black Lake to get closer to the bottom of the falls and found myself marsh-hopping and then rock-hopping to no real advantage.

During high runoff in late June, there's a veil-like "falls" that streams down from the cliffs above Black Lake to the south, but it's blown to mist before it ever reaches the talus.

Loch Vale Trail

Two miles from the Glacier Gorge trailhead, the trail forks. The left fork goes up Glacier Creek to Mills Lake, as above. The right fork climbs up Icy Brook into Loch Vale. The trail continues around the west side of The Loch, the longest lake in Loch Vale. About 3.1 miles from the trailhead you will pass the Andrews Creek trail leading to Andrews Glacier. Continue on the trail up Icy Brook toward Sky Pond and Timberline Falls.

Timberline Falls

(See Glacier Creek and Loch Vale Trail group map, page 23.)

Access: Hike
Rating: ★ ★ ★
Type: Segmented
USGS Topographic Quad: McHenry's Peak (40105 C6)
Trail Miles: 3.3
Altitude: 10,500 feet
Elevation Change: From 9,200 feet, + 1,300 feet

Timberline Falls is a classic segmented falls: narrow at the top, breaking into a series of leaps 70 to 80 feet from the bottom. There the water gathers itself and hustles and burbles on down through the meadow for a relaxing trip through The Loch.

You can see Timberline Falls from the north end of The Loch and at various points along the valley, including from where the trail to the Andrews Creek campsite leaves the main trail. Timberline Falls is 4 miles from the Glacier Gorge trailhead.

If you climb up the rocks to the west of the falls, you can see Sky Pond and Glass Lake, jewellike tarns in a glacier-crafted setting that is incredibly grand and primeval.

Fern Lake Trail

There are five waterfalls to be seen on the trail up Fern Creek. Fern Falls is the only one that is a worthy destination in itself, but the valley stretches from high in the ice-carved heart of the park, sparkling with beautiful glacial lakes, all the way to the bottomlands of Moraine Park. The vistas of Notchtop, Flattop, and Ptarmigan Point are sublime as the trail climbs steadily through talus to a saddle between the Big Thompson River and Glacier Creek.

To reach the Fern Lake trailhead, enter Rocky Mountain National Park at Beaver Meadows and drive to the Moraine Park campground turnoff. Stay on the dirt road into the valley, past the turn to the campground, and all the way to the end of the road. The trail follows the Big Thompson River through Beaver Meadows; there are views through the trees of the river and the Continental Divide.

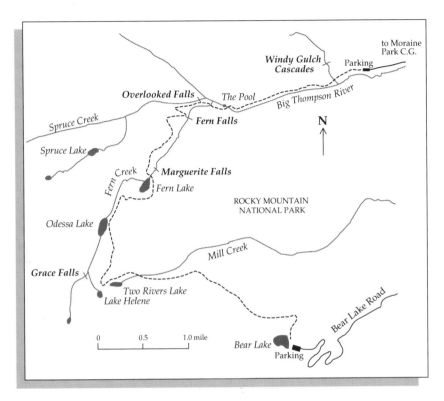

The Fern Lake Trail group of waterfalls
(**#3** on Rocky Mountain National Park drainage map, page 8):

Windy Gulch Cascades
Overlooked Falls
Fern Falls
Marguerite Falls
Grace Falls

Windy Gulch Cascades

(See Fern Lake Trail group map, page 29.)

Access: Hike
Rating: ⌐
Type: Cascade
USGS Topographic Quad: McHenry's Peak (40105 C6)
Trail Miles: .5-mile + .5-mile climb
Altitude: 8,500 feet
Elevation Change: From 8,100 feet, +400 feet

Windy Gulch Cascades is marked on the USGS map of the park, and it's on a park list of waterfalls. Frankly, I don't know why. It's a narrow series of trickling leaps and scours creating a track of moss and brush down the dry, rocky slope. The ability of this small amount of water to cut just a few inches to expose the bare rock illustrates the shallowness of the soil cover here. There is not much water flowing, even in early June.

You must climb the slope without a trail to get to Windy Gulch Cascades, and we found it not worth the effort. But if you want to see for yourself, stroll .3-mile from the Fern Lake trailhead. There's a game trail 100 yards short of the Windy Gulch drainage that climbs the steep, shifting slope of the moraine north to the cascades in less than .2-mile.

Deer scat and the animals themselves are in abundance here, and the hillside provides nice views of the valley of the Big Thompson, and even of the top of Longs Peak.

Overlooked Falls*

(See Fern Lake Trail group map, page 29.)

Access: Hike
Rating: ★ ★
Type: Horsetail
USGS Topographic Quad: McHenry's Peak (40105 C6)
Trail Miles: 2
Altitude: 8,500 feet
Elevation Change: From 8,100 feet, +400 feet

One mile from the Fern Lake trailhead, Arch Rocks looms over the trail. At 1.5 miles, you will pass The Pool, where a bridge crosses the Big Thompson. In another .1-mile, the trail crosses Fern Creek and starts a steep climb between

Fern Creek on the south (left) and Spruce Creek on the north (right). At the end of the first leg of a long switchback, if you step to the edge of the trail about 200 yards above the confluence of Fern Creek and Spruce Creek, you'll see Overlooked Falls on Spruce Creek, 30 to 40 feet down the cliff. It's hard to see because of the trees on the trail's edge, but it's a 20-foot twisting horsetail that seems very wild in its inaccessible gorge.

We gave it this name because it's not marked on any map, and people stay just long enough to catch their breath here, usually overlooking it.

Overlooked Falls (or Spruce Creek Falls) is very noisy and provides a spooky and steep view from the trail above.

Fern Falls
(See Fern Lake Trail group map, page 29.)

Access: Hike
Rating: ★ ★ ★
Type: Tiered
USGS Topographic Quad: McHenry's Peak (40105 C6)
Trail Miles: 3.5
Altitude: 9,000 feet
Elevation Change: From 8,100 feet, +900 feet

Fern Falls pours off the glacial shelf below Fern Lake in two roaring sequential leaps 30 to 40 feet high. It seems as though it ought to be possible to cross the creek below the falls on the jumble of slick wet logs lying across it, but common sense advises against this.

Fern Falls is 2.7 miles from the Fern Lake trailhead. It reminds me of both Ouzel and Lost falls, which is not surprising, because they all occur in similar rock.

This waterfall definitely suffers from its own accessibility. It's right on a very popular trail and consequently has all the signs of overuse. But it's a wonderful destination for a short day hike or a good place to rest on the way to Odessa Lake.

Marguerite Falls
(See Fern Lake Trail group map, page 29.)

Access: Hike
Rating: ★
Type: Cascade
USGS Topographic Quad: McHenry's Peak (40105 C6)
Trail Miles: 3.25 + .2-mile bushwhack
Altitude: 9,400 feet
Elevation Change: From 8,100 feet, + 1,300 feet

Marguerite is another of those waterfalls that seems too inconsequential even to be given a name, much less marked on maps. Maybe there was a time when it served some purpose as a landmark before the present system of trails was established.

Where the falls is marked on the map, Fern Creek bounces down a couple of short drops over a 50-yard stretch. It's hidden deep among the trees and off-trail through many fallen and rotted logs and hidden bogs.

About 3.75 miles from the Fern Lake trailhead (according to the park's literature), and about an eighth of a mile below Fern Lake, Marguerite Falls is easiest to locate by walking downstream from the lake on the east side of the stream. The falls is small and is easy to miss in its intimate, densely wooded setting if you try to reach it by hiking directly downhill from the Fern Lake trail to the stream.

Grace Falls
(See Fern Lake Trail group map, page 29.)

Access: Overnight
Rating: ★
Type: Segmented
USGS Topographic Quad: McHenry's Peak (40105 C6)
Trail Miles: 5
Altitude: 10,300 feet
Elevation Change: From 8,100 feet, + 2,200 feet

Grace Falls may be said to consist of the entire twisting, rocky drop of water from Lake Helene to the wooded marsh below. The "waterfall" is between Notchtop and Little Matterhorn Peak at the foot of a very noticeable rock slide, and is visible from an open stretch of trail at about 10,300 feet on the way from Odessa Lake to Lake Helene. The falls is in the center of the valley and requires about .25-mile of bushwhacking to get close.

When we visited, in late June, the falls' lower stretches were still covered by snow. We were hoping, of course, for a straight leap of hundreds of feet. We'd seen a little bit of the falls poking up from the trail half a mile away, but we couldn't believe this was the falls. The views from the cirque above Odessa Lake are stunning, and in that visual symphony the falls is a "grace" note.

We climbed to Grace Falls on the Fern Creek trail; it's 5.5 miles from the trailhead. It's a shorter hike from Bear Lake (3.25 miles), with an elevation gain of 2,000 feet and loss of 600 feet down to the falls.

Fall River Road and Roaring River

As you drive the 4.5 miles from Estes Park to the Fall River entrance on U.S. 34, you have already begun your trip into terrain sculpted by glaciers. The debris deposited by the oldest Bull Lake glaciers of seventy thousand years ago extends .5-mile east of the entrance.

In Horseshoe Park, 2 miles from the Fall River entrance station is the right turn up Fall River Road to the Endovalley picnic area.

Horseshoe Park was created by ice, and the glaciers virtually filled the entire valley here and carved the valleys of the tributaries to Fall River, including Roaring River and Chiquita and Sundance creeks, down to the 8,000-foot elevation. The greater erosive power of the main valley glacier cut deeper than the tributary glaciers, creating what are called hanging valleys—a drop-off from the tributary valleys resulted in the cascades and waterfalls of today.

About .25-mile up the Fall River Road is a picnic area and a trailhead for the Lawn Lake and Ypsilon Lake trails and the waterfall on Ypsilon Creek. Then .2-mile farther are parking areas and a loop trail created for viewing the results of the 1982 Lawn Lake flood.

Endovalley picnic area is a mile beyond the Roaring River and the flood path. Fall River Road is one way from here to Trail Ridge Road, 8 miles and 3,000 feet of elevation gain from the picnic ground (or you can turn around and drive back to U.S. 34).

Fall River Road is famous for its spectacular views back down the river to Horseshoe Basin and across the valley to the craggy slopes, where unnamed waterfalls dance down Trail Ridge. The mesmerizing colors of aspen and tundra all during the year recommend this trip, although the road is closed in winter.

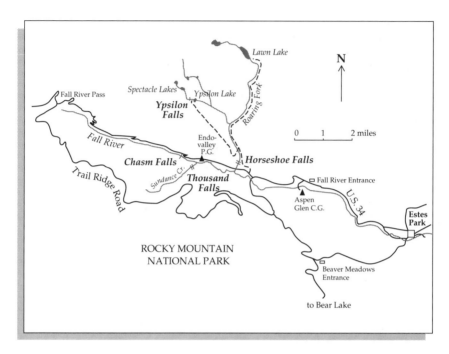

The Fall River Road and Roaring River group of waterfalls

(**#4** on Rocky Mountain National Park drainage map, page 8):

Horseshoe Falls
Thousand Falls
Chasm Falls
Ypsilon Falls

Horseshoe Falls

(See Fall River Road and Roaring River group map, page 34.)

Access: Wheelchair
Rating: ★
Type: Cascade
USGS Topographic Quad: Trail Ridge (40105 D6)
Trail Miles: .1-mile
Altitude: 8,800 feet
Elevation Change: From 8,550 feet, +250 feet

Horseshoe Falls was buried under rocks and mud by a flood in July 1982, when the Lawn Lake Dam burst. The pent-up water scoured the Roaring River valley like an army (a *big* army) of bulldozers. The course of the river is still very steep, cutting over a hundred feet deep in places, but the falls is now merely a steep but not particularly photogenic cascade down the scar of the flood. It could be decades or centuries before the old falls is restored, if ever.

The park has turned the area into a fascinating geological exhibit, creating a walk connecting two parking lots that provides a close-up look at the flood damage. I have not been able to locate any photos of the falls before the flood. The scoured valley of the Roaring River is a startling but unaesthetic reminder of the power of water and the knife of time.

Thousand Falls

(See Fall River Road and Roaring River group map, page 34.)

Access: Bushwhack
Rating: ★
Type: Cascade
USGS Topographic Quad: Trail Ridge (40105 D6)
Trail Miles: .1-mile
Altitude: 9,600 feet
Elevation Change: From 9,400 feet, +200 feet

Thousand Falls is reached (with difficulty) by bushwhacking across the Fall River from Endovalley picnic area. It requires one to ford the stream and climb through heavy fallen timber, and is consequently very isolated.

Drive .25-mile up Fall River from Endovalley picnic area by a road that leaves the west end of the picnic area (the Fall River Road is at the east end). From the end of this short road a trail winds 200 yards along the river.

Thousand Falls is across the Fall River and reached by improvised log crossings. There is an intermittent trail up Sundance Creek that is hidden in the dense underbrush and fallen logs. The falls is a long series of stepped cascades working through underbrush, rocks, and logs to the Fall River. There's no major leap down by the river, but there may well be something more spectacular uphill for those with the curiosity and stamina to look.

Chasm Falls
(See Fall River Road and Roaring River group map, page 34.)

Access: Walk in
Rating: ★ ★
Type: Punchbowl
USGS Topographic Quad: Trail Ridge (40105 D6)
Trail Miles: .03-mile
Altitude: 8,965 feet
Elevation Change: From 8,985 feet, –20 feet

Chasm Falls leaps down about 30 feet into a rock cauldron, making a tremendous noise, then twists and tumbles into a series of lower cascades. There are active cascades above the main leap as well. The falls' chute is deeply eroded and polished by the water action.

Drive up Fall River Road .9-mile beyond the Endovalley turnoff. The road twists through an unmistakable switchback, and the Chasm Falls parking area is just above it.

Chasm Falls is sensational and on a popular road, but it can be solitary late in the day. When tourists are plentiful, the falls' natural feeling of splendid isolation is seriously degraded.

We hiked on snowshoes to this falls in March, but there is nothing to see at that time of year.

Fall River Road is a spectacular one-way uphill trip 9 miles to Trail Ridge, and it's worth a look even if you skip the falls along the way. From near Chasm Falls additional waterfalls can be seen across the Fall River valley on the north slopes of Trail Ridge. You can see another falls near the junction of Fall River Road and Trail Ridge Road.

Ypsilon Falls*
(See Fall River Road and Roaring River group map, page 34.)

Access: Hike
Rating: ★ ★
Type: Tiered
USGS Topographic Quad: Trail Ridge (40105 D6)
Trail Miles: 4.5
Altitude: 10,800 feet
Elevation Change: From 8,600 feet, + 2,200 feet

The Lawn Lake trail begins at a picnic area .25-mile up the Fall River Road from U.S. Highway 34. The trail climbs northwest across the slope to enter and then parallel the Roaring River and its naked gorge.

From a fork in the trail 1.2 miles from the trailhead, the Ypsilon Lake trail crosses and then departs from the Roaring River, leading up the ridge of a moraine covered with lodgepole pine to Chipmunk (small and mirrorlike), Ypsilon, and Spectacle lakes.

At 2.5 miles from Roaring River, the trail comes to the west end of Ypsilon Lake. Where Ypsilon Creek comes down to the lake, you can see Ypsilon Falls' lower leap nestled in the cut of the creek. This is a 15-foot segmented waterfall that gathers immediately into a clear, deep run to the lake, with rocks suited for picnicking or meditating along its banks. This beautiful small falls is not on any map.

The trail continues up into the rocks to the left of the falls, and after a hundred yards you can glimpse the head of a 20-foot second leap when you cross Ypsilon Creek. The entirety of this second leap can be seen only from the north side of the gorge, requiring leaving the trail above the falls and bushwhacking (rockwhacking?) downstream.

Above Ypsilon Falls, the trail climbs to Spectacle Lakes, below the crest of the Mummy Range. The valleys above the falls offer great adventure.

The North Boundary Trail

While most of Rocky Mountain National Park's visitors focus on Trail Ridge, Fall River, Moraine Park, and Glacier Basin, there is another corner of the park that is less-traveled and much less extensively carved up by glaciers. Consequently, the valleys here are V-shaped rather than U-shaped, hilly rather than mountainous, and provide environments somewhat more intimate and

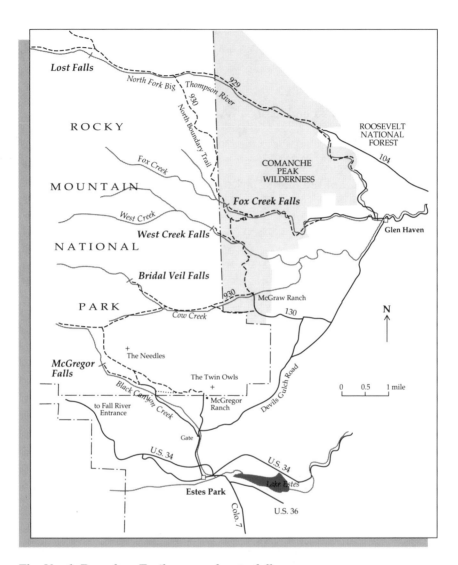

The North Boundary Trail group of waterfalls
(**#5** on Rocky Mountain National Park drainage map, page 8):

McGregor Falls
Bridal Veil Falls
West Creek Falls
Fox Creek Falls
Lost Falls

lower in altitude than the better-known parts of the park. Slopes are more gradual, so that trails plunge straight up and down rather than follow contours.

To get to the falls in this area, go north out of Estes Park on the Devil's Gulch Road toward Glen Haven. A mile from the intersection of highways 34 and 7, there's a gate on the west side of the road going onto the McGregor Ranch, which is now owned and administered by the park. Access by the dirt road west across the ranch is discouraged by a no-trespassing sign because the city of Estes Park's filtration plant draws water from Black Canyon, less than .5-mile below McGregor Falls. McGregor Falls can also be reached from the Twin Owls trailhead, which is inside the park boundary.

About 3.5 miles farther on there's a turnoff to the left, onto County Road 130, which ends in 1.25 miles at what used to be called McGraw Ranch, which is not inside the park. At one time, access to trails from this ranch was restricted. In 1990, arrangements were made to allow for use of the trailhead at the ranch for the Cow Creek and North Boundary trails, although instructions posted at the trailhead indicate that you should notify the personnel in the ranch office that you are leaving your car at the ranch.

Cow Creek is the route to Bridal Veil Falls; or rather, the park's use of that name. This is not the state's largest falls, also called Bridal Veil Falls, which is near Telluride (see page 196), but any bride would still be proud to wear it.

The North Boundary trail, making no compromise with the steepness of the terrain, heads directly up- and downhill to the West Creek drainage and West Creek Falls. A repeat of this exercise leads to a corner of the Comanche Wilderness and Fox Creek Falls, which can also be reached from a trailhead west of Glen Haven.

McGregor Ranch and the North Boundary Trail Area

To get to the falls in this area, start at the intersection of highways 7 and 36 outside of Estes Park. Drive .4-mile toward Estes Park, but instead of turning left into town, take the bypass to Rocky Mountain National Park. In another .5-mile there's a right turn onto Devil's Gulch Road north out of Estes Park toward Glen Haven. All the falls in this group are reached from this road, and mileage is calculated from the turn onto Devil's Gulch Road.

McGregor Falls
(See North Boundary Trail group map, page 38.)

Access: Hike
Rating: ★ ★
Type: Segmented
USGS Topographic Quad: Estes Park (40105 D5)
Trail Miles: 2.7
Altitude: 8,400 feet
Elevation Change: From 8,000 feet, +400 feet

McGregor Falls graces a beautiful cul-de-sac setting that is landscaped with aspen and pine and barricaded in front by massive granite boulders and on the sides by grassy wooded hillsides. The falls, 20 feet high, cascading steeply and then sheeting down a granite slab, is visually distinctive because of a huge iron-shaped rock directly below the falls that the water must twist around.

Although it is not named as such on some maps, McGregor Falls is located about a mile north of the Estes Park filtration plant on Black Canyon Creek. There is a road directly to the plant. A gate on the west side of the road driving onto the McGregor Ranch (less than a mile from Highway 34 on the Devil's Gulch Road) is marked "No Trespassing," and access by the dirt road across the ranch is discouraged because Black Canyon Creek is also the source of Estes Park's water supply. However, McGregor Falls, which is inside the park boundary, can be reached from the Twin Owls trailhead.

About .8-mile from Estes Park on the Devil's Gulch Road, there's a large wooden gate with a sign announcing the McGregor Ranch and museum. Drive through the gate and follow the signs .5-mile to the Twin Owls trailhead.

The right fork from this trailhead provides access to some exciting rock-climbing areas with names like Alligator Drool and No-Purchase-Required. The left fork is marked as the trail to Lawn Lake. Take this trail, which offers great open views of the Continental Divide, a little less than a mile to a gate.

Instead of staying on the trail after climbing or passing through the gate (close it behind you: This is a working ranch), cross down to the dirt road to your left a few hundred yards—you are inside the park boundary at this point. Follow this road into the woods, reaching the filtration plant and the trail to McGregor Falls at about 1.7 miles.

McGregor Falls is just under a mile from this point along the trail, which climbs gently along Black Canyon Creek in the shade of evergreen and aspen groves.

Northern Tributaries to the Big Thompson

Indian Ranch is the trailhead for the North Boundary trail and for the Cow Creek trail.

The North Boundary trail, making no compromise with the steepness of the terrain, heads directly up- and downhill to the West Creek drainage and West Creek Falls. A repeat of this exercise leads to a corner of the Comanche Wilderness and Fox Creek Falls. Farther along, the North Boundary trail intersects the North Fork trail, leading to Lost Falls. We visited all of these waterfalls on one three-day hike in May 1989, using the North Boundary trail. (Lost Falls is more directly reached by using the Dunraven trailhead, described under Lost Falls.)

The Cow Creek trail provides the route to the park's version of Bridal Veil Falls.

To reach the Indian Ranch trailhead, drive along Devil's Gulch Road. At about 4.5 miles from Highway 34 the paved road curves sharply to the right, but if you continue straight ahead onto a dirt road (County Road 130), it ends in 1.25 miles at what used to be called McGraw Ranch, which is not yet inside the park.

At one time, access to trails from this ranch was restricted. In 1990, arrangements were made to allow public access from the trailhead for the Cow Creek and the North Boundary trails. Instructions posted at the trailhead indicate that you should notify the personnel in the ranch office that you are leaving your car at the ranch.

Bridal Veil Falls
(See North Boundary Trail group map, page 38.)

Access: Hike
Rating: ★ ★ ★
Type: Plunge
USGS Topographic Quad: Estes Park (40105 D5)
Trail Miles: 3
Altitude: 8,800 feet
Elevation Change: From 7,800 feet at ranch, + 1,000 feet

From the Indian Ranch trailhead, hike west along Cow Creek. In 2 miles the trail forks. Bridal Veil Falls is a mile up the right fork, which gets steep near the falls.

Bridal Veil is one clean, narrow 20-foot leap that splashes from a rock shelf into a pool. Above this main leap is a series of cascades bounding and sliding in stepped pools down a sloped rock face before climaxing in the falls. The environment of stream above the falls is very intimate and attractive, and the falls were surprisingly solitary the July weekend we visited.

Camping is available by reservation at Rabbit Ears or Peregrine campsites on the way to the falls.

West Creek Falls
(See North Boundary Trail group map, page 38.)

Access: Hike
Rating: ★ ★ ★
Type: Punchbowl
USGS Topographic Quad: Estes Park (40105 D5)
Trail Miles: 1.5
Altitude: 8,150 feet
Elevation Change: From 7,800 feet to 8,600 feet, +800 feet; to 7,980 feet, –620 feet; to 8,150 feet, +170 feet

The North Boundary trail actually follows the eastern boundary of Rocky Mountain National Park. It begins at the Indian Ranch trailhead, described above. The trail goes directly uphill north of the ranch, climbing to the top of a ridge and then plunging down through heavy woods to West Creek in about 1.4 miles.

West Creek Falls is reached by a .6-mile hike up West Creek into an inviting cul-de-sac of sandstone cliffs. The falls' 25-foot single leap drops directly into a clear, deep plunge pool, inviting you to take a swim if you happen to have a wet suit handy.

West Creek Falls is in a beautiful and alluring environment with lots of different viewpoints, swift chutes below the plunge pool, and, unfortunately, many, many ticks in May and June.

Fox Creek Falls

(See North Boundary Trail group map, page 38.)

Access: Hike
Rating: ★
Type: Serial
USGS Topographic Quad: Estes Park (40105 D5)
Trail Miles: 4
Altitude: 8,400 feet
Elevation Change: From 7,800 feet to 8,600 feet, +800 feet; to 7,980 feet, −620 feet; to 8,500 feet, +520 feet; to 8,400 feet, −100 feet

Fox Creek Falls is a series of small leaps and chutes inside Comanche Peaks Wilderness running swiftly down a broad granite shelf for a hundred feet or more. Its main leaps are not more than 5 feet high.

To get to Fox Creek Falls, hike 1 mile farther along the North Boundary trail from West Creek, a total of 3 miles from the Indian Ranch trailhead. When you reach Fox Creek, leave the North Boundary trail and head downstream a few hundred yards over the rocks to Fox Creek Falls.

If you want to avoid West Creek Falls for some reason, Fox Creek Falls can also be reached directly by hiking 2.5 miles up Fox Creek from the end of the dirt road west out of Glen Haven—but there is no trailhead, only a fire-lane turnaround in an area densely occupied by cabins, so parking a vehicle could be a problem.

Lost Falls

(See North Boundary Trail group map, page 38.)

Access: Overnight, bushwhack
Rating: ★ ★ ★
Type: Segmented
USGS Topographic Quad: Pingree Park (40105 E5)
Trail Miles: 7
Altitude: 10,000 feet
Elevation Change: From 7,960 feet, +2,040 feet

Black rocks, an explosive 30-foot leap, and dramatic cascades make Lost Falls memorable. The tumble of rocks creates delightful places to sit and admire the white torrent, the light changing constantly in the mist as the sun moves west around behind the falls. If you climb up behind the falls, you'll discover

Lost Falls

another two major leaps, the entire fall of water descending perhaps 200 feet.

Lost Falls can be reached either from the Dunraven (North Fork) trailhead, or by the North Boundary trail. Dunraven is more direct, and the trail miles above are calculated from the Dunraven trailhead.

To reach the trailhead: From the intersection of Highways 7 and 36 just east of Estes Park, turn toward town on 36 but take the Highway 34 bypass north .5-mile, then turn right (north) on the Devil's Gulch Road and drive through Glen Haven (6.5 miles) to the Dunraven Glade road at 8.2 miles.

Turn left on the Dunraven Glade road and drive 2.25 miles to the trailhead inside Roosevelt National Forest.

Trail 929 reaches the boundary of Rocky Mountain National Park in 4.4 miles, following the North Fork of the Big Thompson River. The North Fork Ranger Station is across the river .9-mile inside the park boundary, and the North Boundary trail joins it from the south. Continue on the North Fork trail past the Lost Falls campsite at 6.7 miles.

Lost Falls is not visible from the trail. When we visited the falls I didn't look at the map carefully enough, and we hiked on up the trail past the campsite a half-hour until, stopping for a rest at a cascade running noisily across the trail, I realized that the falls was far below us on the river; we could hear its thunder.

We hiked back, bushwhacked straight down the slope to the river, and then worked our way along the bank, up the current, for about fifteen minutes, and discovered the falls. More directly, there is a faint trail to the falls from the North Fork trail less than a minute west of the Lost Falls campsite, where the trail and river part company. Be careful—there are no signs.

Rocky Mountain National Park's Western Slope

Mount Cirrus Falls
(See Western Slope group map, page 46.)

Access: Overnight
Rating: ★
Type: Cascade
USGS Topographic Quad: Mount Richtofen (40105 D8)
Trail Miles: 6.4
Altitude: 11,300 feet
Elevation Change: From 9,050 feet, +2,250 feet

Mount Cirrus Falls is below the outlet of Lake of the Clouds, twisting down a jumbled talus slope for hundreds of feet. Even in late September water flow is steady but shows white only in a couple of places when viewed from a distance. At the foot of the falls the water disappears under the talus almost immediately. I would guess the cleft is 200 feet long, and in full flow the falls may make several large leaps. The falls requires a lot of rock-hopping to reach.

Stick around until sunset and you'll find out why they call this the Never Summer Range.

To reach Mount Cirrus Falls, drive north on U.S. 34 to the trailhead of the Colorado River trail, 10 miles past the park's west entrance. The trail heads north out of the parking lot, follows the river up on the bank for a half-mile, then the Red Mountain trail forks to the left. The Colorado River trail continues on up the Colorado to Lulu City and the river's headwaters below La Poudre Pass.

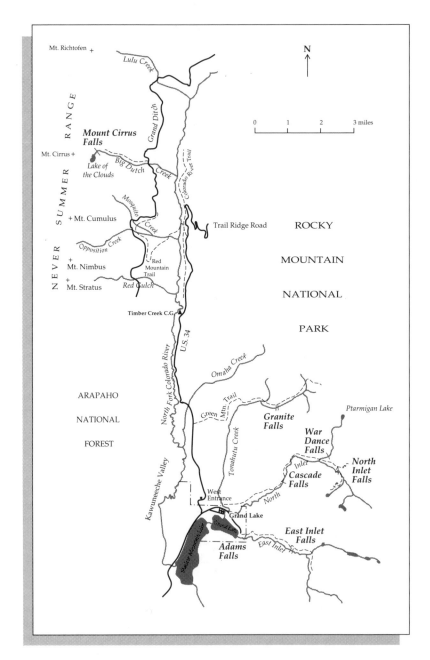

The Rocky Mountain National Park Western Slope group of waterfalls
(**#6** on Rocky Mountain National Park drainage map, page 8):

Mt. Cirrus Falls
Adams Falls
East Inlet Falls
Cascade Falls

War Dance Falls
North Inlet Falls
Granite Falls

The Red Mountain trail crosses the Colorado and heads into the woods on the moraine forming the river's west bank. It climbs this slope heading south for 1.5 miles, when it finally swings back to the north, makes several refreshing stream crossings, and climbs to Grand Ditch and its service road.

Grand Ditch, dug by Asian labor in the nineteenth century, is a water diversion project that was completed in 1900 to carry Never Summer water across the Continental Divide into the Poudre River. The Grand Ditch road marks the 10,186-foot elevation of the ditch, which runs the entire length of the Never Summer Range as clearly as a neon sign. There are plenty of deer and elk in the area, and they use the service road as a wildlife super-highway.

Once on the road, hike north a couple of miles to reach Hitchens Gulch and Big Dutch Creek coming down from Lake of the Clouds. There's a trail heading steeply uphill along Big Dutch Creek past the Dutchtown ruins and scrambling out onto the bare rock at timberline 6.5 miles from the trailhead. The route to the falls above tree line is strictly stone-to-stone for half a mile, but the cliff holding Lake of the Clouds and the jagged cleft of the falls are visible from the rim of the basin.

The trail gets sketchy across the bare rock, but cairns mark the route up into the basin of Lake of the Clouds.

The cliffs framing and surrounding the falls are made of very fine-grained metamorphic rock that fractures in planes, and glaciers have left the cirque between Mount Cirrus (12,787 feet) and Howard Mountain (12,810 feet) a bowl of rock chips ranging in size from butter pats to automobile-size blocks.

Although Mount Cirrus Falls, not marked on any map, may not be a worthy objective in itself, at least not in September, it's definitely worth a trip to see the Never Summers, to check the falls out, and to be in that great rock-filled glacial basin, feeling like an ant in a bowl of Grape-Nuts.

Colorado River Valley Tributaries:
East Inlet, North Inlet, and Tonahutu Creek

The approach by auto to the west side of Rocky Mountain National Park is like an airplane ride; one soars at high speeds through verdant open country, and the unrestricted vistas of Middle Park slowly give way to the exciting, ever-changing views of the western slope of the Front Range, the volcanic Rabbit Ears Range north of Granby, and the distant ramparts of the Park Range. Beyond Granby, Highway 34 heads north from Highway 40 straight for the heart of the park looming invitingly to the east.

The glacier that carved the upper Colorado River valley was over 20 miles long—the longest in the park—extending from La Poudre Pass to Shadow Mountain Lake.

When the glaciers dropped their load in a terminal moraine here, they created a natural dam for the waters of the East and North inlets and Tonahutu Creek, resulting in Grand Lake and Shadow Mountain Lake. The islands at the southern end of Shadow Mountain Lake mark the southernmost extent of the glaciers' crawl.

The waterfalls on the North Inlet and East Inlet trails are reached from Grand Lake. Granite Falls and upper Tonahutu Creek are accessible from Grand Lake, but the upper drainage is most easily reached by using the Green Mountain trail.

The East Inlet

To reach the East Inlet trail, follow the bypass road around the town of Grand Lake all the way to its end, 2.25 miles, to the parking area at the northeast end of Grand Lake, where there are restrooms and a very well used trail up the East Inlet. Most people leaving their cars in this parking lot are headed for Adams Falls. You will leave most of them behind if you continue on up the trail toward East Inlet Falls.

Adams Falls
(See Western Slope group map, page 46.)

Access: Walk in
Rating: ★ ★ ★
Type: Segmented (cascade and punchbowl)
USGS Topographic Quad: Shadow Mountain (40105 B7)
Trail Miles: .25-mile
Altitude: 8,450 feet
Elevation Change: From 8,370 feet, +80 feet

An eighth-of-a-mile hike from the East Inlet trailhead brings you to Adams Falls. The falls consists of an interesting, twisting, steep cascade and leap into a ninety-degree turn through a deep cut in the rock. The surrounding cliffs provide many nice views of the main falls and the secondary 15-foot leap into a pool below it. The roar of Adams Falls is powerful because it cuts so steeply through the rock.

The falls gets many visitors: It's close to Grand Lake, accessible to all ages, and signs to it are easy to follow. The rocks are fun to climb around on but are not for nervous parents with careless children.

East Inlet

East Inlet Falls
(See Western Slope group map, page 46.)

Access: Hike
Rating: ★ ★
Type: Segmented
USGS Topographic Quad: Shadow Mountain (40105 B7)
Trail Miles: 2
Altitude: 8,900 feet
Elevation Change: From 8,370 feet, + 530 feet

As you work your way up the East Inlet, a wall of rock appears to close off the end of the valley ahead. The trail climbs around this wall to the north.

As you climb, you will see glimpses of white water in the East Inlet, but it is hidden from view as the cliffs get higher and the cut of the creek through them gets deeper.

East Inlet Falls is at the end of the valley at the top of this metamorphic

East Inlet Falls

rock barrier. One set of falls is off the trail below the cliffs when the trail turns sharply uphill to the left. Leave the trail and go forward and to the right over and down the rocks to the East Inlet watercourse. The falls are a few hundred feet up the drainage through the woods. There is a faint trail. Stick close to the water and you can't miss the falls.

The main leap of East Inlet Falls crashes 15 feet down off a lip of blackened metamorphic rock. The white water runs swiftly through a narrow defile and disappears over the edge.

There may be some beautiful leaps downstream, but it appears you can't get to them without going into the woods down-valley to work upstream along the East Inlet, if then. You will probably have East Inlet Falls to yourself. There are no signs, and the falls are a ten-minute walk off the trail.

North Inlet Waterfalls

To reach the North Inlet trail, bear left when making the turn off Highway 34 to Grand Lake, using the road that bypasses the central business district. After driving 1.1 miles beyond the turn, you will come to a dirt road that turns sharply uphill to the north, leading in .2-mile to the North Inlet trailhead. This trail goes to Summerland Park, Cascade Falls, War Dance Falls, North Inlet Falls, and other destinations along the west side of the Continental Divide.

Cascade Falls
(See Western Slope group map, page 46.)

Access: Hike
Rating: ★ ★
Type: Segmented
USGS Topographic Quad: Grand Lake (40105 C7)
Trail Miles: 3
Altitude: 8,800 feet
Elevation Change: From 8,500 feet, + 300 feet

Cascade Falls lives up to its name, and the cascades are long, with deep, swirling pools in between leaps. The reach of the cascade is about 80 feet, and it makes a lot of noise. Moss grows like a lawn all over the surrounding woods.

Hiking distance to the falls from the North Inlet trailhead is 3.5 miles. The trail follows an old road for quite a distance, and there are open views of the valley. Then the trail passes through woods and starts to climb up the inlet.

The Cascade Falls campsite is a short distance in the rocks north of the falls—reservations are required for the use of the campsite.

There's a fair amount of traffic along the North Inlet trail, and many campsites along its length. The only times you are likely to have the falls to yourself are early morning and late evening.

War Dance Falls
(See Western Slope group map, page 46.)

Access: Overnight
Rating: ★ ★
Type: Serial
USGS Topographic Quad: McHenry's Peak (40105 C6)
Trail Miles: 7
Altitude: 10,000 feet
Elevation Change: From 8,500 feet, + 1,500 feet

War Dance Falls has many small leaps and long cascades and stretches up the slope from the North Inlet trail to Bench Lake. The top of the falls is indicated 500 feet up Ptarmigan Creek on the USGS map.

On the way up the North Inlet trail to Ptarmigan Creek there are several lovely small falls where North Inlet cuts through the rock. Big Pool, about halfway to Ptarmigan, is deep and inviting but cold enough for polar bears.

Three miles from Cascade Falls there's a bridge crossing Ptarmigan Creek (immediately after the Ptarmigan campsite sign). A faint trail up through the brush on the east side of the creek leads fairly soon to the foot of War Dance Falls. It's a charming segmented falls with one major leap of about 15 feet and many smaller ones.

The trail, such as it is, continues upstream over bush and log high above the water and sometimes right next to it. War Dance continues as many charming little leaps, pools, and cascades.

War Dance Falls

North Inlet Falls

(See Western Slope group map, page 46.)

Access: Overnight
Rating: ★ ★
Type: Segmented
USGS Topographic Quad: McHenry's Peak (40105 C6)
Trail Miles: 7.6
Altitude: 9,500 feet
Elevation Change: From 8,500 feet, +1,100 feet, -100 feet

About .8-mile farther along the North Inlet trail from Ptarmigan Creek there's a fork to Lake Nanita. North Inlet Falls is about .2-mile from the fork, where a large wooden bridge crosses the creek at a chasm. North Inlet Falls pounds over the bedrock, and there's a huge boulder right in the middle of the stream.

Nanita Lake was closed to camping in 1988 when we visited, and the area around the falls and bridge was heavily traveled.

North Inlet Falls made terrific photographs, but the presence of the large wooden bridge compromises any sense of wilderness. The total distance to North Inlet Falls is 7.6 miles from the trailhead near Grand Lake.

Granite Falls

(See Western Slope group map, page 46.)

Access: Overnight
Rating: ★ ★
Type: Cascade
USGS Topographic Quad: Grand Lake (40105 C7)
Trail Miles: 5.7
Altitude: 9,800 feet
Elevation Change: From 8,800 feet, +1,000 feet

Granite Falls is reached most directly by way of the Green Mountain trail, which cuts across a ridge north of Green Mountain to reach Tonahutu Creek from the Colorado River valley.

Drive to the parking area on the east side of Highway 34, 3.75 miles north of the park's west entrance. The trail begins at the south end of the parking lot, and even if you're not headed for the falls, the 2-mile hike over the ridge into Big Meadow is worth the trip.

At Big Meadow, the Green Mountain trail joins the Tonahutu Creek trail, which follows the curve of the creek north and east, heading for Sprague Mountain on the Divide.

Granite Falls is 3.6 miles from the intersection of Green Mountain and Tonahutu Creek trails, a total of 5.2 miles from the Green Mountain trailhead. The trail skirts the length of Big Meadow and provides beautiful open views of the mountains to the northeast. The falls is a long cascade, its main leap less than 10 feet, but the creek drops rapidly 40 to 50 feet over smooth water-reddened granite, with many twists, slides, minileaps, and captivating pools. The falls is close to the trail and there's a sign marking the turn. The trail is popular, and the falls encourages people to linger.

2

The North and South Platte Rivers

The population and history of the North and South Platte rivers' drainages are easily described in terms of transportation—the movement of goods, water, and people.

In 1812, Robert Stuart blazed along the North Platte (in Wyoming) on what came to be known as the Oregon Trail. Captain Benjamin Bonneville followed Stuart's footsteps on his way to the Pacific Northwest in 1834. And the "Great Pathfinder," John C. Fremont, used the North Platte route in 1842 on his first expedition west accompanied by a young scout named Kit Carson.

The South Platte valley was used as a route to the Rockies as early as 1820, when Stephen H. Long's scientific expedition followed its course. The fur trade, established in the 1820s, also followed the South Platte, and the trappers crossed the valley of the North Platte in Colorado to get to the annual mountain man rendezvous farther west on the Green River.

The Platte rivers were named by French trappers, but the land drained by the two great rivers served migratory humans for at least eleven thousand years before the first Europeans arrived. The South Platte drainage contains a dozen archeological sites, including the Lindenmeier Ranch site, one of the most famous Folsom sites in North America.

The South Platte valley now has the greatest concentrations of people in the state. The drainage makes up only twenty percent of Colorado but contains more than sixty percent of its population. This corner of Colorado, which Major Stephen H. Long called in 1820 "almost wholly unfit for cultivation," supports the largest concentration of irrigated lands in the state, growing beets, wheat, corn, barley, and cattle. The transportation of water, of people, and of goods still dictates Colorado's destiny.

The majority of waterfalls in the South Platte drainage are in Rocky Mountain

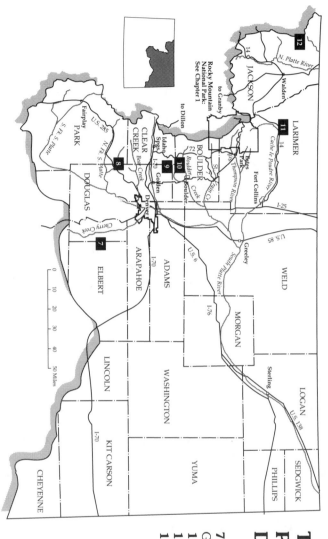

The North and South Platte Rivers Drainage Map

7, 8, 9: Denver Area Waterfalls Group

10: Boulder Area Waterfalls Group

11: Cache la Poudre River

12: North Park Waterfalls Group

National Park. However, there are ten additional falls here, including some close to the state's major urban areas: Denver, Boulder, and Fort Collins (waterfalls near Colorado Springs are described in Chapter 3). There is evidence of human habitation near several of these falls in the form of ancient "No Trespassing" signs.

Denver Area Waterfalls

There are times when seeing a waterfall isn't possible in the mountains because of a job, finances, a flat tire. There aren't many falls for the city-bound. One can go to Confluence Park in Denver, at Fifteenth Street and the South Platte, where the load of boulders and concrete in the middle of the Platte creates a very soothing block waterfall most of the year. There was probably not a falls here when Indians camped at the confluence and gold-hunters forded upstream.

There's a small falls on the Platte near Ruby Hill Park in Denver, just south of the Florida Street bridge.

Several pleasant architectural waterfalls serve the office-bound in downtown Denver, in the sunken plazas on Arapahoe Street between Fifteenth and Seventeenth streets. There are a 5-foot, four-sided falls and granite-lined pool in the lobby of the Denver Water Department, at 1600 West Twelfth Avenue. There are a quadruple plunge and a punchbowl falls pleasing the crowds at Denver's Botanic Gardens.

A bit farther afield, there's a waterfall close to Denver on Cherry Creek, northeast of the reservoir.

Cherry Creek (Castlewood) Falls *
(See Denver Area group map, page 59.)

Access: Wheelchair
Rating: ★ ★
Type: Plunge
USGS Topographic Quad: Castle Rock South (39104 C7)
Trail Miles: .05-mile
Altitude: 6,300 feet
Elevation Change: None

As unlikely as it may seem, you reach Cherry Creek Falls by driving *away* from the mountains, to the verge of the plains in the Black Forest.

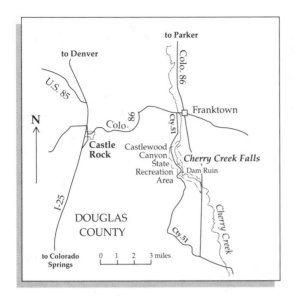

The Denver area group of waterfalls
(**#7** on North and South Platte rivers drainage map, page 57):

Cherry Creek Falls

The falls is a straight leap of about 20 feet, the amount of water varying according to the time of year. The water feeding the creek comes from the plains, not the mountains. The vegetation in and near the cut of Cherry Creek is lush and very different from the scrub brush out of the arroyo. It's a wonderful place to visit to experience autumn color in a strangely surreal environment, inside a crack in the plains.

Cherry Creek Falls is a good example of a falls created by a retreating layer of resistant rock (sandstone) overlying a softer rock (clay). The tumble of large rocks below the leap has been broken from the hard sandstone layer that created the falls. The falls is working its way upstream and will eventually cease to exist. What is surprising is that it exists now, after the flood of water created when the upstream Castlewood dam collapsed, in 1933. It does make one wonder what effect the flood had in shaping the arroyo and in carving the falls.

Cherry Creek Falls is in the Castlewood State Recreation Area, .25-mile west of Franktown on Highway 86. You can reach Franktown by taking Highway 86 east from Castle Rock 7 miles, or by taking Parker Road (Highway 83) south from Cherry Creek Reservoir.

Then take County Road 51, a dirt road beginning at Highway 86, .25-mile

Cherry Creek Falls

west of Franktown. The recreation area entrance is 3 miles south. A daily fee of three dollars or an annual Colorado State Parks pass is required.

Wheelchair-accessible, Cherry Creek Falls is visible from the parking area and well worth the drive. It's one of the falls most easily reached from Denver, and there are many other recreational opportunities within the area as well, including hiking along the canyons of Cherry Creek.

Waterfalls are sparse in the foothills west of Denver. The absence of glaciation here makes the conditions that produce waterfalls relatively rare, especially below 8,000 feet. But where hard and soft rock meet you'll find an exception or two, in the area between Evergreen and Conifer.

Maxwell Falls
(See Denver Area group map, page 62.)

Access: Hike
Rating: ★
Type: Segmented
USGS Topographic Quad: Conifer (39105 E3)
Trail Miles: 1
Altitude: 8,300 feet
Elevation Change: From 7,840 feet, +460 feet

Maxwell Falls is a narrow, steep cascade 20 feet down a black face of moss-covered rocks, nestled in a cozy little defile amidst cliffs deep in the woods of the foothills. The setting has the feeling of the wilderness but is on the foothills' small scale, making it a popular family destination.

The falls are sparse in July but still provide a shady spot out of the heat. The cliffs provide rock climbing for kids, and the falls is popular with dog lovers. The falls is close enough to Denver to make it accessible in winter and summer.

To reach Maxwell Falls, take I-70 to the El Rancho turnoff (exit 252) and drive on Highway 74 to Evergreen.

About .5-mile south of Evergreen, take Brook Forest Road to the right (west). Drive 4 miles to a parking lot at the base of a small dam that is visible from the road. The trail goes up on the west side of the dam. At about 1 mile the trail splits. Follow along the drainage as it turns to the left. The walk to the falls is a few hundred yards.

The falls can also be reached from Conifer. Drive 1 mile toward Evergreen, then take a left turn on Brook Forest Road 5.5 miles to Maxwell Falls picnic ground and Cub Creek picnic ground. The trail heads south from the picnic ground about 1 mile to the falls.

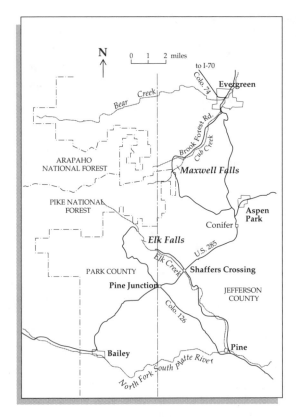

**The Denver area group
of waterfalls**
(**#8** on North and South
Platte rivers drainage map,
page 57):

Maxwell Falls
Elk Falls

Elk Falls
(See Denver Area group map, above.)

Access: Hike
Rating: ★ ★
Type: Segmented
USGS Topographic Quad: Meridian Hill (39105 E4)
Trail Miles: 1
Altitude: 8,710 feet
Elevation Change: From 8,200 feet, +510 feet

Elk Falls

Elk Falls is a 46-foot segmented horsetail coming steeply off the smooth cliffs below Lions Head, just northwest of Chimney Rock, plunging down into the heavily vegetated cut of Elk Creek. The thin but powerful stream of water skims and hisses down the face of a monolithic red wall, then runs away swiftly across and down a broad gravel and boulder terrace fallen from the cliffs.

Drive west on Highway 285 to Shaffer's Crossing. Take the county road north from the highway, bearing left, past the many private cabins hidden in the woods, driving several miles on a northwest heading. There is no public access, so about all you can do is to get as close as possible by car to the falls' location as marked on the quad map and ask permission to cross private property to the Elk Creek drainage. You must also ask permission to go across to the creek and the trail to the falls.

The falls are on private land just outside Pike National Forest immediately east of Lions Head, which is marked on maps and visible from the highway.

There is a road that skirts Lions Head from Pine Junction and comes down almost all the way to the falls from the north to Chimney Rock; but that, too, is on private land, and permission is required to travel in this area.

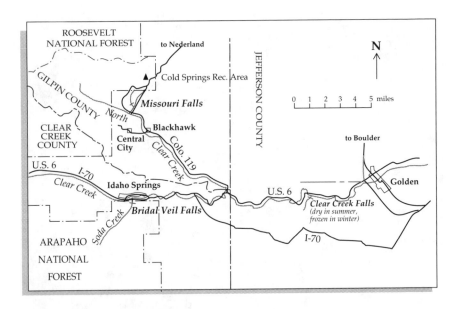

The Denver area group of waterfalls
(**#9** on North and South Platte rivers drainage map, page 57):

Bridal Veil Falls
Missouri Falls
Clear Creek Falls

Bridal Veil Falls

(See Denver Area group map, page 64.)

Access: Roadside
Rating: ★
Type: Horsetail
USGS Topographic Quad: Idaho Springs (39105 F5)
Trail Miles: .1-mile
Altitude: 7,800 feet
Elevation Change: None

Bridal Veil Falls (not to be confused with any of the four other falls in the state with the same name) is visible on the south side of I-70 as you zip through Idaho Springs.

It's easy to get to a more stationary view of the wispy 30-foot horsetail falls. Exit I-70 at the Idaho Springs exit, #241. Drive into town and park near City Hall, right by Clear Creek. There's an old train there for kids to climb on, a trail that crosses under the highway to a viewing point of the waterfall across the creek, and a marker that tells about the waterwheel. The old mill wheel is still spinning, not under the water of the falls, but propelled by another stream on the cliffs to the west.

Missouri Falls

(See Denver Area group map, page 64.)

Access: Walk in
Rating: ★
Type: Tiered
USGS Topographic Quad: Central City
Trail Miles: .1-mile
Altitude: 8,580 feet
Elevation Change: From 8,500 feet, +80 feet

Missouri Falls consists of two small punchbowl falls. The top leap is 5 feet, the bottom 10 feet. The seasonal flow of water is small enough that this falls is sometimes a dribble rather than a plunge. The rock that made the falls is beautifully striated and marbled gneiss turned very red by the water. Missouri Falls is on private land but shows definite signs of much use. Most of the trash is confined to a trash barrel thoughtfully provided by the landowners.

About 1.5 miles past Blackhawk on State Highway 119 there's a dirt road off

to the right that goes up Missouri Creek. About .3-mile from the highway there's
a little shack where a fellow told us he lives in exchange for cleaning up around
the falls. We received permission to see the falls in exchange for help in keeping
it clean. Last time we were there, before gambling was made legal in Central
City and Blackhawk, access hadn't been limited.

Clear Creek Falls *
(See Denver Area group map, page 64.)

Access: Roadside, walk in
Rating: ★ ★ in winter
Type: Serial
USGS Topographic Quad: Squaw Pass
Trail Miles: .12-mile
Altitude: 6,500 feet
Elevation Change: From 6,450 feet, + 50 feet

Clear Creek Falls is not very noticeable if it isn't frozen. We visited it many
years ago and walked up close enough to actually climb into an air pocket
where a natural cave had been formed by the buildup of ice, which extended
a hundred feet down the drainage.

The falls are on the left on the way up Clear Creek Canyon. Head west
4 miles on U.S. 6 out of Golden. Cross Clear Creek on the bridge and pull
over. A trail angles northeast up the slope from the south side of the road.

Boulder Area Waterfalls

There are two waterfalls on the Boulder Creek drainage. One is west of
Boulder and close to State Highway 119. The second is on South Boulder
Creek, west of Eldorado Springs.

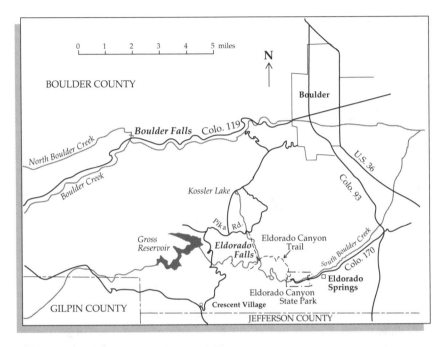

The Boulder area group of waterfalls
(**#10** on North and South Platte rivers drainage map, page 57):

Boulder Falls
Eldorado Falls

Boulder Falls

(See Denver Area group map, page 67.)

Access: Walk in
Rating: ★ ★ ★
Type: Segmented
USGS Topographic Quad: Gold Hill (40105 A4)
Trail Miles: .1-mile
Altitude: 7,050 feet
Elevation Change: From 6,900 feet, + 150 feet

Boulder Falls is just above the confluence of North Boulder Creek and Boulder Creek. It has a total drop of 40 feet amounting to a 20-foot leap and powerful spume splashing into the air. There's a broad rocky space below the falls where tourists sit by the cascades and where rock climbers can be seen rappelling from the cliffs above.

The falls lies in a part of Boulder Canyon called The Narrows, cutting through igneous rock formed 1.7 billion years ago. Middle Boulder Creek has always had more water flowing in it, and its greater eroding strength has cut deeper than North Boulder Creek, creating a hanging tributary valley and Boulder Falls.

Boulder Creek diggings were some of the first manifestations of gold fever in Colorado in the late 1850s. The road from Boulder to Nederland was completed in 1871, and Boulder Falls was famous a century ago as the destination of day-long picnic trips from Boulder City made by wagon before the railroad made its way deeper up Boulder Canyon. Charles G. Buckingham sold the property to Boulder in 1914 for one dollar with the stipulation that it remain a public park.

The waterfall is less than a ten-minute walk from the highway and is therefore very popular. Drive 8 miles west of Boulder on State Highway 119 to the turnout and a decent-sized parking area at the base of the .1-mile trail.

Eldorado Falls*
(See Denver Area group map, page 67.)

Access: Hike
Rating: ★ ★
Type: Cascade
USGS Topographic Quad: Eldorado Springs (39105 H3)
Trail Miles: 4.5
Altitude: 6,450 feet
Elevation Change: From 6,000 feet to about 7,000 feet on trail, + 1,000 feet;
   to falls, -550 feet

Between Boulder and Golden, South Boulder Creek has carved a prominent break in the wall of the foothills at the south end of the Flatirons. Poised here at the entrance of Eldorado Canyon, off Highway 93, 2 miles south of Boulder, is the turn-of-the-century resort town of Eldorado Springs.

The mouth of the canyon beyond the town is private land, but the state of Colorado has created Eldorado Canyon State Park in among the private holdings. A fine trail begins at the end of the public road, Colorado 398, which heads north, uphill from the parking and picnic area and past the first ramparts of the canyon.

The Eldorado trail climbs steep switchbacks up the north side of the canyon and then traverses for a total of 3 miles to a beautiful view of the Indian Peaks and across the top of the foothills. Following the trail another two-thirds of a mile drops you into Eldorado Canyon again, just above the confluence of Woods Gulch and South Boulder Creek.

Eldorado Falls is less than a hundred paces on the other side of South Boulder Creek across a new bridge (built beside a springy, narrow, fun-looking older one) and up a slight slope.

South Boulder Creek makes its way noisily over a great rock pile in three short leaps and a roiling cascade, with a vertical drop of only 17 feet in a 60-foot stretch of water. Since the creek flows from Gross Reservoir, the volume of water is heavy and steady, even in October, and makes a great roar one first hears from the trail high on the other side of the canyon.

A shorter hike would be from the trailhead that is 1 mile to the north on Pike Road (south of the road from Boulder to Gross Reservoir).

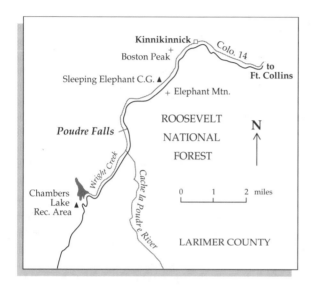

The Cache la Poudre River
(**#11** on North and South Platte rivers drainage map, page 57):

Poudre Falls

The Cache la Poudre River

State Highway 14, which travels the Poudre Canyon from Fort Collins, was originally a trail blazed by William Ashley on his way to a Brown's Park trapper's rendezvous in 1824. It was improved upon by supply trains on their way in 1840 to Fort Davy Crockett. The generally accepted story of the river's name is that a supply train cached gunpowder along the river in 1836 when the wagons got bogged down by snow; but the first recorded use of the name is in 1835, in the journals of Captain John Gannt of the Dodge Expedition. Nevertheless, the Daughters of the American Revolution erected a monument at the location of the supposed cache, near Bellvue.

Poudre Falls
(See map above.)

Access: Walk in
Rating: ★ ★
Type: Tiered
USGS Topographic Quad: Boston Peak (40105 F7)
Trail Miles: .1-mile
Altitude: 8,250 feet
Elevation Change: From 8,350 feet, -100 feet

Poudre Falls is on the Poudre River immediately below State Highway 14, 5 miles northeast of Chambers Lake and 7 miles southwest of Kinnikinnick. A sign on the west side of the road locates the middle of the falls' three separate leaps, which span about a hundred yards altogether.

The first leap is about 15 feet high; the second, 60 yards downstream, is about the same height as the first. The third is the highest, but not by much; its height is difficult to gauge because the gorge is so narrow that it's hard to get any view of it except from directly above.

The entire width of the Poudre at the third leap isn't more than 6 feet. The water has carved a bowl back into the rock and the sound is wonderful, particularly since it's punctuated by the clicking and rumbling of the rocks beating against one another in the plunge pool below the leap.

The falls is right below the highway, but the echoing of the water against the walls wipes the sound of the traffic away almost completely. We visited in October; the water is probably much higher at other times of the year, but at low water the exposed rocks are captivating—jumbled and angular above the riverbed, smooth and rounded where the water has polished them.

Poudre Falls is a rare example of a waterfall on a major river, most of which usually carry so much water they make short work of falls, reducing them to a rapids.

Waterfalls of North Park

The North Platte River originates south of Walden. Only 25 of the river's 618 miles are in Colorado. We know of only two waterfalls in the North Park area: Both originate in the Mount Zirkel Wilderness.

Big Creek Falls

(See North Park group map, page 72.)

Access: Hike
Rating: ★ ★
Type: Segmented
USGS Topographic Quad: Davis Peak (40106 H6)
Trail Miles: 2.5
Altitude: 9,200 feet
Elevation Change: From 9,000 feet, +200 feet

Drive 10 miles north of Walden on State Highway 125 to Cowdrey. Turn left, follow a good dirt road to Pearl for about 17 miles. Turn southwest along the

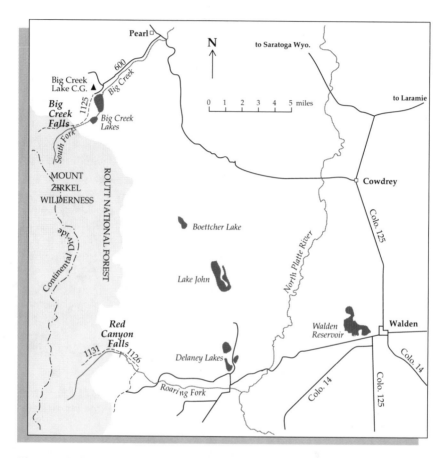

The North Park area group of waterfalls

(**#12** on North and South Platte rivers drainage map, page 57):

Big Creek Falls
Red Canyon Falls

South Fork of Big Creek to the Big Creek Lakes campground. Trails go on either side of the lake, but the most direct route to Big Creek Falls is on the west side of the lake. It's 2.5 miles to the falls and the boundary of the Mount Zirkel Wilderness.

The hike to Big Creek Falls is easy, with only about 500 feet of elevation gain. The falls is at the point where the granites of Mount Zirkel contact the glacial deposits. Great rectangular slabs of the granite illustrate beautifully how the falls cuts its way into the rock; it's almost like a quarry where the tools are ice and water. The falls has small leaps and is more remarkable for its slabs of stone than its flow, although that may be just because we saw it in late October.

If you hike during hunting season, wear something bright orange—the hunters are out in force. We didn't hear much shooting but were told at breakfast in Walden that three moose had been shot "accidentally."

Red Canyon Falls *
(See North Park group map, page 72.)

Access: Hike
Rating: ★ ★
Type: Punchbowl
USGS Topographic Quad: Pitchpine Mountain (40106 F5)
Trail Miles: 3.5
Altitude: 8,500 feet
Elevation Change: From 9,000 feet to 8,800 feet, -200 feet; to 9,200 feet, +400 feet; to 8,300 feet, -900 feet; to falls, +200 feet

Drive west out of Walden south of Delaney Butte and follow the road west into Routt National Forest. Shortly after crossing the forest boundary there's a sign identifying trail 1126, the Grizzly-Helena trail. Follow this trail, which is clear until it meets a dirt road. Walk along this dirt road east (downhill) a few hundred yards to pick up the trail again; or barge north through the trees to a fence line and follow it east to a break in the fence where the trail goes through. The area has been closed to the public long enough that many roads indicated on the topos and national forest map are now just tracks through the grass.

The Grizzly-Helena trail leads 2.5 miles from the entrance road, where you park, through alternating stands of aspen and lodgepole to a ford across the Roaring Fork coming down out of Red Canyon. You can hike up- and downhill

Red Canyon Falls

on a moraine deposited twenty thousand years ago by glaciers that surrounded Mount Zirkel. Red and gray granite cliffs loom to the west. After fording the creek, head upstream a hundred yards or so to the waterfalls.

Red Canyon Falls has a couple of nice leaps with a total drop of about 25 feet. There's a mysterious black plunge pool over 6 feet deep below the first 8-foot leap, and a gorgeous emerald pool at the bottom of the second leap. The area has been camped and visited often in the past but is relatively undisturbed except for the crude black-plastic water diversion to Red Canyon Reservoir downstream from the falls.

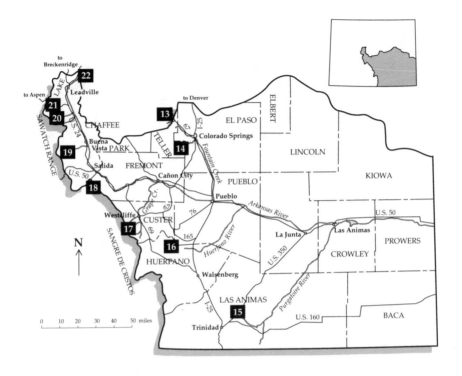

The Arkansas River Drainage Map

13, 14: The Colorado Springs Area Group
15: The Purgatoire River
16: The Wet Mountain Area Group
17, 18: The Rainbow Trail Group
19, 20, 21, 22: The Sawatch Range Group

3

The Arkansas River Drainage

Three hundred and fifteen miles of the Arkansas River flow in Colorado. It drops 5,000 feet in its first 125 miles and leaves the state at its lowest point (3,350 feet) on the Kansas border. The Arkansas originates high in the Sawatch Range, named by the Utes *Saguache*, meaning Blue Land. The Sawatch is the highest and most massive ridge line in the state, running 100 miles from Eagle to south of Monarch Pass, and includes Mount Elbert and Mount Massive, Colorado's two highest peaks.

The Arkansas River drainage contains twenty-five waterfalls, ranging from a world-class waterfall exploited for profit to wilderness waterfalls high in the Sawatch Mountains.

The Colorado Springs Area

Extensive faulting and uplift at the base of Pikes Peak have created ideal conditions for waterfalls. Four are accessible up Cheyenne Canyon, right outside Colorado Springs.

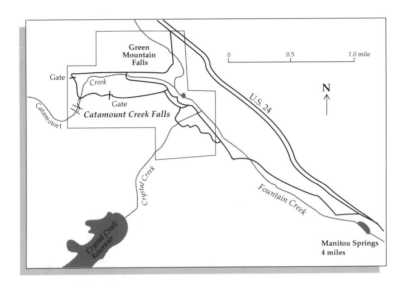

The Colorado Springs area group of waterfalls
(**#13** on Arkansas River drainage map, page 76):

Catamount Creek Falls

Catamount Creek Falls
(See Colorado Springs group map, above.)

Access: Hike
Rating: ★ ★
Type: Cascade
USGS Topographic Quad: Woodland Park (38105 H1)
Trail Miles: .5-mile
Altitude: 8,250 feet
Elevation Change: From 8,050 feet, +200 feet

Green Mountain Falls is the name of an old resort community on U.S. 24 between Manitou Springs and Woodland Park. A town merchant told us that the falls for which the town was named was eliminated when its water was diverted to the Air Force Academy to the north of town.

However, there is still a series of falls on North Catamount Creek in the hills west of town. Both the North and South Green Mountain exits from U.S. 24 (6 miles north of Manitou Springs) lead to Ute Pass Avenue, the main street. Belvedere Avenue intersects Ute Pass Avenue six blocks north of the prominent pond and park in the center of town. Take Belvedere Avenue up the hill to a gate that closes the road to auto traffic. Walk south past this gate on the road .25-mile to a large water tank and bridge, where North Catamount Creek flows under the road. At the north end of the bridge, a trail heads nearly straight uphill along the creek, climbing briskly over rocks and through trees and dense brush. Cascades and small falls extend all along the creek for hundreds of yards, and well-worn side trails lead to several intimate environments. Occasional splashes of surprisingly unobtrusive green paint designate the main trail, which is very steep in its higher reaches, requiring some swinging from root to branch, and is not for the timid.

Seven Falls
(See Colorado Springs group map, page 80.)

Access: Wheelchair
Rating: ★ ★ ★ ★
Type: Tiered
USGS Topographic Quad: Manitou Springs (38104 G8)
Trail Miles: 0
Altitude: 6,800 feet
Elevation Change: + 266 feet to top of falls if you climb the staircase

Seven Falls is the clearest example we've seen yet of a waterfall exploited for profit. You can make your own judgments, but it reminds me of nightmares I've had about waterfalls surrounded by concrete.

If it's any consolation, the Disneyfication of Seven Falls has been going on since at least 1888, when the first wooden steps were installed to allow people to get to it. In the nineteenth century, seeing identifiable shapes in the natural rock formations was a favored sport, and at Seven Falls virtually every rock has a sign telling you what someone thought it resembled. Old newspaper accounts in the gift shop call attention to additional falls up the canyon, but employees at the site didn't know anything about them. Water has been diverted from another stream above the falls to provide a steady flow. In 1992 an elevator shaft was installed in the cliff to allow visitors to ride to the top. There is a steadily rising entrance fee.

The seven falls illustrate different types of horsetail and plunge. Old accounts claim a 750-foot cumulative drop for the seven distinct leaps, but an encyclopedia says 266 feet. Each of the leaps has been given a name, and colored

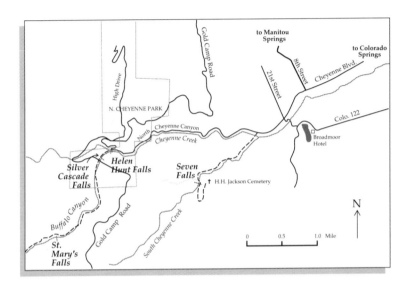

The Colorado Springs area group of waterfalls
(**#14** on Arkansas River drainage map, page 76):

Seven Falls   Silver Cascade Falls
Helen Hunt Falls   St. Mary's Falls

floodlights illuminate the falls at night. You'll see signs advertising the falls all over Colorado Springs. It's the only waterfall in Colorado on a National Geographic list of the world's major waterfalls.

To reach Seven Falls, take I-25 to exit 141 (Manitou Springs), turn left on Eighth Street to Cheyenne Boulevard, then bear right to the turnoff to the falls. You can't miss it for the signs all along the way.

Seven Falls is a well-run commercial operation but almost totally lacks wilderness feeling. There are lots of trout in the ponds below the falls, and you can feed them pellets from vending machines. There's a snack bar in the gift shop. You can climb 185 stairs to view the falls from an adjacent knob (the cable line is not operating due to insurance problems) with another snack bar on top. Or you can climb the 265 steps up the falls past a little asphalt stage reserved for "Indian Dances."

There is a trail 1 mile from the top of the falls that leads to a view of Colorado Springs and the grave of Helen Hunt Jackson. The topmost of the seven falls is named "Ramona," after Jackson's heroine.

Seven Falls

Helen Hunt Falls

Helen Hunt Falls
(See Colorado Springs group map, page 80.)

Access: Roadside
Rating: ★ ★
Type: Segmented
USGS Topographic Quad: Manitou Springs (38104 G8)
Trail Miles: 0
Altitude: 7,300 feet
Elevation Change: None

If you drive up Cheyenne Boulevard beyond the Seven Falls turnoff, you continue into Cheyenne Canyon Park and wind up on a pleasant, steep paved drive to Helen Hunt Falls. It's right by the road, a single 30-foot fall of water down an impressive face of granite. The somewhat conspicuous visitor's information center sells maps, a good selection of guidebooks, and various outdoorsy knickknacks. Youthful attendants in uniform provide information about the many trails in the park.

Children can play in the shallow cascades below the falls. There is a path that leads to stairs above the falls, and some nice cascades a few dozen yards upstream. Hike 200 yards up this steep but well-maintained dirt path above Helen Hunt Falls to Silver Cascade Falls.

Helen Hunt Falls was formerly known and photographed as Ramona Falls, after the character in Hunt's novel by the same name.

Helen Hunt Jackson started writing after being widowed during the Civil War. Since writing novels then was considered "unwomanly," she wrote under the nom de plume Saxe Holm. Her stories were popular, but it was years before the general public discovered that Saxe Holm was Helen Hunt, or H.H. Ralph Waldo Emerson called her the greatest American woman poet.

H.H. contracted tuberculosis and moved to Colorado Springs, where she met and married William S. Jackson, one of Colorado Springs' founders. On a trip to New England, H.H. was stirred by the account of a Ponca chief of the suffering of Indians dispossessed of their lands, and she decided to try to help restore human rights to the Native American. The result of her researches was *A Century of Dishonor*, published in 1881. She sent copies to every U.S. congressman at her own expense.

H.H. was one of the few who protested Colorado's infamous Sand Creek Massacre. She was reviled for her unpopular views, but President Chester A. Arthur appointed her a Commissioner of Indian Affairs. Her observations of the plight of the Indian in Southern California led her to write the novel *Ramona*, which ranked with Stowe's *Uncle Tom's Cabin* as one of the great ethical novels of the nineteenth century.

Silver Cascade Falls
(See Colorado Springs group map, page 80.)

Access: Walk in
Rating: ★ ★
Type: Horsetail
USGS Topographic Quad: Manitou Springs (38104 G8)
Trail Miles: .1-mile
Altitude: 7,600 feet
Elevation Change: +200 feet

You can hike to Silver Cascade Falls on a steep trail from Helen Hunt Falls (see above) or more easily climb down from Gold Camp Road, above, where there is a turnout.

Also known as Spoon Falls, this is a cascade of water sheeting over a long face of smooth granite. In July there is little water flowing down Buffalo Canyon to the falls, which is fed by a different stream than is Helen Hunt Falls.

The water-smoothed rocks around the Silver Cascade are treacherous dry or wet, especially when salted with fine sand. The long roll of rock is probably 200 feet at an angle of nearly forty degrees from the horizontal. An unexpected trip over the cliffs would be extremely unpleasant, and signs wisely suggest staying off the rocks.

Silver Cascade Falls is probably best seen in the spring, when the flow can do more than wet the rock, but there's an overlook at the falls with a nice view of Colorado Springs and the plains beyond Cheyenne Canyon.

St. Mary's Falls
(See Colorado Springs group map, page 80.)

Access: Hike
Rating: ★ ★
Type: Segmented
USGS Topographic Quad: Manitou Springs (38104 G8)
Trail Miles: 2
Altitude: 9,000 feet
Elevation Change: + 1,070 feet

Drive up North Cheyenne Canyon past the Seven Falls turnoff and 2 miles past Helen Hunt Falls (see above) on Forest Road 370. Right through the tunnel there's a trailhead (above Silver Cascade Falls) for trail 624.

This trail follows Buffalo Canyon Creek up its course 1.5 miles to St. Mary's Falls, which is below the impressive face of Stove Mountain. The trail begins at 7,930 feet, and the falls is at 9,000 feet. In July this hike is beautiful, and wildflowers surround the trail. The path is well maintained and easy to follow either to the foot of the falls, or .2-mile farther up to its head. Working directly up the rocks alongside the falls is not recommended for inexperienced climbers.

St. Mary's Falls is a steep, long cascade down a wall of bedrock, spreading out in a series of splashing natural fountains that drop 100 to 120 vertical feet at an angle of seventy degrees from the horizontal. There are beautiful, gentle cascades above the head of the falls.

Nancy and I didn't take the main trail, but we cut off probably half a mile by driving 1.2 miles farther up Forest Road 370 to a turnout where a trail is indicated on the topo map—there are no signs to identify it as such. We made the fairly steep climb up the hill through trees to a saddle (probably not more than 500 vertical feet), then down to the left and across the stream through the woods to meet the main trail. Make sure to mark mentally where this "short-cut" trail comes out at the main trail, or you will certainly miss it on the way down.

The Purgatoire River

In 1528, a Spanish fleet of exploration and conquest wrecked on the U.S. gulf coast. Eight years later, Cabeza de Vaca and three other survivors crawled half-starved into San Miguel de Culiacan, on the Sea of Cortez in Mexico, babbling of a place where gold bells hung in trees and city streets were paved with gold—the Seven Cities of Cibola. Several expeditions were launched by the Spanish to locate and subjugate these fabled cities. One of them, the Coronado expedition of 1840, crossed the Arkansas River, but probably not in Colorado. Another expedition vanished into the canyons of southeast Colorado, leaving behind only a few pieces of rusted armor and the name "El Rio de las Animas Perdidas en Purgatorio." The leadership of this group was assumed by one of its members after he killed his captain, and the accompanying priests refused to go a step farther with a murderer and his followers— the "lost souls in purgatory." The French translation gave the river its present name, the Purgatoire.

You wouldn't expect to find a waterfall in this land of desert canyons, but there is one on Trinchera Creek, tributary to the Purgatoire River.

Trinchera Falls
(See map on page 86.)

Access: Hike
Rating: ★
Type: Punchbowl
USGS Topographic Quad: Trinchera Cave (37104 B1)
Trail Miles: 1.1
Altitude: 5,300 feet
Elevation Change: From 5,590 feet, -290 feet

To get to Trinchera Falls, take U.S. 160/350 east out of Trinidad about 7 miles to the fork where 350 heads to La Junta. Continue on 160 east about

25 miles, cross Trinchera Creek via an old steel bridge to road 127.0, the west entrance to Box CK Ranch. Drive 2 miles north on this road until you come to a road on the right leading to a windmill and a fenced road on the left heading due west, as indicated on the topo map.

Hike about 1 mile on this road west through the juniper-strewn prairie and come to the edge of the canyon/ arroyo of Trinchera Creek. An easy climb down through the rocks leads to the creek. Trinchera Cave is in the wall opposite the end of the trail, across Trinchera Creek. Used by Plains Indians as a rock shelter, it was excavated and backfilled in 1974-76. It's easy to imagine people living along Trinchera Creek. We saw animal tracks in silt on the rocks.

The Purgatoire River
(**#15** on Arkansas River drainage map, page 76):

Trinchera Falls

Following the creek down the canyon over the flat rocks leads to the falls in about an eighth of a mile. It is hidden in the shade of a cluster of boulders.

Trinchera Falls is not more than 10 feet high, but it is the active agent in the creation of a narrow flash-flood-swept canyon in the limestone. The falls has created a plunge pool more than 20 feet deep.

The upper Purgatoire is reminiscent of some places in the Grand Canyon and in the Escalante, a desert in the middle of the high plains over 30 miles from the nearest hills! It's peaceful and isolated and is definitely rattlesnake country.

The Wet Mountain Area

We know of two waterfalls on the east side of the Wet Mountains, southwest of Pueblo. The range's highest peak, 12,234-foot Greenhorn Mountain, is named after the Comanche chieftain Cuerno Verde, defeated by Anza near here in 1779.

Apache Falls

(See Wet Mountain Area group map, this page.)

Access: Hike
Rating: ★ ★
Type: Horsetail
USGS Topographic Quad: Hayden Butte (37104 G8)
Trail Miles: 2.5
Altitude: 8,720 feet
Elevation Change: From 7,200 feet, +1,520 feet

Take the Lascar exit off I-25 (exit 64) and drive west into the foothills below Greenhorn Mountain. The road turns north and dead-ends 8 miles from the interstate at a ranch. A quarter of a mile before the road ends, it crosses Apache Creek and turns uphill past a gate on the left and a no-trespassing sign. Before reaching this posted gate, park on the roadside near the creek and head directly into the brush, following a faint trail, or even the creek. The trail intersects a dirt road going to a rusted metal shack marked on the topo as a mining prospect. Soon you cross through a gated fence and reach the San Isabel National Forest boundary.

Although there is no trail marked beyond this point on the Hayden Butte quad, the national forest map shows trail 1311 continuing up the stream. The national forest map shows the trail turning north after about a mile's hike to meet the Bartlett trail, but we did not notice this turning. The trail to Apache Falls continues through oak, white fir,

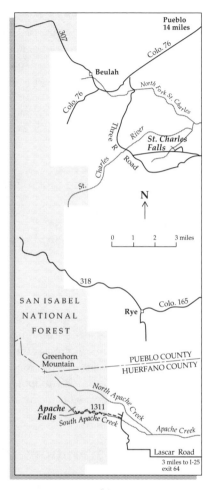

The Wet Mountain area group of waterfalls
(**#16** on Arkansas River drainage map, page 76):

Apache Falls
St. Charles Falls

and aspen along the creek, crossing it ten times after the national forest boundary. After 2.2 miles the creek finally turns north and winds up as a small tributary to Apache Creek, leading directly to Apache Falls in .3-mile or less.

Apache Falls is created by steep granite cliffs at the head of this small tributary, which act as a barrier to further progress upstream. The falls is 102 feet high and in late October was a thin stream spreading and dancing down the rock. When water flow is greater the falls probably plunges much of its height, but there is no plunge pool, so it is possible to get right below the fall of water.

St. Charles Falls *
(See Wet Mountain Area group map, page 87.)

Access: Possibly walk in
Rating and Type: Not visited
USGS Topographic Quad: Beulah (38104 A8)
Trail Miles: Unknown
Altitude: 7,050 feet
Elevation Change: None

This is a falls indicated on the quad as on private land. Drive 18 miles southwest on State Highway 76 from Pueblo, turn south, and follow the road across the St. Charles River. In 4 miles this road passes the Three R Ranch and turns east in another 2 miles to a dirt road leading a quarter-mile to a driveway and ranch across an unnamed tributary to the St. Charles. The falls is .1-mile upstream. Ask permission at the ranch to visit.

Rainbow Trail Waterfalls

There are seven sets of waterfalls on the east face of the Sangre de Cristos. They are all reached from the Rainbow trail, which begins below Music Pass at the southern end of the Grape Creek drainage and traverses the foot of the Sangre de Cristo Range all the way to Salida.

Westcliffe Area

You can reach five waterfalls, or groups of falls, from Westcliffe in the Wet Mountain valley. Westcliffe is 25 miles south of Texas Creek (between Salida and Cañon City on U.S. 50) on State Highway 69, or 50 miles west of Pueblo on Colorado 96.

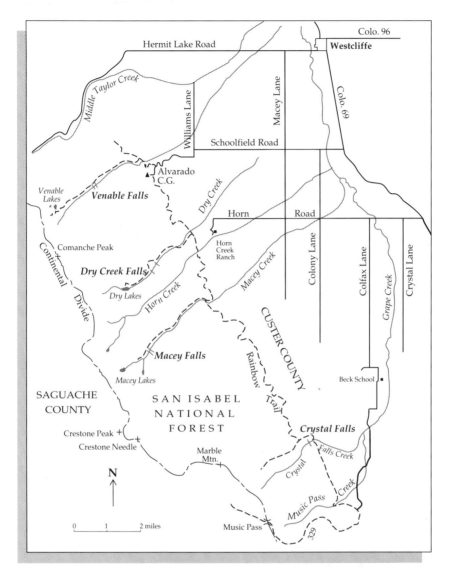

The Rainbow Trail group of waterfalls
(**#17** on Arkansas River drainage map, page 76):

Venable Falls
Dry Creek Falls
Macey Falls
Crystal Falls

Venable Falls

(See Rainbow Trail group map, page 89.)

Access: Hike
Rating: ★ ★
Type: Serial
USGS Topographic Quad: Horn Peak (38105 A5)
Trail Miles: 2.25
Altitude: 11,500 feet
Elevation Change: From 9,050 feet, + 1,450 feet

Venable Falls is a series of long cascades punctuated by its steep passage through shaley dark red stone; there are two main leaps about 100 feet apart, and neither one is more than 15 feet high. The cascade is characterized by steep rocks and the possibility that one can get right down to the water by two or three different approaches.

To reach the falls, drive 3 miles south of Westcliffe on Highway 69. Turn right on Schoolfield Road. At 4.25 miles, turn left, then west again in another .25-mile. Alvarado campground is in the forested hills about 6 miles from the highway.

The Rainbow trail enters the campground at its south end. From the north end, a trail climbs .75-mile to reconnect with the Rainbow trail. The Venable Creek trail begins a short distance to the north.

The hike to the falls heads up the creek through beautiful mixed aspen and spruce. At just over 2 miles the trail makes a sharp switchback, and .1-mile farther a sign points to the left down a spur to Venable Falls.

A series of informal trails parallels the creek on the north side, making it easy to climb from the top of the cascades to the bottom, and there are several viewing points and leaps along the way.

Dry Creek Falls* *

(See Rainbow Trail group map, page 89.)

Access: Hike
Rating: ★ ★
Type: Cascade
USGS Topographic Quad: Horn Peak (38105 A5)
Trail Miles: 2.25
Altitude: 10,800 feet
Elevation Change: From 8,920 feet, + 1,880 feet

Venable Falls

Dry Creek Falls and Macey Falls (see below) are both reached from the Horn Creek Ranch trailhead. Drive 3 miles south of Westcliffe on Colorado 69 and turn right on Schoolfield Road. After 1.75 miles, turn left (south) on Macey Lane. After 2 more miles, turn right (west) on Horn Road. Turn left at Willows Road after 2.25 miles. Drive past the Horn Creek Ranch and go uphill on a road that becomes suitable only for four-wheel-drive vehicles, then ends at a common parking area less than .25-mile from the ranch. Old jeep roads wind up the hill all the way to the Rainbow trail but are blocked to motorized traffic about half a mile below it.

If you're going to Macey Falls, follow the trail closest to the creek, which flows from the southwest. If you're going to Dry Creek, a trail leaving the old road to go directly west is more pleasant hiking than the old road and cuts off .3-mile of hiking back to the north on the Rainbow trail. A sign pointing to the trail says .75-mile, but this shortcut makes it more like .4-mile.

It's another .5-mile to Dry Creek, but the Dry Creek trail starts about an eighth of a mile south of Dry Creek. It's marked only by a blasted tree, a sign advising the Rainbow trail is for horse and foot traffic only, and a perforated metal sign prohibiting motorized vehicles.

The Dry Creek trail is not a good one, and is marked occasionally only by prescription bottles nailed to trees. One crosses Dry Creek and then heads straight up the ridge adjacent to the stream, mostly following what appear to be game trails, climbing 1,400 feet in less than 2 miles. The trail is so faint that at times you might as well be bushwhacking. We came to a level spot on the ridge at about 10,600 feet and saw the upper falls farther up the valley, coming down what looks to be the edge of a cirque between Horn Peak and Little Horn Peak. From there, it was a mile and a half to the upper falls. The lower falls marked on the quad was hidden in the aspen. It was too late in the day for us to approach any closer and still get back to camp while it was light.

Hunters going to Macey Creek said that there is good fishing on the Dry Creek drainage and that it is the roughest trail in the area.

Macey Falls

Macey Falls
(See Rainbow Trail group map, page 89.)

Access: Overnight, but possible as a long day hike
Rating: ★ ★
Type: Serial (cascade and punchbowl)
USGS Topographic Quad: Horn Peak (38105 A5)
Trail Miles: 6
Altitude: 11,100 feet
Elevation Change: From 9,000 feet, +2,100 feet

Drive to Horn Creek Ranch trailhead, described for Dry Creek Falls above. Follow the old jeep road to the Rainbow trail, or take the foot trail that goes toward Horn Creek and then uphill, reaching the Rainbow trail at about the .75-mile mark.

Take the Rainbow trail south over the bridge over Horn Creek. Macey Creek is about 2.7 miles farther along the trail. There's a sign at the creek that says

Macey Lakes is 5 miles, but I think it's mistaken. The falls is more like 2.6 miles up the trail, about .5-mile below the lake. It passes through stunning aspen and fir woods with white fir, Douglas fir, ponderosa pine, Englemann spruce, and even some bristlecone pine down below, as at Dry Creek.

After about 2.25 miles above the Rainbow trail, there is an open area below Copperstain Cliff. The trail then crosses to the left and starts up the rocks very close to the water. You can hear the lower falls there and see the stretch of it a few yards off the trail.

The lower falls is a powerful punchbowl leap of 10 feet into a wild, rocky basin. The upper falls (50 to 60 paces above the lower falls, about 150 feet off the trail) is a twisting 30- to 40-foot cascade into a placid run of water traveling through moss-hung black shale cliffs—not spectacular, but worth stepping off the trail.

Another .5-mile gets you up to Macey Lakes and a view of Mount Adams.

Crystal Falls
(See Rainbow Trail group map, page 89.)

Access: Hike
Rating: ★ ★
Type: Cascade
USGS Topographic Quad: Beck Mountain (37105 H4)
Trail Miles: 3
Altitude: 9,200 feet
Elevation Change: From 9,260 feet, + 140 feet, - 120 feet

Go south on Colorado 69 .4-mile from Westcliffe, and then straight south on Colfax Lane 5.7 miles to a T intersection. Turn left and follow the road south toward Music Pass to a turnout and the beginning of the Rainbow trail.

Crystal Falls is 3 miles up the Rainbow trail, which weaves in and out of spruce and aspen woods with long open stretches overlooking the Wet Mountain valley.

The trail drops down into a copse of aspen and the draw of Crystal Falls Creek. The falls is just a few yards above the trail in a gorgeous moss-hung patch of cliffs that support a large variety of ferns, mosses, and other riparian plants. The dry, cactus-strewn hillsides near the falls are a terrific contrast to the lush green cut of Crystal Falls Creek.

The falls is about 30 feet high and consists of tiered cascades twisting down through the willow and aspen trees over rocks black from water and moss.

Crystal Falls is an easy 3-mile walk—and a good place to make a pleasant halt and consider hiking another 3 miles to Marble Cave.

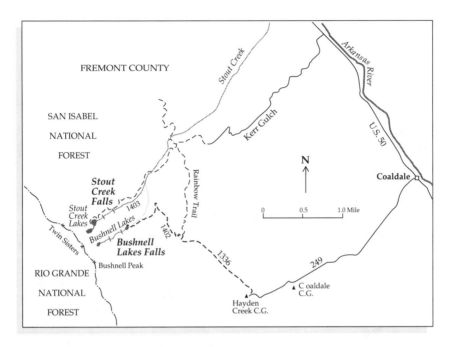

The Rainbow Trail group of waterfalls
(**#18** on Arkansas River drainage map, page 76):

Bushnell Lakes Falls
Stout Creek Falls

Coaldale Area Waterfalls

Two sets of waterfalls off the Rainbow trail are reached from Coaldale, 20 miles south of Salida on U.S. 50. Turn west on Forest Road 249, proceed 4 miles to the Coaldale campground, then another mile to the end of the road at Hayden Creek campground. The Rainbow trail (#1336) starts in the lower portion of the campground, crossing the creek over a good bridge and climbing steeply to the north. A sign says no motorized vehicles over 40 inches wide are allowed.

Bushnell Lakes Falls**
(See Rainbow Trail group map, page 95.)

Access: Overnight
Rating: ★★
Type: Horsetails
USGS Topographic Quad: Bushnell Peak (38105 C8)
Trail Miles: 4.5, 4.75
Altitude: 11,320 feet, 11,600 feet
Elevation Change: From 7,800 feet, +3,520 feet, +3,800 feet

Follow the Rainbow trail 2.5 miles up through aspen and fir to the turnoff to Bushnell Lakes, which are another 2 miles. The trailhead starts at 7,800 feet, so the 3,500-foot climb to the first waterfall (above the lowest of three lakes) is a considerable climb, 1,900 feet of it from when the trail leaves the Rainbow.

After climbing through more aspen, the trail gets very rocky as it turns to the north, but there are good views to the south and at times into the Arkansas valley. There's nowhere to camp until you are off the Rainbow trail and it switches back to the southwest, and there's no ground water until you are almost at the lakes.

When I reconnoitered here in late September it drizzled the whole way up, and the trail turned to mush. By dark I reached near where the trail crosses Bushnell Creek and camped by a limestone outcropping; the ground was uneven and stony, but it was the driest I could find. The lower falls is visible for some distance as the trail drops out of some burnt timber to cross a rocky open stretch, and as you approach you can see the whole bowl of the glacial valley below Bushnell Peak and the southernmost of the "Twin Sisters."

The next morning the sky was clear, and the sun was shining on the snow dusting everything liberally right down to timberline. As the sun threatened to rise and I cooked breakfast, a fog rose in the lower valley and moved up, topping the peaks by the time I'd headed up toward the lake fifteen minutes from my camp.

The lowest of Bushnell Lakes is actually two small lakes, appearing from above like a giant's footprint. Lower Bushnell Falls is a noisy 60- to 70-foot horsetail that rushes down a forty-five-degree slope where gneiss contacts the Leadville limestone from below. The night had frozen my rain fly to the tent, and it took the half-frozen water flow a few hours to get real noisy; the falls was reflected in the stillness of the glacial "footprint" and surrounded by snowy rocks and mountains and rich autumn colors.

I hiked up the snow-covered rock to Upper Bushnell Falls, which is less impressive, just 20 to 30 feet of small leaps through a narrow defile in the rock. The overall setting covered with snow was more interesting.

Stout Creek Falls**
(See Rainbow Trail group map, page 95.)

Access: Overnight
Rating: ★ ★ ★
Type: Horsetail
USGS Topographic Quad: Bushnell Peak (38105 C8)
Trail Miles: 7.5, 8.0
Altitude: 11,200 feet, 11,440 feet
Elevation Change: From 7,800 feet, +3,400 feet, +3,640 feet

Access to Stout Creek Falls is from the Hayden Creek campground (see Bushnell Lakes access, above). Hike on the Rainbow trail past the Bushnell Lakes trail (#1402) 5 miles to the Stout Creek trail (#1403) at 8,800 feet (600 feet below the Bushnell Lakes fork). The waterfalls are straight up Stout Creek 3 miles for 2,800 feet in elevation gain.

I wanted to see both Bushnell Lakes Falls and Stout Creek Falls on the same trip. Starting at Bushnell Lakes, hiking back down to the Rainbow trail and on to Stout Creek and then up that drainage was at least 7.5 miles. The drainages are only a kilometer apart on the map!

I'd thought about bushwhacking to Stout Creek from the upper falls but decided after an hour of perilous step-by-step over rocks covered by snow that discretion would be best served by repairing to camp and fixing my gaiters and putting on a pair of dry socks.

I took a lower route, going down the grassy slopes of the rain forest along Bushnell Creek, skirted a rockfall, and headed back up the Stout Creek drainage, but too soon, for in no time I was stumbling down the steep slopes and encountered limestone cliffs, although I did glimpse Lower Stout Creek Falls along the way. I made my way down the hill, crossed the stream, and climbed through the grass and willows to the falls, which is a very striking 100-foot horsetail, brilliant against the granites and gneisses, surrounded by the limestone cliffs and bathed in radiant fall color. The fog kept playing peekaboo with the sun all day, but it was warm enough to have erased the snow above the lower falls up to timberline. In the sunlight, the Stout Creek valley seemed more open and more colorful in general than Bushnell Creek.

Upper Stout Creek Falls is a few minutes above the lower falls through the tundra, a broad stepped horsetail 30 to 40 feet high.

The tundra above the lower falls was rich with color in late September, and I was tempted to go on above the upper falls for a view of the lakes and the Twin Sisters at the same time, but the fog was rolling back in, hinting that I go back to camp.

I followed the trail down the valley a little too far, almost to the confluence of Bushnell and Stout creeks. I entered the woods, crossed the creeks, and would have headed off totally wrong, except that I checked my compass and realized I was starting east instead of north toward my camp on Bushnell Creek.

The hike uphill through the woods seemed interminable, especially since I didn't know for sure whether I was actually in the right drainage until I came out onto the rocks about .25-mile from camp. The woods are lush, wet, and mossy but easily passed through for the most part by way of game trails. Finding your way with a compass through the woods with no landmarks to sight by certainly gives you an appreciation for a well-established trail. I would actively discourage bushwhacking without a compass in this terrain.

It appears that Stout Creek can be reached directly via the Kerr Gulch road 3.6 miles north of Coaldale and across BLM land to within 2.5 miles of the lower falls. Kerr Gulch, if it's passable, could also provide access to the Bushnell Lakes trail at no greater distance than from Hayden Creek.

The Sawatch Range

The spine of the Sawatch twists from Eagle nearly to Saguache, where its tail fans into the Cochetopa Hills. If its head is the Holy Cross area (described in Chapter 7), then its upper torso is the Collegiate Peaks Wilderness and its lower torso is the cluster of 14,000-foot peaks, including Mount Princeton (not in the Collegiate Peaks Wilderness), Mount Antero, and Mount Shavano.

The Sawatch and Mosquito ranges were formed by the uplift of a single enormous domelike anticline with a slight sag in the middle. The Arkansas River valley splits the two ranges topographically.

Repeated faulting and igneous activity are evidenced by Princeton Hot Springs and Poncha Springs, where water bubbles up through the fissures and cracks. Similar geothermal activity is responsible for the deposition of all the precious minerals that were so sought after in the 1800s up and down the range.

The Southern Sawatch—Buena Vista to Salida

As we describe the waterfalls of the Sawatch, we'll move up the Arkansas River to its headwaters, following the footsteps of "The Great Pathfinder."

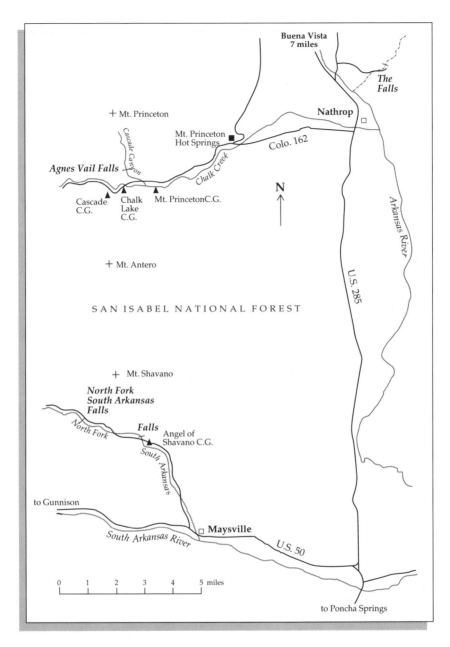

The Sawatch Range group of waterfalls
(**#19** on Arkansas River drainage map, page 76):

North Fork of the South Arkansas Falls
Agnes Vail Falls
The Falls

But not too closely, we hope, since Fremont had a rather notable failure later in his career (see page 118).

North Fork of the South Arkansas Falls* *
(See Sawatch Range group map, page 99.)

Access: Bushwhack
Rating: ★
Type: Horsetail
USGS Topographic Quad: Garfield (38106 E3)
Trail Miles: .03-mile
Altitude: 10,200 feet
Elevation Change: None

Drive to Maysville, 7 miles west of Poncha Springs on U.S. 50. Turn north (right) up Forest Road 240. Drive 4 miles to the Angel of Shavano campground. A quarter of a mile beyond the campground the road crosses the North Fork of the South Arkansas, and we're told that there is a nice falls up the creek a little from this crossing.

A waterfall is indicated on the Garfield quad another 2.2 miles farther upstream. This is created by the North Fork of the South Arkansas flowing over a rounded block of granite and sliding 10 feet or so into the creek. The drop of the falls is buttressed by pink cliffs about 30 feet high.

The falls is 20 or 30 yards north of the road, and there are no signs to assist in locating it. Try to note where the road comes close to the creek, running level with it, 2 miles from the campground. The road leaves the stream to climb the rocks, then comes back to the stream again, running more swiftly as it approaches the falls.

The road to the falls is paved nearly halfway, and though it's rough at times, it does not require four-wheel-drive.

North Fork of the South Arkansas Falls

Agnes Vail Falls

(See Sawatch Range group map, page 99.)

Access: Hike
Rating: ★ ★
Type: Segmented
USGS Topographic Quad: Mount Antero (38106 F2)
Trail Miles: .5-mile
Altitude: 9,300 feet
Elevation Change: From 8,715 feet, +585 feet

Drive 8 miles south of Buena Vista (6 miles from the intersection of U.S. 24 and U.S. 285) on U.S. 285 to Nathrop. About .3-mile south of Nathrop, turn west on County Road 162 past Mount Princeton Hot Springs, between Mount Princeton and Mount Antero.

There's a turnout opposite Chalk Creek campground about 9 miles from U.S. 50. Take the trail going straight north from the turnout up into Cascade Canyon .5-mile to Agnes Vail Falls.

Even in late October the stream has a decent little flow, and the showers and slides angling 75 feet down the cliff are captivating.

The surrounding chalky cliffs are very sheer and the rock is rotten, but it's easy to get higher on the wall for a nice view of the falls. The area is well used in summer. The falls' gorge gets sunlight only in the middle hours of the day, when the sun is directly south.

Agnes Vail was the name of a famous Colorado mountaineer who died on Longs Peak during a technical climb.

There is also a long cascade on Chalk Creek marked on the quad just west of the trailhead, but a view can be obtained only by trespassing on private property and sliding down a very steep streambed wall.

The Falls

(See Sawatch Range group map, page 99.)

Access: Walk in
Rating: None
Type: Dry
USGS Topographic Quad: Buena Vista East (38106 G1)
Trail Miles: .1-mile
Altitude: 8,000 feet
Elevation Change: None

We visited The Falls twice, and it was bone dry both times. Water has been diverted from Arnold Gulch, above, so the name is purely ironic, now and in perpetuity, even though many maps identify it prominently.

A mile and a half north of Nathrop on U.S. 285, there is a group of cabins and signs associated with rafting outfitters, and a turn onto Chaffee County Road 300. Drive across the bridge and turn right onto County 301, then take the second left turn into a blind canyon. There's a gulch cutting uphill to the left, near hills used for target practice, the designated location of The Falls.

The Middle Sawatch and Collegiate Peaks Wilderness

Two hundred and fifty square miles in the center of the Sawatch Range were designated the Collegiate Peaks Wilderness in 1980. The awesome view of the Sawatch from U.S. 285 as you approach Buena Vista from Trout Creek Pass is one of the state's grandest, most memorable mountain vistas, dominated by Mount Princeton. Look northwest across the Arkansas and you can easily pick out the remaining Collegiate Peaks—Mount Yale, Mount Harvard, Mount Columbia, and Mount Oxford—all over 14,000 feet. Three other fourteeners are in the wilderness area: Mount Belford, Missouri Mountain, and Huron Peak.

Three of the four waterfalls in the Collegiate Peaks are inside the wilderness boundary. Only one can be seen from a road, two require trail hikes greater than 4 miles, and one is a quarter-mile bushwhack. We'll describe them in order by access from U.S. 24, south to north, moving toward Leadville and the headwaters of the Arkansas.

Bedrock Falls

(See Sawatch Range group map, page 104.)

Access: Overnight
Rating: ★ ★
Type: Cascade
USGS Topographic Quad: Mount Harvard (38106 H3)
Trail Miles: 8
Altitude: 11,200 feet
Elevation Change: From 8,960 feet, +2,240 feet

Bedrock Falls is a series of broad slides over granite sparkling in the sunlight, and it provides a pleasant setting for a rest and a snack. Unfortunately, it takes 8 miles of hiking to get to, so it should be a *light* snack.

Drive to the settlement of Princeton, 18 miles north of Buena Vista on U.S. 24,

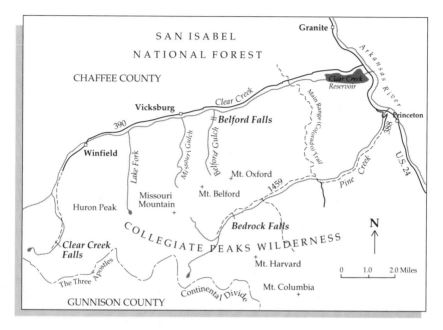

The Sawatch Range group of waterfalls
(**#20** on Arkansas River drainage map, page 76):

Bedrock Falls
Belford Falls
Clear Creek Falls

4 miles south of Granite. Drive west up Forest Road 388 to a gate at the Pine Creek trailhead about .25-mile from the highway.

The Pine Creek trail follows a road for 2 miles, then climbs up the drainage into some mixed lodgepole and aspen woods. In another 1.5 miles it intersects the Colorado Trail and crosses Pine Creek into a long, level valley and proceeds another mile before coming to H. Littlejohn's cabins at the foot of Mount Harvard.

The cabins were built in 1881. Littlejohn took over the claim in the 1920s and lived there, mining bismuth and trapping bobcats until he died in 1951. His cabins were named in the National Register of Historic Places in 1978.

The cabin is boarded up, but the mule barn and the forge across the creek, at the foot of the trail to Mount Harvard, are still open and usable for shelter. Someone graciously left a hammock in Littlejohn's yard, and you can grab a wink or two in between hiking groups.

Another mile up Pine Creek from the cabins is Bedrock Falls, right by the trail. It consists of a shallow dancing slope of water over granite boulders, and slides across 60 feet with a drop of maybe 20 feet, unremarkable as a destination in itself. The valley above the falls, with its views of Oxford, Belford, and Harvard, is spectacular.

I was impressed by the ruin of a large bristlecone pine and its progeny about .5-mile downstream from Littlejohn's place, isolated in a valley otherwise rimmed with spruce and lodgepole pines.

Belford Falls

(See Sawatch Range group map, page 104.)

Access: Roadside or bushwhack
Rating: ★
Type: Segmented
USGS Topographic Quad: Mount Harvard (38106 H3)
Trail Miles: .5-mile bushwhack
Altitude: 9,600 feet
Elevation Change: Road is at 9,400 feet

Belford Falls can easily be seen from Forest Road 390, 6 miles west of Clear Creek Reservoir. It's a long, steep cascade down the hillside, including what appears to be a 30-foot main leap, surrounded by deep woods. A hike closer might be fun, but you'd have to cross Clear Creek's marshes.

To see the falls, drive 1.5 miles south of Granite on U.S. 24 and turn west, taking 390 past Clear Creek Reservoir toward the old mining settlements of Vicksburg, Rockdale, and Winfield. If you wish to see more of the Collegiate Peaks Wilderness than is possible from a car, drive on to Winfield to reach the trail up the valley of the Three Apostles.

Clear Creek Falls*
(See Sawatch Range group map, page 104.)

Access: Hike
Rating: ★
Type: Plunge
USGS Topographic Quad: Winfield (38106 H4)
Trail Miles: 4.25
Altitude: 11,200 feet
Elevation Change: From 10,600 feet (at Banker Mine), +600 feet

Clear Creek Falls is on an unnamed tributary to the South Fork of Clear Creek. It's an unremarkable 10-foot plunge partly hidden from the trail by deep woods, but the trail to Lake Ann takes you into the valley of the Three Apostles, the center of which is Ice Peak (13,951 feet).

Drive west on 390 from Clear Creek Reservoir, 1.5 miles south of Granite on U.S. 24. It's 11 miles of well-graded road to Winfield, a half-mile to the beginning of a gravel four-wheel-drive section. Banker Mine is 1.6 miles from Winfield; a gate marking the Collegiate Peaks Wilderness boundary is a half-mile farther. It's about 2.5 miles from the mine to the falls.

Snyder Falls
(See Sawatch Range group map, page 107.)

Access: Bushwhack
Rating: ★ ★
Type: Punchbowl
USGS Topographic Quad: Mount Elbert (39106 A4)
Trail Miles: .25-mile
Altitude: 9,710 feet
Elevation Change: From 9,760 feet, −50 feet

Snyder Falls is a beautiful 15-foot aquamarine plunge hidden deep in flat, stream-scoured sandstones. The rocks channel the entire flow of water into a cut 6 feet wide, then drop it into a deep aqua-colored pool that takes a few turns and then spreads out onto shallow cascades. The sandstone is bright orange and creates wonderful flat surfaces to walk (or lounge) around on.

Two miles north of Granite on U.S. 24 and 13 miles south of Leadville, State Highway 82 goes west to Independence Pass and Aspen. The highway

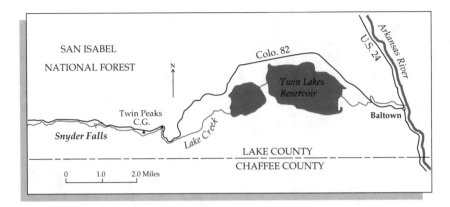

The Sawatch Range group of waterfalls
(**#21** on Arkansas River drainage map, page 76):

Snyder Falls

goes past Twin Lakes to Parry Peak and Twin Peaks campgrounds. The highway gets very close to Lake Creek .8-mile beyond Twin Peaks campground, then starts climbing. On this slope, there's a turnaround overlooking the creek. Park here.

There is no trail to the falls to speak of. You have to bushwhack downhill through fallen timber. Follow the course of the creek upstream as best you can through woods strewn with logs felled by beavers in the marsh between the river and the road.

I'm sure that there are times when high water would prevent, or at least recommend against, trying to reach Snyder Falls. We visited in October, lingering as a full moon rose over the purple haze concealing Independence Pass. Unfortunately, we stayed too long, and when exploring for a shortcut to the road at twilight, I stepped up to my waist into a beaver pond, thinking its yellow leaf-strewn surface solid ground. I might have disappeared completely except for grabbing a tree in my fear of being unearthed—in perfect condition—a thousand years hence by archaeologists.

Snyder Falls

The Headwaters of the Arkansas

The Arkansas River rises in the Sawatch Range north and west of Leadville from the drainages of Tennessee Creek, Halfmoon Creek, and the East Fork of the Arkansas. The East Fork curls up just below Fremont Pass, named for the famous explorer who led a government expedition in 1845 up the Arkansas, over the pass, and on to California.

The city of Leadville, 2 miles above sea level, was founded in 1877, and in two years was the second largest city in the state. Placer gold-mining claims had been worked in the area from 1860. The Leadville boom began in 1878, when Horace Tabor grubstaked George Hook and August Rische and they found the Little Pittsburg in the great ore body beneath Fryer Hill. The population of Leadville grew from 200 in 1877 to 5,000 in 1878 to 14,820 in 1880. Silver-mining was its main focus until the crash of 1893, which sent Horace and his wife, Baby Doe, spinning into legend.

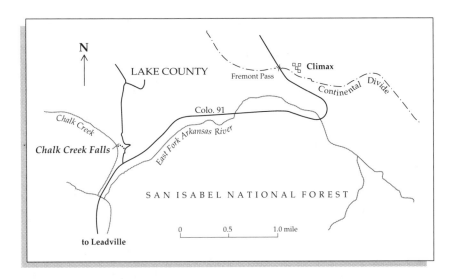

The Sawatch Range group of waterfalls
(**#22** on Arkansas River drainage map, page 76):

Chalk Creek Falls

Chalk Creek Falls*
(See Sawatch Range group map, above.)

Access: Walk in
Rating: ★ ★
Type: Plunge
USGS Topographic Quad: Climax (39106 C2)
Trail Miles: .125-mile
Altitude: 10,800 feet
Elevation Change: None

Cars whiz down the straight side of the hairpin just below Fremont Pass, glad to escape the spectacle of the molybdenum mountain that Climax ate. But there is a waterfall hiding out of sight less than a quarter-mile off the road.

It was late April when we visited, and there was still plenty of snow just below 11,000 feet. We worked our way up the drainage using islands of dry ground where the trees had kept the snow from piling up. But there was a level and dry route, of course, following the 10,800-foot contour to the falls from where Chalk Creek crosses under the highway. As usual, we went up the hard way to find out what the easy way is.

On the Climax quad there's a road heading north 3 miles below Fremont Pass. A hundred yards up this road, head straight west into a break in the rocks on the east side of Chalk Creek. Walking through this break you will come to the lip of a hollow carved by Chalk Creek as it hooks to the south. Chalk Creek Falls is high on this bend.

When we saw it, Chalk Creek Falls was a 35-foot leap pounding through an inverted cone of ice onto sandstone. The falls was like a gravity hammer beating inside the cone of ice. The creek eats at the upthrust cliff, saws into it, and creeps farther around the corner, the better to be hidden from the road.

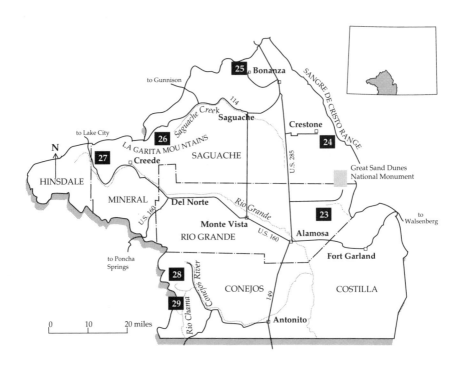

The Rio Grande River Drainage Map

23, 24: The Sand Dunes Area
25, 26: The Cochetopa Hills Area
27: North of Creede
28, 29: The South San Juan Wilderness Area Group

4

The Rio Grande River Drainage

Over a third of the 7,700-square-mile Rio Grande drainage doesn't flow openly into the Rio Grande at all. Snowmelt from the San Juans to the west, the Cochetopa Hills to the north, and the Sangre de Cristos to the east flows into aquifers underlying the north end of the San Luis Valley. Eighty miles wide and a hundred miles long, the San Luis Valley is thought to be a great depression created by the Rio Grande Rift, a gigantic crack deep in the earth's crust caused by continental drift. As the valley sank, the volcanoes of the San Juans tipped their hats in response. Volcanic ash and debris blocked the water's exit from the valley, resulting in over 13,000 feet of sand and gravel deposited in the basin. If the gravels were removed, the hole would be twice as deep as the surrounding mountains are high. The rift and subsequent mountain-building shaped a container and lined it with sand; the mountains on all sides filled it with snowmelt, creating artesian springs.

The Rio Grande basin contains twenty waterfalls. Our descriptions will follow the rim of the valley counterclockwise, starting near the Sand Dunes, moving north into the Sangre de Cristos, west to the Cochetopa Hills, to the La Garita Mountains, then south down the Continental Divide to the South San Juan Wilderness and the Rio Chama.

113

The Sand Dunes Area

As the last ice age came to a close twenty thousand years ago, the glaciers encircling the Sangre de Cristo and San Juan mountains began to melt. As the climate got drier, the valley floor dried up and the Sand Dunes developed, nestling below Mosca, Medano, and Music passes on the west side of the Sangre de Cristos. Winds funneling over these passes drop tons of fine sand carried across the Rio Grande valley from the west. The dunes now cover 40 square miles and reach heights up to 800 feet. Zebulon Pike recorded seeing the dunes when he stumbled over Medano Pass into the valley in the winter of 1806. He built a substantial stockade on the Conejos River complete with a moat and 12-foot-high walls while waiting for the Spanish to come and arrest him.

Zapata Falls

(See Sand Dunes Area group map, page 115.)

Access: Hike
Rating: ★ ★
Type: Serial
USGS Topographic Quad: Twin Peaks (37105 E5)
Trail Miles: 2
Altitude: 9,400 feet
Elevation Change: From 7,800 feet at highway, +1,600 feet

Zapata Falls is hidden deep in a limestone cleft and tumbles noisily down several hundred feet to a couple of 15- to 25-foot leaps. Its upper reaches are difficult to see without actually climbing into the cleft, but you can peer down into it from precarious moss-lined perches along the trail. At its base you can clamber up a short wall and walk through the water right into the *sanctum sanctorum:* the final leap and a sheet of ice creating a stone icebox.

There are ranch roads that reach the falls, and a jeep trail, which is on land owned by the state or the BLM, is indicated all the way to Zapata Falls. Other trails and roads up to the falls or up its drainage are on land owned by the Zapata Ranch, and no trespassing signs are in abundance.

According to a BLM newsletter, a recreation area highlighting the falls is being developed, but a phone call to the San Luis Valley Information Center produced only a suggestion to check for directions at the Great Sand Dunes Golf Course or at the Zapata Ranch headquarters for more specific directions.

We took a four-wheel-drive road on BLM land past the radio towers visible from Highway 150 about 10.4 miles north of U.S. 160. We drove 3 miles on the four-wheel-drive road and then parked and plunged directly east into the piñon forest, finding an old campsite and the beginning of a relatively clear trail that got better closer to the falls. It climbs over a ridge and joins trail 852 (marked on the Rio Grande National Forest map and on a sign near the falls). Trail 852 leads down to Zapata Falls by way of a steep but negotiable trail.

When we left the falls, we retraced our steps to the old

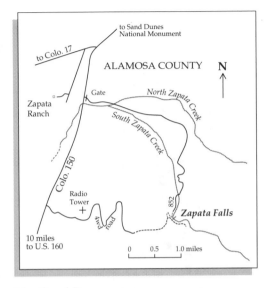

The Sand Dunes area
(**#23** on Rio Grande River drainage map, page 112):

Zapata Falls

campsite and headed into the woods to the cruiser, but we went off in the wrong direction and got lost. There were no landmarks visible until we sighted the radio towers and realized how far off our course we'd gone. We finally found our road almost 1.5 miles *below* the truck, after snaking all over the hill.

¡Estupido! We should have taken bearings when we left our vehicle, instead of trying to surmise them later. California Peak would make a good reference point. Knowing which direction is north helps.

Zapata Falls

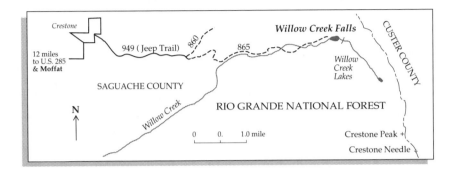

The Sand Dunes area
(**#24** on Rio Grande River drainage map, page 112):

Willow Creek Falls

Willow Creek Falls
(See Sand Dunes Area group map, above.)

Access: Hike
Rating and Type: Not visited
USGS Topographic Quad: Crestone Peak (37105 H5)
Trail Miles: 5
Altitude: 11,600 feet
Elevation Change: From 8,080 feet, +3,520 feet

Willow Creek Falls is a 30- to 40-foot leap on the creek entering the lower Willow Creek lake. Drive to Crestone, 12 miles west of Moffat. A dirt road leaves the southeast end of Crestone half a mile to the Rio Grande National Forest boundary. Trail 949 starts at the boundary at 8,080 feet, crosses South Crestone Creek in 1.5 miles and over 800 feet of elevation gain. The trail forks here: Trail 860 heads up South Crestone Creek; trail 865 crosses to the Willow Creek drainage in a mile (and another vertical 800 feet), then follows the creek another 2.5 miles to the lake and falls in the basin between Kit Carson Peak (14,165 feet) and Mount Adams (13,391 feet).

The Cochetopa Hills Area

The basalts and andesites that underlie the Cochetopa Hills were deposited near the beginning of the volcanic activity that created the San Juans. The granites and gneisses of the Sawatch Range to the north predate the hills by a billion years. Cochetopa Pass at 10,067 feet provides a route from the San Luis Valley into the drainage of the Gunnison.

John C. Fremont's 1848 expedition that conducted an unofficial search for a railroad route across Colorado attempted to leave the San Luis Valley via the much higher San Juans. An amusing all-mule menu describes that year's Christmas dinner, but Fremont's overestimation of his expertise cost the lives of eleven men and a hundred animals. Fremont had to retreat south to Taos, and the remainder of his party was saved by the assistance of some friendly Indians and four horses. More men were lost when they attempted to recover the scientific equipment that had been left behind.

Fremont's later, 1853 expedition meekly followed John Gunnison's path across the state, leaving the San Luis Valley successfully in winter by way of Cochetopa Pass.

Antora Creek Falls*
(See Cochetopa Hills Area group map, page 119.)

Access: Hike and bushwhack
Rating and Type: Visited, but falls hidden under snow
USGS Topographic Quad: Bonanza (38106 C2)
Trail Miles: 2
Altitude: 11,600 feet
Elevation Change: From 10,600 feet, + 1,000 feet

Antora Creek flows from the base of Antora Peak (13,269 feet) into Brewery Creek, which flows into Kerber Creek, which in turn flows into San Luis Creek, which empties into the aquifers of the northern San Luis Valley.

Drive west out of Villa Grove 12 miles on LL56 toward the old mining community of Bonanza. Take a left turn onto road 46PP, which climbs 1.5 miles before crossing the Slaughterhouse Creek drainage, then proceeds another 1.25 miles, where there's a clear dirt road up to the left (west). This twists its way in a mile to the Antora Creek drainage, and travel here is not recommended without four-wheel-drive. A much fainter dirt track leaves this four-wheel-drive road after 150 yards, cutting west to the creek about .8-mile higher on the drainage—good for hiking but impassable even with four-wheel-drive.

When we visited in late May the ground was still patchy with snow above 10,200 feet, and a trail was not in evidence near the creek. We finally resorted to climbing out of the drainage up the south-facing slope to get out of the snow and were able to get into walkable snow at about 11,000 feet. There were many noisy cascades along the way, the water shooting out from underneath pads of ice. The falls indicated on the map was still buried under 3 to 4 feet of snow. The stillness below the Continental Divide is wonderful here, but if you visit in early spring, take a lunch, wear your gaiters, and waterproof your boots.

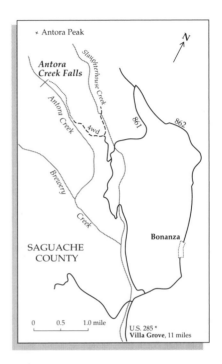

The Cochetopa Hills area
(**#25** on Rio Grande River drainage map, page 112):

Antora Creek Falls

The Cochetopa Hills area
(**#26** on Rio Grande River drainage map, page 112):

Saguache Falls

Saguache Falls

(See Cochetopa Hills Area group map, page 120.)

Access: Hike
Rating: ★ ★
Type: Fan
USGS Topographic Quad: Halfmoon Pass (37106 H7)
Trail Miles: 4.5
Altitude: 10,760 feet
Elevation Change: From 10,060 feet, +700 feet

Although Saguache Creek is in the Rio Grande drainage, to get to Saguache Falls you must cross over the Continental Divide from the Gunnison drainage, 8 miles south of Cochetopa Pass.

State Highway 114 crosses the Cochetopa Hills via North Pass 41 miles from Gunnison and 37 miles from Saguache. Five miles northwest of North Pass, head south from Colorado 114 to meet Forest Road 750—the Cochetopa Pass road. Drive .8-mile east toward Cochetopa Pass, then turn south on Forest Road 787. (If you would like to follow Fremont's route from Saguache, your turn south will be 5 miles west of Cochetopa Pass on 750.)

Drive 13 miles, nearly to the Stone Cellar campground. Just beyond the grave marker of one Private Jacob Sattler (died 1881, no explanation given), leave the road to the campground and drive southwest up the Middle Fork of Saguache Creek, 5.5 miles on occasionally good dirt road (a high clearance or four-wheel-drive vehicle is recommended) to the hillside trailhead.

Trail 744 drops off the hill and down to the streambed, where the ground is marshy. You must ford the creek, though rock-hopping shortens time in the water. The trail follows Middle Saguache Creek upstream, providing broad views of the La Garitas and the Continental Divide.

At 4.5 miles, topping a brief climb, trail 744 comes to within 20 to 30 yards of the limestone cliffs cut deeply by the creek, creating Saguache Falls just above the confluence of the Middle Fork and Benito Creek. The 100-foot wall of rock blocks the valley, and Benito comes down as a long cascade into a lush greensward of fern and cinquefoil. Saguache Falls is a 50-foot fan that is 30 feet wide at the bottom, where it flows into a plunge pool. Broad stone platforms across the falls provide sublime views in every direction.

There is quite a nest of roads honeycombing these hills—a Rio Grande National Forest map will be helpful to anyone trying to navigate this area.

North of Creede

Creede was a late entry in the annals of Colorado mining. In 1891 Nicholas Creede discovered the Amethyst lode in the narrow canyons where the San Juans and the La Garita Mountains press close together, and the area produced 5 million ounces of silver in 1892 alone. The glory was short-lived, however. Silver prices had been falling since 1873, when the government stopped minting dollars out of it. The mints of India closed in June of 1893, staggering communities around the world dependent on silver for their prosperity. The Panic of 1893 ensued.

Unlike many other boomtowns, Creede survived. It was well situated in the Rio Grande valley, serving as a conduit carrying miners and their supplies over Stony Pass to Silverton. The upper Rio Grande proved hospitable to settlers, and the mines produced lead, zinc, and gold as well as silver.

The highway to Creede loops over the top of the caldera of a collapsed volcano. West of Creede, a huge down-dropped block 20 miles long and 4 wide has created a broad valley, which the Rio Grande, entering from the west, meanders through. In the midst of this valley, extensive faulting, from the collapse of the Creede volcano, has resulted in sudden sharp increases of stream grade and, as a consequence, waterfalls. There is a cluster of four falls on North and South Clear creeks, 20 to 23 miles west of Creede on Colorado Highway 149. We'll describe them as you approach them from Creede.

Lower South and Lower North Clear Creek Falls * *
(See North of Creede group map, page 123.)

Access: Walk in
Rating: ★ ★
Type: Horsetail and tiered
USGS Topographic Quad: Hermit Lakes (37107 G2)
Trail Miles: .05-mile
Altitude: 9,420 feet, 9,390 feet
Elevation Change: From 9,490 feet, -70 feet, -100 feet

These waterfalls are at the junction of South Clear Creek and North Clear Creek. There are actually three separate leaps on South Clear Creek between 10 and 30 feet high.

The hike to the falls is only a few hundred feet beyond the end loop of South Clear Creek campground, about 21 miles from Creede on State Highway 149.

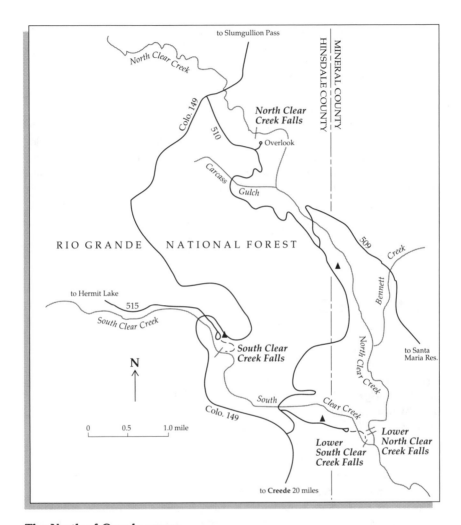

The North of Creede group
(**#27** on Rio Grande River drainage map, page 112):

Lower South and Lower North Clear Creek Falls
South Clear Creek Falls
North Clear Creek Falls

In mid-May, when we visited, the campground was closed, and it required an easy half-mile walk past the campground entrance to reach the trail to the falls. This trail leaves the end of the campground loop, heads downhill, crosses South Clear Creek and then a little piece of marshy ground on a plank footbridge. When the trail forks, the right fork leads south 10 or 20 yards to Lower South Clear Creek Falls. The steep hillside at its head makes it hard to see the water any way except from directly above. South Clear Creek takes a short leap of 15 feet, then cascades a hundred feet or more to join North Clear Creek.

The left fork in the trail takes you to the lip of the chasm overlooking North Clear Creek. You have to climb down the rocks to a level where a little cul-de-sac in the cliffs overlooks the main leap, which is close to 30 feet. The sheer depth of the canyon heightens the noise and makes it seem very profound. While I photographed the water and tried to reach a perilous viewpoint, it started to snow.

There are three additional leaps a short distance up the canyon.

South Clear Creek Falls
(See North of Creede group map, page 123.)

Access: Walk in
Rating: ★ ★ ⸜
Type: Plunge
USGS Topographic Quad: Hermit Lakes (37107 G2)
Trail Miles: .2-mile
Altitude: 9,650 feet
Elevation Change: From 9,720 feet, -40 feet

The turnoff to South Clear Creek campground is 2 miles north of the falls described above, on State Highway 149, 23 miles from Creede. A trail begins at the campground and is marked by a sign. It goes over a hill and down a stairs to provide nice views from above and at the base of South Clear Creek Falls, only five minutes and .2-mile from the parking area.

The falls is a clean 60-foot leap from the edge of the sand-colored tuff amphitheater to boulders below. The surroundings are trail-marked, but not too badly, and it's possible to get right up to the water as it spreads over the rock at the foot of the falls.

North Clear Creek Falls
(See North of Creede group map, page 123.)

Access: Wheelchair
Rating: ★ ★ ★ ★
Type: Segmented
USGS Topographic Quad: Hermit Lakes (37107 G2)
Trail Miles: 0
Altitude: 10,000 feet
Elevation Change: None

About 4.5 miles north of South Clear Creek Falls on State Highway 149, Forest Road 510 heads south .8-mile to a turnoff for a viewpoint overlooking North Clear Creek Falls. This and the other Clear Creek waterfalls mark the southern edge of the volcanic tuffs of the main San Juan volcanic sequence.

The lip of the canyon on the south side of the creek has a fenced viewing area, and it's possible to walk around on the rocks to the head of the falls.

North Clear Creek Falls is a real stunner dramatized by the flat serenity of the marshland above. North Clear Creek comes suddenly to a split in the earth and pounds its way a hundred feet down into the chasm on its way to the Rio Grande. The surrounding cliffs provide open views from several directions, and you can see the San Juans to the west over the head of the falls.

Staring all that water in the face for a couple of days in a row is like staring into the blind eyes of eternity. It is unsettling to see everything as transient, unfixed, flowing. There were times when it seemed the rock was flowing and the only things steady were a column of white water and its standing wave.

The South San Juan Wilderness Area

In 1952, the last Colorado grizzly was reportedly killed near the Rio Grande Pyramids in the Weminuche Wilderness. In 1979, the last Colorado grizzly was killed (again) by a guide, who said he was defending himself, with a hand-held arrow, this time in the South San Juan Wilderness near the headwaters of the Navajo River.

The Navajo is in the San Juan basin and flows to the Colorado in Utah. The Rio Chama is the next drainage east, on the other side of the Continental Divide. It meets the Rio Grande north of Santa Fe.

The southern San Juans are several thousands of feet lower than the peaks around Silverton and Telluride. Glaciation to the 8,000-foot level has created

North Clear Creek Falls

a vast rolling tundra cut deeply by many rivers with waterfalls, including those on two of the tributaries to the Rio Grande—the Conejos River to the east and the Rio Chama to the southwest. Thirty-two miles of the Conejos River have been deemed eligible for the National Wild and Scenic Rivers system.

These mountains receive 24 inches of moisture a year (compared to the San Luis Valley's 7 or 8 inches) and provide habitat for bald eagle, peregrine falcon, bighorn sheep, and reputedly have excellent trout fishing as well.

Long continuous hikes across the tundra are possible, but we'll describe three separate approaches. Seven falls are reached from Cumbres Pass, where the Cumbres & Toltec Railroad crosses the Continental Divide between Chama, New Mexico, and Antonito, Colorado. Four waterfalls are reached by driving into New Mexico and crossing back into Colorado to reach the Rio Chama. One solitary waterfall can be reached most directly from Platoro Reservoir.

Cumbres Pass Access to the Victoria Lake Area

Drive to Cumbres Pass, 34 miles from Antonito on Highway 17. There's a train depot at the pass, and a road heading north toward Trujillo Meadows Reservoir. Drive 1.6 miles, turn left onto road 118.2, a four-wheel-drive road that intersects (but does not cross) the Los Piños River in another 2.1 miles. The road was muddy but passable for another .75-mile in mid-June, when we visited.

This serendipitous route suggests side trips to several groups of falls, the last one 14 miles from the trailhead. We have so far visited only the first described—look us up when you get to Cañon Escondido.

Rio de Los Piños Falls *

(See South San Juan Wilderness Area group map, page 128.)

Access: Hike
Rating: ★ ★
Type: Plunge
USGS Topographic Quad: Cumbres (37106 A4)
Trail Miles: .5-mile, 4.5 without four-wheel-drive
Altitude: 10,800 feet
Elevation Change: From 10,600 feet, +200 feet

Four-wheel-drive will get you up to 4 miles, then you hike the road to within .25-mile of the falls, assuming that there isn't snow on the road, which starts at 10,200 feet. The trail starts at about 10,600 feet.

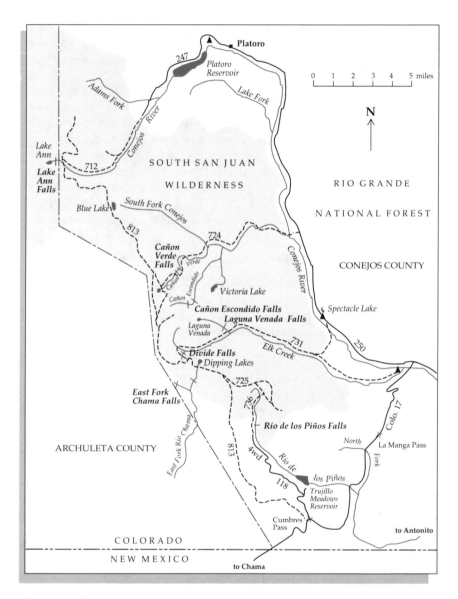

Platoro

247

Platoro
Reservoir

Lake Fork

Adams Fork

Conejos River

0   1   2   3   4   5 miles

N

Lake
Ann

Lake
Ann
Falls

712

SOUTH SAN JUAN

WILDERNESS

RIO GRANDE

NATIONAL FOREST

Blue Lake

South Fork Conejos

813

724

Cañon
Verde
Falls

Verde

Conejos River

CONEJOS COUNTY

Cañon Escondido

Victoria Lake

Spectacle Lake

Cañon Escondido Falls
Laguna Venada Falls

Laguna
Venada

731

250

Divide Falls

Elk Creek

Dipping Lakes

East Fork
Chama Falls

725

736

Rio de los Piños Falls

North

La Manga Pass

Colo. 17

ARCHULETA COUNTY

East Fork Rio Chama

813

4wd

Rio de

los Piños

Fork

118

Trujillo
Meadows
Reservoir

Cumbres
Pass

to Antonito

COLORADO

NEW MEXICO

to Chama

The South San Juan Wilderness Area group
(**#28** on Rio Grande River drainage map, page 112):

Rio de Los Piños Falls	Cañon Escondido Falls
Divide Falls	Cañon Verde Falls
Laguna Venada Falls	Lake Ann Falls

Neither the quad nor the forest service maps appear to be accurate about how to get up the river, although road 118, in one incarnation or another, seems to be the answer. A string of interconnected roads frays at the river, where there are fire rings and camping spots but no trail. Keep working up the river on 118. After crossing a couple of small creeks, it climbs a steep hill, where we were stopped from driving farther by snow.

Even though Los Piños Falls is marked on neither the quad nor the forest service map, it is impossible to miss. The river arcs to the northeast before heading up into the cliffs, and the falls comes down through a long shelf of finely compacted volcanic ash that wraps around the head of the valley. The trail climbs this shelf just to the west of the falls, whose sound dominates the bowl.

Rio de Los Piños Falls is about 35 feet high and 10 to 12 feet broad, pouring over the ledge in a lacy but powerful leap, the sound echoing in the rocks that enclose it. There's another small falls entering the river just to the west, and the two together make a green, lushly vegetated area in the rock slide. It's possible to get right up to the falls at the margin, where the sound is over-powering.

About 1.5 miles beyond Rio de Los Piños Falls, trail 736 meets the La Manga Stock Driveway, trail 725. It's another 4 miles northwest to the largest of Dipping Lakes (11,241 feet) and the intersection with trail 731 (coming up from Elk Creek). The total hiking distance (with four-wheel-drive) to this juncture is about 6 miles, almost 5 miles less than by taking the trail directly up Elk Creek from the Conejos River.

Divide Falls*

(See South San Juan Wilderness Area group map, page 128.)

Access: Overnight and bushwhack
Rating and Type: Not visited
USGS Topographic Quad: Victoria Lake (37106 B5)
Trail Miles: 10
Altitude: 11,000 feet
Elevation Change: From Dipping Lakes, -242 feet

Half a mile down trail 725 below Dipping Lakes, take trail 731 a half-mile as it starts down into the Elk Creek drainage. It crosses an unnamed drainage about 120 feet above a falls marked on the Victoria Lake quad, which we've named Divide Falls because the Continental Divide is a mile and a half west.

Laguna Venada Falls*

(See South San Juan Wilderness Area group map, page 128.)

Access: Overnight
Rating and Type: Not visited
USGS Topographic Quad: Victoria Lake (37106 B5)
Trail Miles: 10.5
Altitude: 10,600 feet
Elevation Change: None

If you continue down into the Elk Creek valley from Divide Falls, in 4 miles the trail (731) crosses a creek, unnamed, that flows down from Laguna Venada ("veined lake" in Spanish?). A falls is marked on the quad .3-mile and 400 feet in elevation higher on this creek. No trail is indicated, and the contour lines are very close indeed.

Total hiking distance to Laguna Venada Falls (or a view of them, at least) from the Los Piños trailhead is 10.5 miles. Trail 731 continues on down Elk Creek 7 miles to the Conejos River near Forest Road 250 and Spectacle Lake. Trying to see Laguna Venada Falls and Los Piños Falls on the same trip is a minimum 17-mile hike, assuming you had a car to station at each end.

The crossroads below Dipping Lakes, where 731 and 725 (and 813) intersect, is 11.5 trail miles from the Conejos River, 6.5 from the Los Piños trailhead. There is no easy way to get there, which is one of the things recommending it.

Cañon Escondido Falls* *

(See South San Juan Wilderness Area group map, page 128.)

Access: Overnight and bushwhack
Rating and Type: Not visited
USGS Topographic Quad: Victoria Lake (37106 B5)
Trail Miles: 11.75 (10 + 1.75 bushwhack)
Altitude: 11,480 feet, 11,200 feet
Elevation Change: From crossroads (11,400 feet) to 12,080 feet, +680 feet; to upper falls, -600 feet; to lower falls, -880 feet

Trail 813 comes up Wolf Creek from Cumbres Peak to meet the La Manga trail (725) between Los Piños Falls and Dipping Lakes. Leaving the intersection of 725 and 731, it becomes the Continental Divide trail, heading northwest a mile across the tundra to 12,080 feet at the Divide, which it follows for a mile and a half. About 3.25 miles from the intersection it forks near Trail Lake. Trail 724 goes down Cañon Escondido ("hidden canyon") for .7-mile before it heads east to Laguna Venada (the lake, not the falls). If you leave the trail and continue on down the Cañon Verde drainage, waterfalls are indicated at 11,480 feet and 11,200 feet, 1.3 and 1.6 miles of bushwhacking, respectively. I'd think about leaving my pack back up at Trail Lake (11,983 feet). There is no trail indicated on the quad to Cañon Escondido Falls.

Cañon Verde Falls* *
(See South San Juan Wilderness Area group map, page 128.)

Access: Overnight and bushwhack
Rating and Type: Not visited
USGS Topographic Quad: Victoria Lake (37106 B5)
Trail Miles: 14 from Los Piños, 7 from Conejos River
Altitude: 10,800 feet, 10,900 feet
Elevation Change: From Trail Lake at 11,983 feet, -1,183 feet, -1,283 feet

From Trail Lake, trail 813 continues along the Continental Divide between 11,000 feet and 12,000 feet 2 miles to Green Lake (we're now 11.25 trail miles from the Los Piños trailhead). The trail forks again, and trail 726 heads down Cañon Verde to two waterfalls marked at 1.3 and 1.4 miles from Green Lake. You've lost a lot of elevation to get here. You're about 14 miles from your trailhead—maybe you'd like to continue on down the green cañon about 7 miles to the Conejos River, where you've cleverly left a car with a cooler full of beer.

The Chama River
Drive over Cumbres Pass 7 miles toward Chama on Highway 17. Turn right on the national forest access, which becomes road 121. You cross back into Colorado from New Mexico, then drive to the campground entrance, just over 5 miles, at 8,478 feet. From this campground, road 738 is shown crossing the Chama and following it upstream. This is not a road but a reasonably good trail, and it provides access to four waterfalls, three of them high on the cliffs of the southern San Juans.

The South San Juan Wilderness Area group
(**#29** on Rio Grande River drainage map, page 112):

Chama Basin Maverick Falls   West Fork Chama Falls
East Fork Chama Falls   Chama Lake Falls

Chama Basin Maverick Falls
(See South San Juan Wilderness Area group map, page 132.)

Access: Hike
Rating: ★
Type: Horsetail
USGS Topographic Quad: Archuleta Peak (37106 A5)
Trail Miles: 1.7
Altitude: 9,000 feet
Elevation Change: From 8,748 feet, +252 feet

From the campground it's a 2-mile hike to the first crossing of the Chama, which in early June, when we visited, was too swollen to ford. We could see one of the waterfalls on the East Fork of the Chama, 3 miles away. There were very few people in evidence, and the valley is beautiful, both open to the sky and enclosed by the mountains simultaneously, light bouncing all around. Chama Basin Maverick Falls is a smallish horsetail hidden in the aspen up a secondary drainage 1.7 miles from the campground.

To get to the falls on the East Fork, a ford of the Chama is necessary, but trail 740 follows the West Fork to two falls without crossing the river.

If the cliffs at the end of the valley are any indication, access to all of the falls at the head of the valley may be strictly for views-at-a-distance.

East Fork Chama Falls* *
(See South San Juan Wilderness Area group map, page 132.)

Access: Overnight
Rating and Type: Not visited
USGS Topographic Quad: Archuleta Peak (37106 A5)
Trail Miles: 5
Altitude: 10,800 feet
Elevation Change: From 8,748 feet, +2,012 feet

Two miles past the ford that stymied us in early June (see above) the trail curves to follow the West Fork of the Chama. Two waterfalls hang in the cliffs 2 miles farther north, on the branched ends of the East Fork. In a mile and a quarter you can climb 600 feet to the 10,000-foot level and should then be in view of the falls. We haven't tried it yet, but save us a rock to sit on.

West Fork Chama Falls *
(See South San Juan Wilderness Area group map, page 132.)

Access: Overnight
Rating and Type: Not visited
USGS Topographic Quad: Archuleta Peak (37106 A5)
Trail Miles: 6.7
Altitude: 11,200 feet
Elevation Change: From 8,748 feet, +2,452 feet

Chama Lake Falls *
(See South San Juan Wilderness Area group map, page 132.)

Access: Overnight and bushwhack
Rating and Type: Not visited
USGS Topographic Quad: Archuleta Peak (37106 A5)
Trail Miles: 6.8
Altitude: 10,800 feet
Elevation Change: From 8,748 feet, +2,052 feet

Two falls are on the cliff of the north and west prongs on the West Fork of the Chama. It's about 6.7 miles from the campground (see above) to the end of trail 740. It would logically continue onto the tundra above tree line, perhaps to meet the Continental Divide trail beyond Chama Lake, but this is where the trail meets the boundary of a portion of the Tierra Amarilla Grant, which is still privately held.

The waterfall on the western prong of the West Fork is about 400 feet higher than the one on the north prong, which is on the drainage from Chama Lake.

Lake Ann Falls *
(See South San Juan Wilderness Area group map, page 128.)

Access: Overnight
Rating and Type: Not visited
USGS Topographic Quad: Summit Peak (37106 C6)
Trail Miles: 5.5
Altitude: 11,600 feet
Elevation Change: From Platoro Reservoir at 9,970 feet, +1,630 feet

This waterfall is briefly mentioned in a guidebook to the South San Juan Wilderness. Take County Road 247 north of Platoro Reservoir to the wilderness boundary, about 6.5 miles from the Mix Lake campground. Trail 712 goes 5.5 miles up the Middle Fork of the Conejos to intersect the Continental Divide trail (11,360 feet) directly below Lake Ann (11,910 feet). Lake Ann Falls is on the Middle Fork below the lake, 240 feet above the trail.

This falls is 9 miles on trail 813 from Green Lake, mentioned earlier in descriptions of falls reached from Cumbres Pass.

The San Juan and Dolores Rivers Drainages Map

30: The Navajo River Group
31: The Blackhead Peak Area Group
32, 33: The San Juan North of Pagosa Springs Group
34: The Piedra River Drainage
35: The Vallecito Reservoir Area
36: The Silverton Area
37: The West Dolores River Group
38: The Cortez-Durango Area

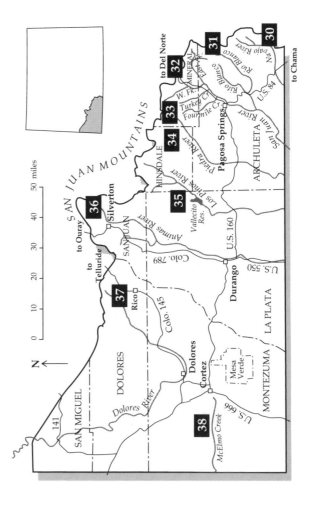

5

The San Juan and Dolores Rivers Drainages

Fathers Silvestre Velez de Escalante and Anastasio Dominguez left Santa Fe, then in Mexico, in late July of 1776, intending to find a route to the missions of Monterey in California. They followed a river they named the Rio Chama into Colorado and then headed west toward a river the Navajo called *Powhuska,* the "mad" river. Escalante and Dominguez called it San Juan.

Escalante and Dominguez also named the River of Our Lady of Sorrows— the Dolores. They named the Animas Perdidas (River of Lost Souls), Rio de Los Piños (River of Pines), Piedra (River of the Rock Wall), and Rio Blanco (White River)—all of which drain into the San Juan. And they all contain water-falls. In fact, there are more falls in the San Juan drainage than in any other drainage in the state.

The San Juan Mountains are the largest range in Colorado, covering more than 10,000 square miles, and contain thirteen of the state's fifty-three over-14,000-foot peaks. The slope of the southeastern side of this range is so steep that the San Juan's 86 miles in Colorado drop the river 6,000 feet from its origin to the Colorado-New Mexico border.

Although there are plenty of waterfalls on both the eastern and western slopes of the San Juans, the southeast has more. The south- and east-facing slopes are

137

those most stressed and eroded by the daily cycles of warming and freezing that reduce great mountain ranges eventually to sand and clay—with a little help from gravity, of course. (Anyone hiking the range knows it has *plenty* of gravity.)

The San Juans have history to spare, too. The northeasternmost outpost of the native Chacoan culture was established at Chimney Rock, west of Pagosa Springs. Mesa Verde is only 60 miles west and was kept in contact with Chimney Rock by a series of watchfires on mesa tops that extended all the way to Chaco Canyon.

Gold was discovered (by white men, at least) in 1870 near Silverton and was produced—along with silver, lead, iron, zinc, salt, lime, uranium, and vanadium—from mines near Rico, Telluride, Ouray, and many other small towns that no longer exist. Marie Curie extracted radium from ores mined near Rico.

But however rich its past, what dominates the San Juan drainage today is the majesty of the mountains, the wildness of the rivers, the depth of the snows, and the beauty of the wilderness. The Weminuche is the state's largest designated wilderness area, with 401,600 acres. The Lizard Head and South San Juan Wilderness areas also drain into the San Juan. They, too, have their share of white falls of water (*cascadas blancas*).

Waterfalls in the San Juan
and Dolores Rivers Drainages

We have documented fifty-five waterfalls in this portion of the state. Most of them require some hiking—and even backcountry bushwhacking—to reach. There are exceptions, however; waterfalls along Highway 160 south of Wolf Creek Pass, including Treasure Falls, are easily accessible.

Each drainage has its share. There's a cluster of falls on national forest land on the Navajo River, but they are inaccessible because of the wishes of private landowners.

Many falls are clustered near Pagosa Springs on the East and West forks of the San Juan, on Rio Blanco, and on the Piedra.

There are clusters north of Vallecito Reservoir on the Los Piños River requiring hikes each way of 12 or 15 miles. A couple of falls on the Animas near Silverton are easy to see from the highway.

Another cluster extends from a roadside falls south of the old mining town of Dunton to one nestled below a glacial lake at the foot of Mount Wilson.

And there is even one falls where you'd least expect it—west of the town of Cortez and glimpsed, no doubt, by some little group of Mesa Verde Anasazi as they made their way to Aunt Tillie's in Hovenweep. They left their truck tires in McElmo Creek.

The Navajo River

This group of five falls is located up the Navajo River valley outside the "town" of Chromo. Included in the group is one of the five "Bridal Veil Falls" named in maps of Colorado. There are also a couple of falls in a place called "Vampire Valley" on the East Fork of the Navajo. The enticement of the place is frustrated, however, by the fact that the whole valley—at least the east side of it—is privately owned. It was part of the Tierra Amarilla land grant and is now broken up into several large-acreage ranches.

The most direct route, Colorado 29, heading north from Chama directly to Archuleta County 382 west of Chromo, was closed, so we drove the 22 miles to Chromo on U.S. 84 toward Pagosa Springs, then east on 382 up the Navajo.

Access to the falls in the valley of the Navajo would be possible if access to the national forest were. But the ranchers in the area have a person stationed in a building along the road to discourage visitors. He came out as we approached in our vehicle, making it clear that we were to stop to be refused permission to enter. At least we weren't greeted by someone carrying a shotgun! The area is pretty enough that I can understand landowners wanting to protect it—or hoard it, depending on your point of view.

The drive, I have to say, was sublime. This country is very solitary, a combination of peaks and mesas, and you sense you're on the imaginary line where Colorado and New Mexico meld. The overall feeling is one of bucolic isolation. This is a place where people ranch and live, not recreate.

Anyhow, the upshot is that Nancy and I couldn't get to any of the falls. I hope you have better luck.

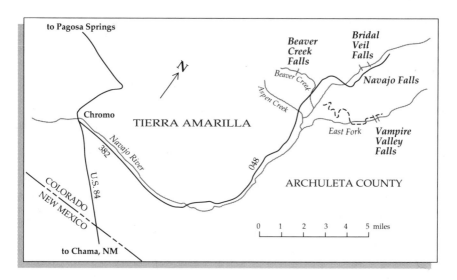

The Navajo River group
(**#30** on San Juan and Dolores rivers drainages map, page 136):

Beaver Creek Falls
Bridal Veil Falls
Navajo Falls
Vampire Valley Falls

Beaver Creek Falls*
(See The Navajo River group map, above.)

Access: Steep cliffs
Rating and Type: Not visited
USGS Topographic Quad: Elephant Head Rock (37106 B6)
Trail Miles: No trail indicated
Altitude: 9,300 feet
Elevation Change: From 8,300 feet, + 1,000 feet

Fifteen miles east out of Chromo on 342, about half a mile past Elephant Head Rock, the road crosses Beaver Creek. The waterfall is indicated on the quad a thousand feet above the road and about a mile to the west in the national forest. The falls may be visible from the road, or from Fall View Lake. The falls is on national forest land, but the road is not.

Bridal Veil Falls
(See The Navajo River group map, page 140.)

Access, Rating, and Type: Not visited
USGS Topographic Quad: Elephant Head Rock (37106 B6)
Altitude: 8,960 feet

One of five "Bridal Veil" falls in Colorado, this one is just off Forest Road 048 18.5 miles northeast of Chromo. The quad indicates a spur off the main road that gives access to the falls. We didn't get within 4 miles of this point because the road is on private land.

Navajo Falls *
(See The Navajo River group map, page 140.)

Access: Hike or bushwhack from road
Rating and Type: Not visited
USGS Topographic Quad: Elephant Head Rock (37106 B6)
Trail Miles: .3-mile
Altitude: 8,780 feet

This falls is just south of Bridal Veil Falls on the Navajo River. No trail access is indicated on the quad.

Vampire Valley Falls **
(See The Navajo River group map, page 140.)

Access, Rating, and Type: Not visited
USGS Topographic Quad: Elephant Head Rock (37106 B6)
Trail Miles: Unknown
Altitude: 9,400 feet, 9,560 feet

This falls is marked on the quad up the East Fork of the Navajo River south of Elephant Head Rock. There are jeep trails indicated right to the falls area winding over Johnson Mountain, but who knows how passable? Hiking seems possible from "Upper Camp" near 048 over Johnson Mountain and up the river to the falls. Ranchland prevents access.

The Blackhead Peak Area

Blackhead Peak is a 12,495-foot peak west of Pagosa Springs that dominates this stretch of the San Juans just south and east of Wolf Creek Pass. The volcanic rock of this area created waterfalls west and east of the peak. Both sides are accessible from U.S. 84 by good dirt roads.

Both sides of Blackhead Peak drain into the San Juan. The Rio Blanco drains from the eastern valley between Blackhead Peak and the Continental Divide. This isolated valley contains five notable waterfalls on four separate tributaries to the Rio Blanco.

On the west side of Blackhead Peak is the origin of the Rito Blanco, easily confused with its larger cousin, the Rio Blanco, to which it is tributary. Two waterfalls are at the upper end of the Rito Blanco.

The Rio Blanco valley is the more remote of the two, and its falls are therefore more difficult to get to.

Rito Blanco Falls**
(See Blackhead Peak Area group map, page 143.)

Access: Hike
Rating: ★ ★
Type: Horsetail and segmented
USGS Topographic Quad: Blackhead Peak
Trail Miles: .25-mile
Altitude: 10,200 feet, 10,600 feet (two falls)
Elevation Change: From 10,360 feet to lower falls, -160 feet; to upper falls, +240 feet

Both waterfalls on the Rito Blanco are reached by driving south on U.S. 84 from its junction with U.S. 160 east of Pagosa Springs, just outside of town. A quarter of a mile south of this junction County 302 heads west, becoming Forest Road 662. About 6.3 miles from 84 take a right onto Forest Road 665.

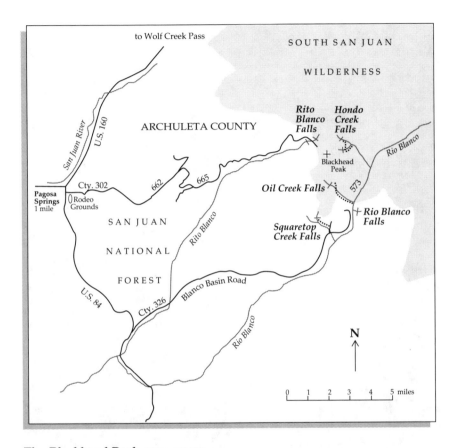

The Blackhead Peak area group
(**#31** on San Juan and Dolores rivers drainages map, page 136):

Rito Blanco Falls
Squaretop Creek Falls
Oil Creek Falls
Hondo Creek Falls
Rio Blanco Falls

Lower Rito Blanco Falls

The end of the road, which is easy for passenger cars to negotiate, is 17.4 miles from U.S. 84. The road climbs to the 10,000-foot level and enters into a bowl bounded by Nipple Mountain and Blackhead Peak. The topo and forest service maps show the road ending here, although it has been graded beyond this westernmost point.

The drainage that the road crosses at the south end of the valley is the drainage containing the falls. The upper falls can be seen from the road in a deep crevice in the rock, north and east and above the road across a steep meadow. There's a faint trail, but the falls is easy to reach directly—a hike of .25-mile and an elevation gain of 250 feet up the steep lower slopes of the cliffs. The drainage cut was still filled with packed snow at the time of our visit (mid-June), so we could climb right up the snow in the stream drainage to the falls—albeit with the caution always called for on snow bridges of any kind. The cut is deep and the rock not well consolidated, so be careful.

The upper falls is a straight leap of 30 to 35 feet turning into a fan of spray inside a narrowly carved slot in the rock. The snow in the cut prevented us from seeing the bottom of the leap.

The falls is situated on steep cliffs of conglomerate eroding nearby into grotesque pinnacles and columns.

The lower falls is reached by hiking about the same distance downstream (.25-mile) from the road. Following the water—not too closely—provides an easy route to the falls, but there's no trail. Steep, vegetated hillsides make the approach worthy of caution, but a good view of the falls can be had without much danger.

The falls is another straight leap of 50 feet, although it's joined at top and bottom to a narrow white stream of churned water, making the total height close to 60 feet, all enclosed in an amphitheater decorated with moss. Downstream a few yards the rock changes from the rough conglomerate to something harder, and there is another small falls on the main creek and also on the one entering steeply from the north, creating a noisy, nurturing environment.

The high aspen-framed meadows below Blackhead Peak are very pretty, but the marshiness at the end of the road did not entice us to stay. There are campsites, but no campgrounds, all along the road.

The Rio Blanco Valley

All the falls in the valley of the Rio Blanco (white river) are reached by taking U.S. 84 south from its junction with U.S. 160 just east of Pagosa Springs. Drive about 8 miles to the intersection of 84 with Archuleta County 326 (Forest

Road 657); named the Rio Blanco Basin Road, this is a dirt road crossing south of Squaretop Mountain to reach the valley of the Rio Blanco.

One falls (Squaretop Creek) can be seen from the road if you drive nearly to the bridge over Rio Blanco and look back east toward the base of Squaretop Mountain. The others are on drainages tributary to the Rio Blanco and accessible only by trail 573 into the South San Juan Wilderness.

Squaretop Creek Falls *
(See Blackhead Peak Area group map, page 143.)

Access: Bushwhack
Rating: ★ ★
Type: Horsetail
USGS Topographic Quad: Harris Lake (37106 B7)
Trail Miles: .5-mile
Altitude: 9,200 feet
Elevation Change: From 8,220 feet, +980 feet

The falls on Squaretop Creek is a broad slide of water down a smoothly eroded cliff face, visible if you look west from the road leading into the valley of the Rio Blanco. The total fall is 200 to 300 feet of slide down the cliff with twists, intermediate pools, and fans to a short leap and a fan 50 feet to the cascades. The hillsides all around the base of the falls are very steep, offering loose footing at best on granular rock eroding in upended slabs. It's tough to get a good view, but there are several nice alternative views, including one of the "knot" in the falls. It's possible to make your way down to the bottom of the last leap.

Access is pretty much by bushwhack, since the slope of Squaretop Mountain is a steep, heavily eroded and lushly overgrown environment. Stay out of the bottom of Squaretop Creek drainage.

From U.S. 84, drive 13 miles on the Blanco Basin Road—County 326 (see Oil Creek, Hondo Creek). Just over 13 miles in, there's a sign indicating the Rio Blanco trail; just beyond there's another sign on a left-hand turn for the Rio Blanco access. About .3-mile up the access road there's a left-hand turn that goes less than .1-mile to some old fire rings in a grassy turnaround. A dirt track leads toward Squaretop Creek Falls but then fades out.

There's a faint trail to the south that meets an old road and a trail from and to the creek (the official Rio Blanco trail), but none of these go to the falls, which requires bushwhacking through dense forest and underbrush for about .5-mile. Any trails there disappear in the density of the brush near the creek.

There is no discernible trail to the falls except the occasional game trails above the creek that follow the contours of the hill.

We decided to take a compass heading (105 degrees east) back directly through the woods rather than follow the drainage, and, amazingly, came out exactly at the truck in half the time it took us to get to the falls.

Squaretop Creek Falls can be seen from the main road, as can the Rio Blanco valley, where the mouths of the Oil Creek and Hondo Creek drainages are very obvious. The Rio Blanco valley is vast and seems perfectly pastoral, as green as Ireland at sunset. It's a lot easier to see from the road than by bush-whacking, but the orienteering was fun, despite the work.

Oil Creek Falls*
(See Blackhead Peak Area group map, page 143.)

Access: Hike
Rating: ★ ★
Type: Segmented
USGS Topographic Quad: Blackhead Peak (37106 C7)
Trail Miles: 3 (1.5 + 1.5 bushwhack)
Altitude: 9,400 feet
Elevation Change: From 8,220 feet at trailhead, + 1,180 feet

Oil Creek Falls is a broad segmented rush of white down the cliffs of probably 200 feet, with a split lacy leap at the top of 60 feet. Unfortunately, you have to make your way up the rocky and washed-out streambed of Oil Creek, crossing many times as it penetrates the sheer, crumbling walls of the canyon with not a trail in sight.

To get to the falls, take the Rio Blanco access road (see Squaretop Creek Falls access information, above). Ignore the dirt road to the left at the .3-mile mark and continue on toward the Hare Ranch boundary (at about .5-mile). Fifty yards before the Hare Ranch fence there are faint turnouts to provide access for hikers to the Rio Blanco trail, which parallels an irrigation ditch just uphill from the access road. We drove in a total of .9-mile, unloaded our packs, and then parked the truck back outside the private property (marked by a gate announcing the Hare Ranch) in a pullout on national forest land.

The Rio Blanco trail threatens to get mixed up with some old dirt roads, but keep straight ahead on the trail, staying out of the valley and ignoring the roads. The Oil Creek drainage is about 1.3 miles up the trail, and you can't miss it. Rio Blanco below Oil Creek, and the Oil Creek drainage itself, have

been heavily flooded, reminding me of the result of the Lawn Lake flood—
like the passage of a bulldozer as big as a football field. We camped near the
confluence in the aspen and spruce woods, contemplating the difference between the rain-forest green of the wood and the barren gravel and boulder-
beach quality of the flooded area.

There is no trail up the creekbed. Rock-hopping and stream-hopping skills
are called for all the way up the drainage, because Oil Creek carves its gorge
deeply into the rock on its way down to the Rio Blanco. We climbed up the
slopes of Oil Creek on the north side, just short of a small falls where the canyon
became impassable (at about 1 mile), and worked through thigh-deep under-
growth to get up where we were directly across from Oil Creek Falls.

Hondo Creek Falls **
(See Blackhead Peak Area group map, page 143.)

Access: Hike
Rating: ★ ★ ★
Type: Plunge (West Fork) and segmented (North Fork)
USGS Topographic Quad: Blackhead Peak (37106 C7)
Trail Miles: 4.5 (plus .25- and .5-mile bushwhacks)
Altitude: 10,200 feet, 10,400 feet
Elevation Change: From 8,220 feet at trailhead, + 1,980 feet, + 2,180 feet

The falls on Hondo Creek (West Fork) is three evenly spaced straight leaps,
the highest on the northwest wall being about 230 feet. The falls on the North
Fork is 50-foot fans of water that are not as dramatic as the three on the West
Fork.

The access to these falls is via the Rio Blanco trail (see Squaretop Creek
Falls and Oil Creek Falls access information). Oil Creek is at the 1.5-mile mark,
then the trail continues along the cliffs high above the river. A falls not marked
on any map can be seen across the canyon. It's 60 to 70 feet high, easily seen
from a switchback at about 1 mile from Oil Creek.

At 3 miles from the trailhead, the trail turns up the Hondo Creek drainage,
staying high above the creekbed on the hill because, as is the case with all the
streams in this area, the creek cuts very deeply, creating steep valleys and gorges.

The trail was badly gouged by animal traffic when we were on it, and there
was a fair amount of deadfall across the trail.

We got to the crossing of the West Fork of Hondo Creek, but the amount
of runoff made the ford impossible, especially after it rained and hailed for
half an hour. But it isn't necessary to ford the creek to get to the falls.

From the hillside above the confluence of the North and West forks of Hondo Creek, head southwest paralleling the West Fork, bushwhacking along the edge of the trees. It's possible to see the troika of long veil-like leaps at the head of the valley ten minutes off the trail. I saw them over the fleeing hind ends of some elk I surprised by being in that neck of the woods in the first place.

It was possible in mid-June to cross the West Fork across a snow bridge and then bushwhack or follow game trails straight north overland to the north drainage and then work upstream to within sight of the North Fork falls. Stay up in the woods where the slopes are not too steep. This crossing to the North Fork is fairly easy but not especially rewarding, unless you are just looking for a place to be totally alone.

The trail back to camp was horribly slick and sloppy.

Rio Blanco Falls *

(See Blackhead Peak Area group map, page 143.)

Access: Hike
Rating: ★
Type: Plunge
USGS Topographic Quad: Blackhead Peak (37106 C7)
Trail Miles: 2
Altitude: 8,600 feet
Elevation Change: From trailhead at 8,220 feet, +380 feet

This is the 70- to 80-foot plunge from the cliffs on the east side into the Rio Blanco from an unnamed tributary, which is visible from a switchback on the Rio Blanco trail.

The San Juan North of Pagosa Springs

The casual Colorado tourist, laboring by car up the ridge of the San Juans on Highway 160 out of Pagosa Springs on the way from Durango to Alamosa, for example, would get the definite impression that waterfalls are plentiful in this part of the state. And the impression would be correct. This is the backbone of the San Juans, and the thousands of feet of volcanic rock erode in great, deep canyons and are split by hundreds of faults that have thrown mountains of rock up and down. The heavy snowfall and resultant snowmelt of the region complete the recipe for making waterfalls by the dozen, and the heavenly chef has whipped up a pantryful.

Moving north on Highway 160 from Pagosa Springs, there are waterfalls up the drainages of Fourmile Creek, Turkey Creek, the East Fork of the San Juan River, the West Fork of the San Juan, and on Wolf Creek and four of its tributaries.

West Fork of the San Juan River

There are nine waterfalls indicated on the topographic quads covering the West Fork valley. None of them is named—nor are they especially worthwhile destinations in themselves—but the constant voice of the water contributes its spirit to the wildness of the valley. The falls on the upper stretches of the West Fork are difficult to distinguish from one another because miles of the river are one continuous cascade and the trail up the drainage stays hundreds of feet above the stream.

There are seven falls on the South River Peak quad; two are in the Saddle Mountain quad.

The West Fork of the San Juan is reached from U.S. 160 about 7 miles south of Wolf Creek Pass or 14.5 miles north of Pagosa Springs and .5-mile south of the Treasure Falls pullout. Forest Service Road 648 drops into the valley, passes the Wolf Creek campground in half a mile, then moves on into the valley, providing a wonderful view back to the east of Treasure Falls. At the 2-mile mark the road narrows and makes its way up the west side of the drainage. There's a parking area and turnaround at just beyond 2.5 miles, and there's a lovely little falls visible from the parking lot that is not marked on any map.

West Fork Falls 1 and 2
(See San Juan North of Pagosa Springs group map, page 151.)

Access: Hike
Rating: ★ ★ ★
Type: Segmented
USGS Topographic Quad: Saddle Mountain (37106 D8)
Trail Miles: .15-mile (1 mile + bushwhack)
Altitude: 8,040 feet, 8,800 feet
Elevation Change: From 8,080 feet to first falls, -40 feet; to view of second falls, +760 feet

The first falls indicated on the quad, West Fork 1, is reached from the parking area. Head toward the West Fork into a small clearing, then walk upstream on

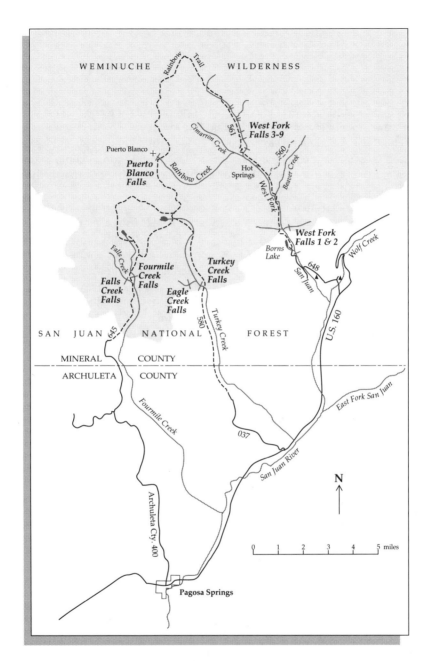

The San Juan north of Pagosa Springs group
(**#33** on San Juan and Dolores rivers drainages map, page 136):

West Fork Falls 1 & 2
West Fork Falls 3–9
Falls Creek Falls
Fourmile Creek Falls

Turkey Creek Falls
Eagle Creek Falls
Puerto Blanco Falls

a path that used to have a "Do Not Enter" sign posted on a chain. This path leads down to a view of the falls within five minutes. This is a wonderful segmented falls, arcing and leaping about 40 feet, round and noisy and white, followed by stair-stepped cascades, a broad fan, and a narrow chute before the water turns back into a river. The mist whips around the rocks like a ghost playing hide-and-seek.

From the parking area, the road passes through a gate onto the private property near Borns Lake. To reach the West Fork trail, also called the Rainbow trail, hike through the gate and up the road, following signs that eventually point your way through the Borns Lake community. We got confused by the signs and were chastised by a resident for wandering around in her pile of empty cans, as though that's what we wanted to do. Just stay on the road until it's clear, about .25-mile past the gate. The trail turns right, heading toward the river, then skirts the lake and heads on upstream.

West Fork 2 is on the cliffs opposite the trail at about 1 mile but requires a walk through the woods to see. It's a straight leap of 50 to 60 feet to the river and is visible through the trees from an open meadow just down the trail from the footbridge inside the wilderness boundary—pretty but inaccessible.

West Fork Falls 3-9
(See San Juan North of Pagosa Springs group map, page 151.)

Access: Overnight
Rating: ★ ★
Type: All types
USGS Topographic Quad: South River Peak
Trail Miles: 4.9, 5.6, 5.9, 6.5, 6.6, 6.8, 6.8
Altitude: 9,220 feet, 9,640 feet, 9,840 feet, 10,120 feet, 10,200 feet, 10,400 feet, 10,440 feet
Elevation Change: From 8,080 feet, + 2,260 feet to highest falls on quad

The West Fork trail is used mostly by fishermen and backpackers hiking to the natural hot springs at the 4.7-mile mark. The trail crosses the West Fork at mile 2.9, where fording used to be very difficult during spring runoff; however, the crossing is now made over a very sturdy wooden bridge. At 4.25 miles the trail passes the Beaver Creek trail.

A large camping area has developed in the meadows above a hot springs at the 4.7-mile mark. Timber is scarce, but the area is reasonably well kept. On the other hand, we were there in early June, when the outfitters couldn't get their horses through to the hot springs yet.

The hot springs is a small rock-enclosed pool below the spring; there is a larger rock-walled pool right at the edge of the West Fork that is surrounded even in early June by small yellow flowers, with nice views up and down the river. Clothing is optional.

We saw West Fork 3 up in the cliffs to the north just after crossing the log across the West Fork at mile 5.25, half a mile beyond the hot springs. West Fork 3, a bridal-veil leap of 60 to 80 feet, is striking in its cliffside isolation, and I wanted to try to get up to the falls, although the terrain surrounding it is extremely rough. I tried to get to it from where the trail levels out at 10,000 feet after innumerable switchbacks climbing from the crossing of the West Fork (9,120 feet). I cliffed-out just above and out of sight of the leap. A safety rope would be a very good idea for anyone willing to risk a closer look. I got a good view of some bighorn sheep from above, and of West Fork 4, which is a double leap at right angles, approximately 25 and 15 feet, easily seen looking northeast through the trees from a little path leading from the level spot at 10,000 feet to the crest of an outcrop that overlooks the entire valley to the south.

The remaining falls on the South River Peak quad are dotted along a stretch of about a mile and a half, over which the river drops from 10,440 feet to 9,220 feet. In early June, parts of the trail were still covered with snow punctuated by deer and bighorn sheep tracks.

We had a picnic lunch as we perched in the dense forest above West Fork 6 and West Fork 7, about 6 miles from the trailhead. These are great rushes of water over a 30-foot chute and a vigorous 20-foot leap. There's also a sinuous, stringlike falls coming down the mountainside opposite. The cliffs are stark and gray but profusely wooded.

Another .25-mile up the trail there are views from the trail of West Fork 8 and West Fork 9, a very broad 6-foot leap and a shooting cascade below it, also about 6 feet. More striking in its way was a small falls coming down the slope the trail was on, climaxing in two deeply sloped channels in the rock serving as chutes for the water, and beautifully and starkly lit by the sunlight.

On the way back I scrambled down the slope to photograph West Fork 5, which is a short leap followed by stepping-stone braids.

I suspect there are more falls than those marked on the quads, but the woods are too dense to see through, and the slopes are perilous and steep.

Fourmile and Turkey Creeks

Fourmile Creek and Turkey Creek are the first two major tributaries to the West Fork of the San Juan north of Pagosa Springs. Fourmile Creek's waterfalls are reached from Pagosa Springs; Turkey Creek is reached from Highway 160 in just over 7 miles north of town.

Fourmile Creek Trail

There are two waterfalls on the Fourmile Creek trail—one actually on Fourmile Creek, the other (reached first on the trail) nearby on Falls Creek, a tributary to Fourmile Creek. Both are reached by taking Fifth Street north out of town. Continue on this road (County 400), which becomes Forest Road 645, 12.5 miles to the trailhead of trail 569. You'll pass the old Cade Ranch just before reaching the trailhead's large parking area.

Falls Creek Falls *

(See San Juan North of Pagosa Springs group map, page 151.)

Access: Hike
Rating: ★ ★ ★
Type: Tiered
USGS Topographic Quad: Pagosa Peak (37107 D1)
Trail Miles: 3.3
Altitude: 10,000 feet; viewpoint at 9,600 feet
Elevation Change: From 9,000 feet, +600 feet

Magnificent Falls Creek Falls consists of an initial leap of 60 to 70 feet, a second leap of 160 feet or more, and a rippling fall over a rounded slab of hard black rock creating a shower 50 feet high. A trail goes up to the cliff wall (wear your raingear), and it's possible to get behind the falls, which is always a great thrill. The temperature back there is about 20 degrees less than the temperature in the shade surrounding the falls.

The falls is high enough that the wind moves the sheet of falling water from side to side, and the veiling and furling of the water is mesmerizing, as are the white pulsations of spuming water on the boulder at the base, making it look like milk streaming down from the sky.

The hike to this and Fourmile Creek Falls is on a clear trail perfectly suited to families with children. After leaving the trailhead parking area and climbing over a hill, the trail drops into the valley of Fourmile Creek and affords views of Eagle Mountain (12,007 feet) and the broad aspen slopes of the Weminuche. You can see a falls deep in the folds of rock below Eagle Peak (12,137 feet) from a point high along the trail about 1 mile from the trailhead, but it is soon lost to sight in the folds of rock and is not to be confused with the falls farther along the trail.

The trail follows Fourmile Creek without much elevation gain, and Falls Creek Falls is visible from the trail for the last half-mile.

The trail crosses Falls Creek right below Falls Creek Falls, heading up through twisted volcanic rock past Fourmile Creek Falls (see below) and eventually to Fourmile and Turkey Creek lakes, where it joins the Turkey Creek trail on its way to the Continental Divide.

Fourmile Creek Falls *
(See San Juan North of Pagosa Springs group map, page 151.)

Access: Hike
Rating: ★ ★ ★
Type: Plunge and horsetails
USGS Topographic Quad: Pagosa Peak (37107 D1)
Trail Miles: 3.4
Altitude: 9,800 feet
Elevation Change: From 9,000 feet, +800 feet

Less than .2-mile beyond Falls Creek Falls, the trail climbs to the top of Fourmile Creek Falls, which is a segmented falls divided at the top into three distinct falling streams, including a 130- to 150-foot leap.

The trail crosses above this falls, but it's possible to drop from the trail steeply down the hill for a little closer view through the bushes. However, the terrain near the base is very roughly overgrown and prevented me from reaching the base of the falls. Fourmile Creek Falls is not as accessible as Falls Creek Falls, but the noise is fabulous, and either one would make a suitable destination by itself. That they are together is a surfeit of riches. The hike is less than 3.5 miles, requiring about one and three-quarter hours—each way—to see both waterfalls, and is consequently fairly popular. Both falls are inside the Weminuche Wilderness.

The Turkey Creek Drainage
To reach Turkey Creek, drive 7.3 miles north of Pagosa Springs on U.S. 160 and turn left onto the Jackson Mountain road (Forest Road 037). Follow this good gravel road 4 miles to the trailhead at the end.

Fourmile Creek Falls

Turkey Creek Falls
(See San Juan North of Pagosa Springs group map, page 151.)

Access: Overnight
Rating and Type: Not visited
USGS Topographic Quad: Saddle Mountain (37106 D8)
Trail Miles: 5.3
Altitude: 9,080 feet
Elevation Change: From 8,300 feet, +780 feet

Eagle Creek Falls
(See San Juan North of Pagosa Springs group map, page 151.)

Access: Overnight
Rating and Type: Not visited
USGS Topographic Quad: Saddle Mountain (37106 D8)
Trail Miles: 5.5
Altitude: 9,480 feet
Elevation Change: From 8,300 feet, +1,180 feet

Puerto Blanco Falls
(See San Juan North of Pagosa Springs group map, page 151.)

Access: Overnight
Rating and Type: Not visited
USGS Topographic Quad: Palomino Mountain (37107 E1)
Trail Miles: 12.5
Altitude: 11,715 feet
Elevation Change: From trailhead, +3,415 feet

Nancy and I have not yet visited this area, but according to Dennis Gebhardt's *Backpacking Guide to the Weminuche Wilderness,* the 18.6 miles along this trail to the Continental Divide is some of the most beautiful in the wilderness.

The Saddle Mountain quad indicates a falls on Turkey Creek below the trail .2-mile after it crosses Turkey Creek. Gebhardt says there are "extremely beautiful" falls below the trail, but it's unclear if this is the falls he is referring to. Another .2-mile along the trail should bring you around to a view of Eagle Creek Falls, 500 feet up the Eagle Creek drainage to the west.

According to Gebhardt, who gives a good description of the trail all the way to the Divide, there is another "spectacular waterfall" at the 12.5-mile mark flowing right from the top of Puerto Blanco Mountain. Puerto Blanco ("white door") refers to a white porphyry ridge separating Rainbow and Puerto Blanco creeks.

Turkey Creek is the legendary route by which the Spanish first ascended to the Divide, and two-hundred-year-old Spanish blazes have supposedly been found marking the route.

East Fork of the San Juan

Silver Falls
(See San Juan North of Pagosa Springs group map, page 159.)

Access: Roadside
Rating: ★ ★ ★
Type: Segmented horsetail
USGS Topographic Quad: Wolf Creek Pass (37106 D7)
Trail Miles: 0
Altitude: 8,600 feet
Elevation Change: From 8,180 feet, +420 feet

Silver Falls is braided into three leaps at the top; the main leap is about 30 feet and there are huge, steep braided cascades another 100 feet and then steep white water for about 200 yards. Very spectacular in the bright sunlight. Silver Falls is in the national forest, just inside the boundary.

We first tried to reach Silver Falls in late April, but about 3 miles up the road there were three boulders in the road and a huge, impassable gouge where an even larger boulder had bounced its way across and into the creek. You could mark its passage hundreds of yards down the slope, across the road, and right into the East Fork. A month later we took the East Fork road, noting that the place where house-size boulders had been deposited a month ago was already patched. The boulders were wading patiently while the millennia began the task of eroding them into beach sand.

To get to the falls, take Forest Road 667 11 miles below Wolf Creek Pass, past the East Fork campground and about 7 miles up the East Fork of the San Juan. After about 2 miles there's a sign advising the next 5 miles of passage are on private property. The first ford of a tributary washing across the road (about 1.5 miles from right-of-way sign) was crossable in the VW Dasher we were driving at the time, but the second ford, at about 2 miles, was not. But fortunately, that's the drainage of Falls Creek and the location of Silver Falls.

The falls was not visible from the road on the west side of the ford but most likely is from the road on the east side. It's also likely there's a turnout and

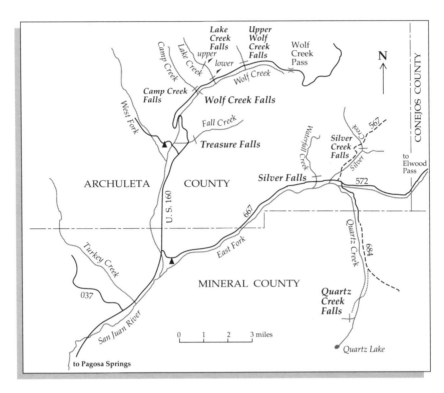

The San Juan north of Pagosa Springs group
(**#32** on San Juan and Dolores rivers drainages map, page 136):

Silver Falls
Silver Creek Falls
Quartz Creek Falls
Treasure Falls
Camp Creek Falls

Wolf Creek Falls
Lower Lake Creek Falls
Lake Creek Falls
Upper Wolf Creek Falls

possibly an outhouse on the other side of the drainage. (I saw a family at the foot of the falls on the other side.)

There is another waterfall indicated on the 1:100,000 topographic map, titled "Antonito." Continue a mile east on Forest Road 667 past Silver Falls, crossing Silver Creek. Trail 567 climbs up into the Silver Creek drainage toward Silver Pass over the Continental Divide. About 1.5 miles along the trail, it separates from the Silver Creek drainage. The falls is up the drainage another .25-mile.

The forest service office in Pagosa Springs, which has a good inventory of maps and useful information, as well as very helpful and knowledgeable rangers, says that there is a falls near Elwood Pass, which is 8 miles farther on 667, becomes a jeep road crossing the Divide, and then deposits you at Platoro Reservoir on the east slope. Check with the rangers in town first for road condition information and more specific directions to the falls.

There is also a falls on Quartz Creek indicated on the San Juan National Forest map.

Quartz Creek Falls*
(See San Juan North of Pagosa Springs group map, page 159.)

Access: Bushwhack
Rating and Type: Not visited
USGS Topographic Quad: Blackhead Peak (37106 C7)
Trail Miles: 6.5, including 1.2 bushwhack from south; about
  4, half-bushwhacking, from north
Altitude: 9,800 feet
Elevation Change: From 9,100 feet, +700 feet

Access may be possible from the road to Rito Blanco Falls (Forest Road 665), adding 4.3 miles to Quartz Lake at 12,000 feet and 1.2 miles down the drainage. Possibly the best route would be to take Forest Road 684 south from Silver Creek (see Silver Falls access) to the end of the road. Trail 571 climbs southeast toward Summit Peak (13,000 feet). After a mile and a half or so, at 9,100 feet Quartz Creek enters from the south. There is no trail indicated up the creek, but there is a falls up Quartz Creek indicated on the map another 2 miles into the South San Juan Wilderness.

How passable is Quartz Creek? We haven't done either of these, so this is the kind of speculation you get into before you've actually hit the trail. I asked the rangers, but they didn't know anything about it. Since there's no trail up Quartz Creek—maybe there's a very good reason one is lacking?

The Wolf Creek Pass Area

There are five falls that are reached directly from U.S. 160 in less than a dozen miles below Wolf Creek Pass (not including the little tumbles past the highway), including the most famous, Treasure Falls. So we'll start the description of falls in this part of the state by moving north on 160 from Treasure Falls and climbing toward the pass.

Treasure Falls

(See San Juan North of Pagosa Springs group map, page 159.)

Access: Wheelchair
Rating: ★ ★ ★
Type: Plunge
USGS Topographic Quad: Wolf Creek Pass (37106 D7)
Trail Miles: .2-mile
Altitude: 8,560 feet
Elevation Change: From 8,200 feet at turnout, +200 feet to bottom of falls

Treasure Falls is visible from U.S. 160; it's 11.75 miles below Wolf Creek Pass. The falls is 105 feet high, a straight leap of Falls Creek to a swift cascade that flows under a footbridge, which provides a closer look at the falls.

There is a turnoff on 160 opposite the Wolf Creek campground, restrooms, a paved .25-mile interpretive trail leading to a close-up view of the falls, and a bridge where you can stand in the middle of the stream. The falls is actually visible from the road if you slow down enough coming around the curve downhill from Wolf Creek to look at it. The key to locating the turnout area is that it is less than .25-mile below the viewpoint turnout at the huge double hairpin on the highway, which provides an overall view of the valley of the San Juan River.

The falls is a direct plunge down the rocks and is best seen in the glory of its setting by taking the road downhill from the highway to the West Fork campground, half a mile down 160 from the Treasure Falls turnout. Drive out into the valley of the West Fork and look back at Treasure Falls in the evergreen cliffs and mountains. At the falls, expect a steady stream of visitors in summer.

Camp Creek Falls *
(See San Juan North of Pagosa Springs group map, page 159.)

Access: Bushwhack
Rating: ★
Type: Segmented
USGS Topographic Quad: Wolf Creek Pass (37106 D7)
Trail Miles: .1-mile
Altitude: 9,560 feet
Elevation Change: From 9,400 feet, + 160 feet

Camp Creek Falls is a single leap of 25 feet cradled in an area of dark volcanic rock that is easy to see from the highway but difficult to get to because of jumbled barriers of rock, vegetation, and water.

Camp Creek crosses U.S. 160 at a runaway-truck ramp 4.5 miles below (south of) Wolf Creek Pass. The falls is visible from the highway and is reached by hiking uphill from the runaway-truck ramp.

Wolf Creek Falls *
(See San Juan North of Pagosa Springs group map, page 159.)

Access: Bushwhack
Rating: ★ ★
Type: Tiered
USGS Topographic Quad: Wolf Creek Pass (37106 D7)
Trail Miles: .2-mile
Altitude: 9,200 feet
Elevation Change: -200 feet

Wolf Creek Falls is a tiered falls in two leaps of about 35 feet each that fall into green plunge pools, one directly on the heels of the other, with the entire mass of the water of Wolf Creek crashing down. The noise is deafening, and the water froths pure white in the roar. The falls is visible from the highway looking southeast down toward Wolf Creek at a point opposite the Camp Creek runaway-truck ramp.

Opposite the ramp there is a dirt road that curves to the south and ends in a bulldozed turnaround. Reach the falls by going directly southeast over the grassy slope surrounding the bulldozed area and head down into the trees. After intersecting the stream, skirt the riverbank to the falls. The surrounding dirt and gravel slopes are dangerous to walk on, and too dangerous to allow one to get right up to the falls.

The slopes are steep down and back to the highway. Bushwhacking tolerance is required. The distance to the falls is an eighth of a mile and takes less than fifteen minutes. Don't take awkward children or careless adults on the hike.

Lower Lake Creek Falls*
(See San Juan North of Pagosa Springs group map, page 159.)

Access: Hike
Rating: ★
Type: Segmented
USGS Topographic Quad: Wolf Creek Pass (37106 D7)
Trail Miles: .2-mile
Altitude: 9,200 feet
Elevation Change: From 9,180 feet, +20 feet

The falls is right at the highway, a leap of 15 to 20 feet to a cascade that constricts immediately to enter a culvert under Highway 160 3.5 miles south of Wolf Creek Pass. It's visible from the road if you're quick, know where it is, and can enjoy seeing it at 40 miles per hour.

There is no space to pull off the road, so you have to park on either end of a length of guard barrier just above the turnoff to Falls Creek and Treasure Mountain. You'll have to walk 100 yards along the road to reach the falls. The falls is pretty but despoiled by the highway. If it's any consolation, eventually it will erode the highway away, or retreat into the mountain, back in the woods.

There are two more falls up Lake Creek but I was too bushed to whack to them .7-mile. It looks like an easy hike once you get up the hill cut through by the highway.

Upper Wolf Creek Falls*
(See San Juan North of Pagosa Springs group map, page 159.)

Access: Visible from road
Rating: ★ ★
Type: Plunge
USGS Topographic Quad: Wolf Creek Pass (37106 D7)
Trail Miles: Steep cliff, .2-mile
Altitude: 10,400 feet
Elevation Change: From 10,100 feet, +300 feet

Upper Wolf Creek Falls is a streamlined 60-foot leap in a classic wild-falls

Upper Wolf Creek Falls

setting. Enormous, solidly geometric boulders surround the stream of water, the steep slopes sweep down to the ribbon of froth and flood, and evergreens stand all around like a constant appreciative audience while the water continually throws itself into mist.

Upper Wolf Creek Falls is on an unnamed tributary to Wolf Creek 2.1 miles south of the pass. The stream flow is hidden from the highway by a deep, vegetated ravine, but the top of the falls is visible from the road looking north-northwest and only requires a seven-minute hike, climbing a couple hundred feet, to reach a close, clear view of the falls. There's no trail, but I stayed fairly high on the slope, out of the drainage, then followed deer tracks across the slope through the trees for a good view of the falls. You can get up close if you don't mind sliding down the loose slope into the creek.

The Piedra River Drainage

Piedra Falls
(See Piedra River Drainage map, page 166.)

Access: Hike
Rating: ★ ★ ★ ★
Type: Plunge
USGS Topographic Quad: Pagosa Peak (37107 D1)
Trail Miles: .2-mile
Altitude: 8,400 feet
Elevation Change: From 8,240 feet, + 160 feet

In May, the entire spring runoff of the East Fork shoots through a 6-foot-wide slot at Piedra Falls and plunges 30 feet into a white and yellow cauldron of air and water. The water screams and hisses as it thunders. The mist and thrown water drench like thrown buckets of water and, despite my poncho, soaked me immediately. The falls has a truly disorienting power. Several viewpoints offer something like shelter from the onslaught, and we tried to take pictures under an umbrella.

To get to Piedra Falls, drive west from Pagosa Springs on U.S. 160 2 miles to the top of the hill and the intersection with Archuleta County 600 (Forest Road 631), which is marked by a national forest access sign. Turn right and drive north on 631 past Stevens Field and Sullenburger and Hatcher reservoirs, across the rollling hills curling at the feet of the Weminuche into the network of the tributaries to the Piedra.

Stay on 631 across the bridge over the Piedra, which is about 20 miles from

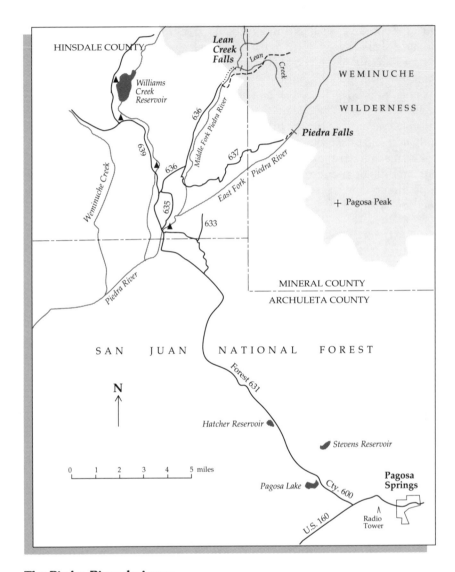

The Piedra River drainage

(**#34** on San Juan and Dolores rivers drainages map, page 136):

Piedra Falls
Lean Creek Falls

Highway 160. Take Forest Road 636, which veers off to the right: Prominent signs identify it as the Middle Fork Road. In another 2 miles there's a sharp right turn onto Forest Road 637. Stay on 637 until it ends at a flat spot below Rock Mountain right at the edge of the East Fork of the Piedra.

To get to the falls, follow the East Fork upstream on the west side, picking up a faint trail through a copse of aspen and spruce directly to the base of Piedra Falls. This requires fifteen minutes or so of hiking. The falls is hidden deep in the cliffs and is covered by the woods, so you hear it before you can see it.

Some portions of 637 are pretty rough, but there are terrific views all along the route of the mountains behind Pagosa, of the valley in between, and of the San Juans from the south. The valley of the Piedra provides a great valley hideaway, and apparently it is much used. There were several trailers full of campers near the end of the road along the East Fork. Piedra Falls is not visible from the road, but there is a small falls stringing down the cliffs near the end of the road. The distance from Pagosa is about 22 miles.

Lean Creek Falls
(See Piedra River Drainage map, page 166.)

Access: Hike
Rating: ★ ★
Type: Horsetail
USGS Topographic Quad: Cimarrona Peak (37107 E2)
Trail Miles: 1.1
Altitude: 8,600 feet
Elevation Change: From 8,400 feet, + 200 feet

We discovered Lean Creek Falls on the list at the national forest office in Pagosa Springs. The forest service's directions to the falls recommend a visit only during times of low water, since part of the hike requires walking up the streambed in a close-walled canyon. It sounded exciting, and it was.

We got to Pagosa Springs in late October around 4:00 P.M., but we didn't get to the trailhead until 5:20. Although we got to the narrows just below the falls by 6:10, that was when the sun set, and we had to turn around and find our way back to the truck before the dark stranded us in the woods.

When we went back the next morning to try again, we went up the west side of the Middle Fork without bothering with the trail marked on the map on the east side.

To get to Lean Creek Falls, take Piedra Road (Forest Road 631) north from Highway 160, which is 2 miles west of Pagosa Springs. Stay on 631 until it meets 636, then take 636 4 miles more to the end of the road in a meadow

Piedra Falls

surrounded by hunter's camps. The trailhead into the Weminuche is clearly marked. A trail goes east across the river and starts to climb into the wilderness toward Palomino Mountain and the Continental Divide trail, but it never approaches the falls.

It's more direct, and ultimately easier, just to stay on the west side and work up through the open spaces in the fir and pine woods (Englemann and ponderosa), up the smooth-rocked remnants of the old streamcourse of the Middle Fork, and once or twice down to the streambed itself. The volcanic palisades on either side of the river constrict the valley into a funnel. A fairly persistent trail starts out in the level ground above the floodplain but is then forced by the closing mouth of the funnel to skirt the cliffs at the base, once or twice disappearing into the riverbed itself.

Once inside the narrows, it's necessary at a couple of spots to climb from rock to rock in the middle of the stream.

At 1.1 miles you can see the falls from the west side of the Middle Fork through the trees; it's just below the confluence of the Middle Fork and Lean Creek. It's possible to cross the Middle Fork almost as soon as you see the falls but easier on rocks a few yards upstream.

Lean Creek Falls tumbles 60 feet over the cliffs into a pool, then cascades another 100 yards to the confluence with the Middle Fork. Its white wilderness-crooked grin peeks at you through the spruce and stripped-down aspen. It smoothes patiently the sponge-rocked lava until grass gathers like an audience around the pool. Then the fall's whiteness recollects itself before whispering its way out of the glowering dark palisades of the rock river. We made our way out of the cliffs through alternating sunlight and snowflakes.

The Vallecito Reservoir Area

There are eight or nine waterfalls north of Vallecito Reservoir, on the Los Piños River and on the Lake Fork of the Los Piños. The hikes to these falls are relatively long, and we have not yet visited the area.

To get to the Pine River trailhead for both of these areas, drive to Vallecito Reservoir on Florida Road (County 240) from Durango or Vallecito Road (County 501) north from Bayfield. Five miles beyond the dam you will reach the Vallecito Forest Service Work Center. Head right onto Forest Road 602 around the northern end of the reservoir, then northeast to Pine River campground another 7.2 miles, where the Pine River trail (523) begins.

Dennis Gebhardt's A Backpacking Guide to the Weminuche Wilderness says this trail is favored by outfitters and is heavily used, especially after July 4.

The trail is on private property the first 5 miles. Don't give the Granite Creek Ranch any reason to deny access. You enter the Weminuche Wilderness at about mile 3.8. At mile 5.8, the Pine River trail meets the Emerald Lake trail (#528, see below).

Los Piños River Falls * * * * *
(See Vallecito Reservoir Area map, page 171.)

Access: Overnight
Rating and Type: Not visited
USGS Topographic Quad: Emerald Lake (37107 E4)
Trail Miles: 9 to 19
Altitude: 9,080 feet, 9,600 feet, 9,120 feet, 9,320 feet, 10,230 feet
Elevation Change: From 7,910 feet to first falls, + 1,170 feet; to uppermost falls, + 2,300 feet

After passing the intersection of the Emerald Lake trail, the canyon of the Los Piños narrows for the next 2 miles, and Gebhardt says there are many nice cascades and small falls below the trail. The canyon opens up at mile 7.5, providing suitable camping spots.

There is a double falls in the cliffs to the east coming down Falls Creek at mile 9. A third of a mile farther along the trail another falls comes down from the east. Flint Creek and the Flint Creek trail (#527) are at the 11.75-mile mark. Gebhardt confirms the existence of a "tremendous" falls on the Los Piños itself, half a mile beyond Flint Creek.

The Pine River trail continues on to the Continental Divide, and Gebhardt says there's yet another "miniature Niagara Falls" at the Rincon La Osa trail (mile 19).

Lake Creek Falls * * * *
(See Vallecito Reservoir Area map, page 171.)

Access: Overnight
Rating and Type: Not visited
USGS Topographic Quad: Emerald Lake (37107 E4)
Trail Miles: 13.8
Altitude: 10,950 feet, 10,950 feet, 11,050 feet, 11,600 feet
Elevation Change: From 7,920 feet to lowest falls, + 3,030 feet; to uppermost falls, + 3,680 feet

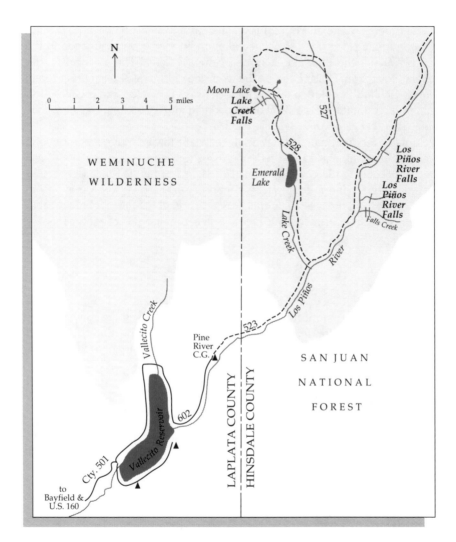

The Vallecito Reservoir area
(**#35** on San Juan and Dolores rivers drainages map, page 136):

Los Piños River Falls
Lake Creek Falls

The Emerald Lake trail (#528) is reached at 8,360 feet by hiking 5.5 miles along the Pine River trail (#523, see above). At mile 9.5 is a junction in the trail between Little Emerald Lake and Emerald Lake. There's a noisy falls coming down from Dollar Lake on the west side of Emerald Lake during spring runoff. Gebhardt's guide to the Weminuche says Emerald Lake is Colorado's second largest natural lake (279 acres), a mile and a half long by half a mile wide, 248 feet deep, and heavily used.

Continue around Emerald Lake on the east side toward Moon Lake. Beyond Emerald Lake, at mile 11.2, the trail crosses to the west side of Lake Creek then back again to the east side at mile 12.2. In another half-mile is a big falls on Lake Creek, and a double falls is marked on the quad on a tributary to Lake Creek from the west. The trail crosses beneath the falls on Lake Creek, then crosses again at mile 13.8 below a falls running out of Moon Lake.

The Silverton Area

There are two falls in the Silverton area we know of, although there are undoubtedly many more hidden in the high peaks circling the town. One is on Burns Gulch, a tributary to the Animas, north of Silverton on the road toward Engineer Pass. The other is on Lime Creek, a tributary to the Animas River south of Silverton.

Burns Gulch Falls *
(See Silverton Area map, page 173.)

Access: Roadside
Rating: ★
Type: Horsetail
USGS Topographic Quad: Handies Peak (37107 H5)
Trail Miles: 0
Altitude: 10,800 feet
Elevation Change: None

We glimpsed Burns Gulch Falls while driving toward Silverton after a hike into the Big Blue Wilderness from Engineer Pass. Burns Gulch is on private property on the east side of the Animas River 9.5 miles north of Silverton on Colorado 110 (Forest Road 586) and 2 miles north of the old mining town of Eureka. The falls is a horsetail leap of 30 to 40 feet and is visible from the road. There is a bridge across the river about half a mile north of the falls.

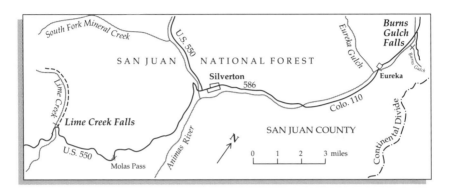

The Silverton area
(**#36** on San Juan and Dolores rivers drainages map, page 136):

Burns Gulch Falls
Lime Creek Falls

Lime Creek Falls
(See Silverton Area map, above.)

Access: Roadside, walk in
Rating: ★ ♪
Type: Block
USGS Topographic Quad: Snowdon Peak (37107 F6)
Trail Miles: .03-mile
Altitude: 10,725 feet
Elevation Change: None

Lime Creek Falls is a small 10-foot leap visible in a cut set back 50 yards from the highway as U.S. 550 passes over Lime Creek. There's a trail approaching from the highway and a turnout right below the drainage, making it easy to pull off for a longer look. And it provides a nice view of the steeper cascades below the road.

Take U.S. 550 south of Silverton about 10 miles. The highway curves very sharply in toward the mountainside to make a hairpin at Lime Creek, and there's a long stretch of wide shoulder for parking just below the bridge over the creek.

The West Dolores River

The valley of the West Dolores River provides access to the Lizard Head Wilderness from the south. There are waterfalls visible from the road to Dunton, and a short mile's hike into meadows carpeted with flowers brings you to two more isolated falls. For stronger hikers and backpackers, this valley offers hiking and climbing of the most rigorous sort—including Mount Wilson, Wilson Peak, and El Diente—and more than repays every effort. The secluded waterfalls below Navajo Lake similarly reward the persistent.

Dunton can be reached either from Dolores or from Colorado 145, 5 miles south of Lizard Head Pass.

From Dolores, drive 11 miles north on Colorado 145. Two miles before reaching Stoner, take a left up Forest Road 535. Aspen cover both sides of the valley most of the 20 miles to Dunton, with Mount Wilson and El Diente looming prominently to the north.

To get to this area from Telluride, drive 5 miles south of Lizard Head Pass on Colorado 145. Take a right on Forest Road 535 opposite the turnoff to Cayton campground. This dirt road, impassable in wet weather, climbs a series of switchbacks steeply uphill and then crosses miles of rolling meadows to enter the forest. You pass the Navajo Lake trailhead at mile 6, Burro Bridge campground at mile 7, and arrive in Dunton at mile 8.5.

Eagle Falls
(See West Dolores River group map, page 175.)

Access: Wheelchair
Rating: ★ ★
Type: Plunge
USGS Topographic Quad: Dolores Peak (37108 G1)
Trail Miles: 0
Altitude: 9,000 feet
Elevation Change: None

We've visited this falls twice. In late April it was completely frozen. Eagle Falls plunges 30 feet off the edge of the cliffs that are visible from the road a half-mile below the town of Dunton. There may be a trail up to the falls after the mine property, which is littered with machinery, immediately below the road, but when we first visited the hillside was covered with snow.

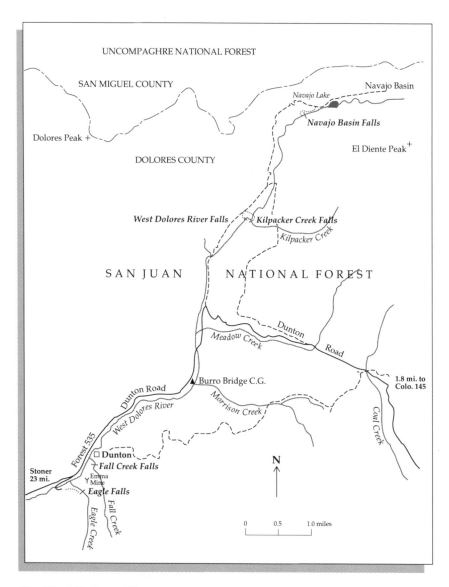

The West Dolores River group

(**#37** on San Juan and Dolores rivers drainages map, page 136):

Eagle Falls
Fall Creek Falls
Kilpacker Creek Falls
West Dolores River Falls
Navajo Basin Falls

We visited this falls again in July 1990, but at this time of year the falls was completely dry. Looks like it could be quite impressive at the right time of year.

Fall Creek Falls *
(See West Dolores River group map, page 175.)

Access: Roadside or hike
Rating: ★
Type: Plunge
USGS Topographic Quad: Dolores Peak (37108 G1)
Trail Miles: .1-mile
Altitude: 8,920 feet
Elevation Change: From 8,900 feet, + 20 feet

Fall Creek Falls is on private property associated with the old mining town of Dunton, which once flourished as a funky resort replete with hot springs. It closed in 1988, but the owners have established a caretaker in one of the cabins, who allowed me to walk up to the falls, frozen in April.

We visited again in July, and the falls flowed freely, a single 20- to 25-foot plunge that is visible from the bridge into Dunton. It's a shame this place is now closed to the public.

If you're not satisfied with the view of the town and falls from the road, walk across the bridge, staying on the road, and ask the caretaker for permission to walk up to the falls. He probably will not be overjoyed to see you.

The road to Colorado 145 east from Dunton is not plowed, and we were informed that it would not open, even in a drought year, until mid-May. When we visited the valley in July, we drove into Dunton this way.

The Navajo Lake Trail

There are three waterfalls on the upper West Dolores drainage, although the Dolores Peak 15-foot quadrangle indicates only two. One cluster of two falls is 1.75 miles up the Navajo Lake trail. The third falls is in the woods below Navajo Lake.

The hike up Navajo Basin is sometimes stiff, sometimes steady; getting up to Navajo Lake is a grind, but in July the flowers are spectacular the whole way. The national forest literature says that Navajo Lake is the most popular destination on the West Dolores—not a great place to go to get away from people. I concur, although during the week the folks aren't oppressive.

Kilpacker Creek Falls*
(See West Dolores River group map, page 175.)

Access: Hike and bushwhack
Rating: ★ ★
Type: Twin plunge
USGS Topographic Quad: Dolores Peak (37108 G1)
Trail Miles: 1.75
Altitude: 9,900 feet
Elevation Change: From 9,340 feet, +560 feet; ±20 feet for the bushwhack

Kilpacker Creek Falls is about 25 feet high and is divided into two leaps by a rock in the middle. It is very lovely, with no pool to speak of. It's tempting to try to reach this from West Dolores River Falls (see below), but it's easier to cross the West Dolores *above* the confluence with Kilpacker Creek. Once you get to the rest spot in the trees above the confluence (at 9,900 feet), go on a few yards farther, cut right and a little downhill off the trail, cross the West Dolores at any of several log-strewn stretches, and hike south through the woods to the falls—all in all taking about ten minutes from the trail. Kilpacker and West Dolores make a mildly strenuous day hike from Burro Bridge campground or Dunton.

West Dolores River Falls*
(See West Dolores River group map, page 175.)

Access: Hike and bushwhack
Rating: ★ ★
Type: Plunge and block
USGS Topographic Quad: Dolores Peak (37108 G1)
Trail Miles: 1.75
Altitude: 9,820 feet
Elevation Change: From 9,340 feet, +560 feet to 9,900 feet on trail;
 -80 feet to falls from trail

West Dolores River Falls is about 24 feet high, a single wide leap to a cascade below, and hidden at the bottom of a hill by deep woods. This falls, on the West Dolores River, is not marked on the Dolores Peak quad. Kilpacker Creek Falls is marked immediately upstream of the confluence of the two streams.

West Dolores River Falls

West Dolores River Falls is the falls you hear from the trail: Go down the hill 30 or 40 yards from the resting spot in the trees at 9,900 feet. Circle back to the left to approach the falls. The easiest way to see Kilpacker Creek Falls is by climbing back up to the trail first, not by trying to work through the dense woods upstream (see Kilpacker Creek Falls).

Navajo Basin Falls*
(See West Dolores River group map, page 175.)

Access: Hike and bushwhack
Rating: ★ ★ ★
Type: Segmented
USGS Topographic Quad: Dolores Peak (37108 G1)
Trail Miles: 4.5 (4.3 hike + .2-mile bushwhack)
Altitude: 10,920 feet
Elevation Change: From 9,340 feet, + 2,060 feet, −480 feet

You can see Navajo Basin Falls across the valley from the trail at around the 3.5-mile mark (10,600 feet) just before hitting the steep switchbacks up to Navajo Lake. The falls consists of a single leap of about 15 feet and two broad 6-foot platform sprays below over a stretch of 50 yards, and a steady, steep cascade at the bottom. The vegetation is wild, the setting gorgeous, the falls a beauty. There are also mock falls above and below, since the terrain below this glacial lake is rocky and steep.

There are breathtaking views including the lake, the basin, and Gladstone Peak up the trail ahead to the east. El Diente (14,159 feet) embraces the north side of the lake, and the western limb of Wilson Peak looms to the south. Coyotes howl at night, and you might even see one if you're quick.

To get to the falls, follow the trail .25-mile from the lake, then drop to the left off the trail where it veers away from the watercourse. When you hit the streamcourse, follow it downstream until the top of the falls becomes obvious. Circle around and down; do not attempt to climb directly down the cliffs.

Our hike to the falls below Navajo Lake was punctuated by rain immediately followed by hail and a tremendous thunderstorm, then by intermittent rain and showers, and then by cocktails before dinner chilled with fresh salmon-egg-sized hail.

Navajo Basin Falls

The Cortez-Durango Area

McElmo Falls
(See Cortez-Durango Area map, page 182.)

Access: Hike
Rating: ★ ★
Type: Plunge
USGS Topographic Quad: Cortez (37108 C5)
Trail Miles: .25-mile
Altitude: 5,900 feet
Elevation Change: From 5,910 feet, +40 feet, -60 feet

Scoured pale sandstone spreads the flow of water above and below McElmo Falls, which plunges in a single, clear stream from the edge of a wide sandstone bench about 25 to 30 feet high.

The falls comes as a complete surprise in the desolate eroded arroyos and canyons surrounding Cortez. In contrast to the arid canyon all around, moss abounds near the falls, and there is a strong sense of isolation despite the nearness of town. The creek runs a little murky, reminding me of the South Platte. Some foam at the bottom of any falls is natural, but this creek has that street-drainage odor of urban rivers. There are a few tires in the stream, partially spoiling the natural canyon environment. We visited in April; I would expect the flow of water to be highly variable.

Drive 2.5 miles south on U.S. 666 from its intersection with U.S. 160, west of town. U.S. 666 passes a dirt road to the west that heads north of Sleeping Ute Mountain onto the Ute Reservation. The county airport is immediately southwest of this intersection.

Turn right and take the dirt road for a quarter-mile; then turn right onto a dirt road that curves to the east to become someone's driveway. Climb straight north up to the lip of a reservoir bordered by natural stone terraces. Turn left and walk west on a dirt track skirting the south end of the reservoir. Cross the reservoir inlet and head across country north-northeast to McElmo Creek. Then follow the creek's shallow drainage to the west. About a quarter-mile from the reservoir the falls drops out of the dry, sand-scoured canyon environment into a grassy amphitheater carved by the creek. You can make your way down to the bottom of the amphitheater by climbing down the muddy banks west of the falls.

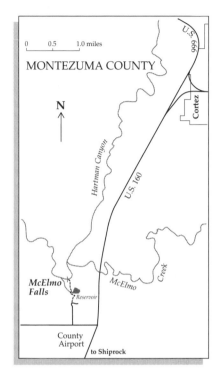

The Cortez-Durango area
(**#38** on San Juan and Dolores rivers drainages map, page 136):

McElmo Falls

McElmo Falls is on private land but probably oft-visited by local youth. There is some evidence of foot traffic, mostly above the falls. Only the local dogs paid us any heed—at a distance, I'm glad to say.

Falls Creek Falls*

Access: Roadside
Rating: ★
Type: Horsetail
USGS Topographic Quad:
   Durango East (37107 C7)
Trail Miles: 0
Altitude: 6,800 feet
Elevation Change: None

This is a small falls on private property—it's in someone's backyard, in fact. And although its presence is no doubt pleasant for the owners, the signs they've erected to discourage trespassing clearly indicate others would like to have a little piece of this private paradise.

The falls is not worth visiting—too many homes nearby and not very much water, just a pleasant trickle down the rocks. We're including it because it's marked on the quad, but it does not appear on any of the maps in this chapter.

The falls flows from the cliffs adjacent to a county road west of Highway 550 that is about 4 miles north of Durango.

McElmo Falls

The Gunnison, San Miguel, and Uncompahgre Rivers Drainages Map

39, 40: The San Miguel River Group
41: The Telluride Vicinity Group
42, 43, 44: The Ouray Vicinity Group
45, 47: The Big Blue Wilderness Group
46: The Lake City Vicinity Group
48, 49, 50, 51, 52: Waterfalls North and West of the Gunnison River
53, 54, 55: The Escalante Canyon Vicinity Group

6

The Gunnison, San Miguel, and Uncompahgre Rivers Drainages

Don Juan Maria de Rivera led a gold-hunting expedition in southern Colorado between 1761 and 1765. As a mark of his passage, he carved a cross into a cottonwood tree at the confluence of the Gunnison and Uncompahgre rivers. Fathers Escalante and Dominguez (mentioned in the introduction to Chapter 5) recorded seeing Rivera's cross when they arrived at the confluence in 1776.

The Uncompahgre is named after the Ute word *ancapagari*, meaning "hot-water springs." In Escalante's account of his expedition, he says it was "by the Yutas called the Anacapagari (which according to the interpreter means Laguna Colorado) because near its source there is a spring of red water, hot and tasting bad."

Anyone who has spent a pleasant hour in the hot springs in Ouray is mighty grateful for that bad-tasting water. Escalante himself probably wouldn't have minded climbing into it if he'd known about it.

The Uncompahgre originates in Lake Como, north of Silverton, but the reference to Laguna Colorado ("red lake") makes sense if you've ever driven up

185

U.S. 550 south of Ouray and gone over Red Mountain Pass. The rock in the bottom of the entire length of Red Creek has been stained by the deposition of iron oxide, commonly a sign of mineralization—the hydrothermal process by which all the minerals mined in the Rockies were pressure-cooked into the rocks. Escalante was not impressed by the presence of minerals. He called the Uncompahgre the Rio de San Francisco.

The Gunnison, on the other hand, was named after Captain John Gunnison, of the U.S. Army, who is best remembered for: 1. shooting his own horse in the head during a bison-hunting trip, and 2. dying in Utah, along with the rest of his expedition, at the hands of a Paiute war party in 1853 while he was making his ablutions. He should have stayed in Colorado.

The first European settlers in the Gunnison basin were gold-seekers who came up the Arkansas River and over the Continental Divide, founding Tincup in the Sawatch as well as Crested Butte and Gothic in the Elk Mountains. Nestled in the San Juans south of the Gunnison River, they sought gold and silver near Telluride, Ouray, and Lake City. More than a few of these pioneers met their ends in these mountains, even though they prudently avoided partying with the Paiute in Utah.

Most of us just wander around the beautiful Victorian homes and storefronts in these mountain towns, sniff at the mine tailings, and imagine the struggles of the men and women who made their lives among the unforgiving slopes of broken rock. As they passed, they left monuments, markers, and ruins that serve today, as Rivera's cross once did, as cenotaphs of hope.

The Elk Mountains are geologically unlike the San Juans. They are composed of thrusted and metamorphosed Paleozoic sediments that are ten times as old as the volcanic rocks of the San Juans. But both ranges cradling the Gunnison River were subjected to the grinding of glaciers down to the 8,000-foot level, and the net result, for our present purposes, was very similar. The Uncompahgre is tributary to the Gunnison; the famed confluence is now under the waters of Blue Mesa Reservoir.

The San Miguel is tributary to the Dolores, which never meets the Gunnison. We include the falls of the San Miguel in this chapter because the river originates near Telluride, which is only 10 miles from Ouray as the crow flies, if crows flew over the 13,000-foot ridge that separates the towns.

In this chapter we describe waterfalls to the west and south and inside Ouray; a cluster of falls around Telluride, including the state's highest; falls in the Uncompahgre and Gunnison national forests; in the Lizard Head, West Elk, and Big Blue wildernesses; and in the Black Canyon of the Gunnison.

The San Miguel River

There are at least fifteen waterfalls on the streams tributary to the San Miguel within a forty-minute drive of Telluride. Despite the growing popularity of the town, it is still possible to find places tucked away in the nearby San Juans where you can have more than a moment by yourself.

There's one highway in and out of Telluride, a spur of Colorado 145. Three miles west of town, 145 heads west toward Placerville and the intersection with Colorado 62 from Ridgway; or you can turn south toward Lizard Head Pass and, ultimately, the town of Dolores.

If you take the turn toward Lizard Head, following the course of the South Fork of the San Miguel, there is a falls you can see from the road along the way, and close-up views are also possible.

Lake Fork Falls* *
(See San Miguel River group map, page 188.)

Access: Hike
Rating: ★ ★ ★
Type: 2 horsetail falls
USGS Topographic Quad: Mount Wilson (37107 G8)
Trail Miles: 200 yards
Altitude: 8,750 feet, 8,910 feet
Elevation Change: Minimal

Lower Lake Fork Falls is 180 to 190 feet high, including a 100-foot main leap and a 50- to 60-foot horsetail immediately below that, with an emerald green pool at the base of sheer cliffs. The best viewpoint is from along a ridge walk to the north about 50 yards. The narrow, sheer, knifelike cut of the canyon makes this location scary and spectacular. If you're subject to vertigo, forget it. There is a smaller companion falls upstream.

To get to this delightful falls near the mountain community of Ames, drive south on Colorado 145. The road to Ames is on the north side of the curve of Ophir loop, 7 miles south of the turn to Telluride.

Near the 6-mile point, Colorado 145 drops down off the hills into the valley of the South Fork of the San Miguel. About half a mile before the sharpest point of the loop, still quite high on the curve, you can see a waterfall almost directly south on the other side of the valley. It may be hard to see through the trees.

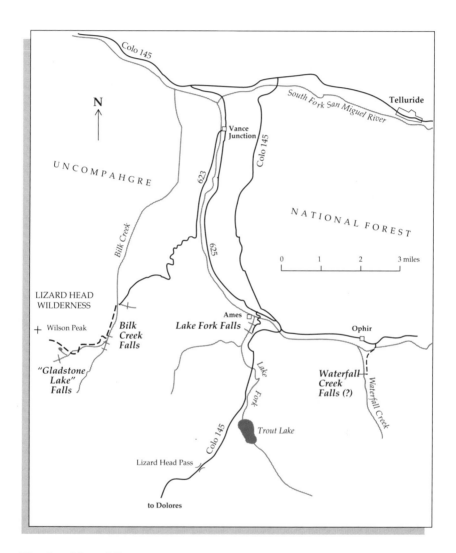

The San Miguel River group

(**#39** on Gunnison, San Miguel, and Uncompahgre rivers drainages map, page 184):

Lake Fork Falls
Waterfall Creek Falls
Bilk Creek Falls
Gladstone Lake Falls

The San Miguel River

In another half-mile down the hill, there's a dirt road turning sharply down and to the southwest. At the bottom of the hill (.5-mile) turn left to cross the Howard Fork and reach Ames. There's a large power generating station there, one of the first and oldest hydroelectric stations in Colorado. Turn up the short, steep hill to your left, passing the house with excitable dogs.

Keep on this narrow dirt road. It winds up through the aspen on its way to a mine on the slope below the highway. In .3-mile, just downhill from a powerline transformer, there's a small sign nailed to a tree pointing the way along a dirt track toward the Lake Fork, where the waterfalls are.

Follow this track less than a hundred yards to a turnaround. At the south end of the turnaround, a trail takes you on a nine- to ten-minute walk across the old streamcourse of the Lake Fork to the falls.

You can reach a second, smaller falls upstream on the Lake Fork by going another .25-mile up the dirt road beyond the sign and turnoff to the lower falls, just past some old buildings posted on the right. The road switchbacks steeply up to the left, but there's a narrow turnaround in sight of the mine buildings, and the top of the upper falls is visible from the road. Scramble a short distance downhill to see and hear the whole falls. Upper Lake Fork Falls has a 35-foot main leap split in two. There are also two taller, thinner leaps on the same rock face.

We tried to get to these falls in late March once, but the snow was too deep even to cross the short distance to the lower falls without snowshoes.

If the road is dry, four-wheel-drive is not necessary, but good traction and clearance are recommended. On one summer trip to the Telluride area, a friend in a passenger car drove over a rock on the road down to Ames from the highway and shredded a tire.

While you're in the neighborhood, you might want to check out the town of Ophir, and even take a hike in search of a falls on Waterfall Creek.

Waterfall Creek Falls *
(See San Miguel River group map, page 188.)

Access: Hike
Rating and Type: Not visited
USGS Topographic Quad: Ophir (37107 G7)
Trail Miles: Not on map
Altitude and Elevation Change: Unknown

We reconnoitered this falls on the basis of a benchmark located on the quad that says "waterfall" at 9,974 feet. The name of the creek, and this benchmark, led us to think there might be a falls, and a woman living in Ophir told us there is a falls up one of the drainages on the south side of the Howard Fork, but she wasn't definite about which. The benchmark is marked half a mile up Waterfall Creek. The trail begins at the road a quarter-mile past downtown Ophir, goes downhill across the Howard Fork at about 9,720 feet, then veers a little west to climb the Waterfall Creek drainage. It was too late in the day for us to verify the woman's testimony.

Wilson Mesa Waterfalls

West of Telluride, Highway 145 goes through the valley at the foot of the San Miguel Mountains, which include Wilson Peak, Sunshine Mountain, and Dolores Peak. At the base of this ridge of peaks is broad, forest-covered Wilson's Mesa, site of many a Telluride Chamber of Commerce photo. There is a trail crossing the mesa from east to west inside Uncompahgre National Forest, and dirt roads drive up the drainages onto the mesa from several points along 145. There are several waterfalls up the Bilk Creek drainage, and one up Fall Creek. We'll start with Fall Creek, farthest west from Telluride.

Fall Creek Falls *
(See map on page 191.)

Access: Hike
Rating: ★ ★
Type: Horsetail
USGS Topographic Quad: Little Cone (37108 H1)
Trail Miles: .75-mile
Altitude: 9,000 feet
Elevation Change: From 8,840 feet at road, + 160 feet

Eleven miles west of Telluride on 145 and 1.5 miles east of Placerville, there's a sign indicating national forest access up Fall Creek, and a road sign for Road 57p (indicated as number 18 on the national forest map). Follow this 6.75 miles until it crosses a small drainage on the left, about 1.25 miles below Woods Lake.

There is a trail indicated as starting on the west side of the creek, but it's easiest to pull off at the turnout into a camping area in the woods just past the drainage.

Cross the creek and follow a faint game trail up the drainage. Try to stay in the open areas, although following this game trail is often a lot like pure bushwhacking. Just follow the curve of the creek, and in about twenty minutes (.5-mile) you come to a wall of organ-pipe volcanic rock about 30 feet high, and the segmented falls that tumbles over and down it very prettily.

The whole drainage is choked with fallen trees covered with moss, and the cliffs near the falls are beautifully decorated with streams of moss. Passage through the brush in October, when there is a light dusting of snow on the ground, may be easier than when the vegetation is at its lushest and most impenetrable.

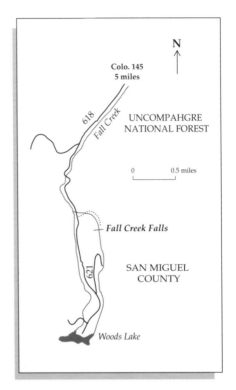

The San Miguel River group
(**#40** on Gunnison, San Miguel, and Uncompahgre rivers drainages map, page 184):

Fall Creek Falls

The Bilk Creek Drainage

There are five waterfalls on the Bilk Creek drainage. None of them are named, so we designate them by order of occurrence as you hike up the trail. The usual approach to these falls would be either up the drainage from Colorado 145 on 624, up Bilk Creek; or via 623, south and west from Vance Junction and also reached from Colorado 145.

Highway 623 is shown on the quad and the national forest map as crossing the South Fork of the San Miguel to meet Highway 625 3 miles south of Vance Junction, but that crossing doesn't appear to exist any longer. There's a bridge crossing the South Fork just south of the Vance Junction schoolhouse. Highway 623 then follows the South Fork upstream 3 miles on the west side of the stream and turns uphill as indicated on the map and climbs through the woods to the slopes of Wilson Mesa.

Highway 623 goes all the way to the wilderness boundary, where it meets trail 409 coming up Bilk Creek. Highway 623 seems in good condition most of the way, having been used to supply the mines in the basin. There were a couple of washed-out spots, and we did not try to drive our passenger vehicle beyond the abandoned, weathered ranch buildings right by the road about 2 miles from the wilderness boundary and trailhead marker. We saw others who did go farther in their four-wheel-drives, but there were no vehicles at the trailhead, and we couldn't tell how far up this road the four-wheelers went.

The ranch buildings are still privately owned. Please show respect for the owners' willingness to let people cross their land by leaving the ruins unmolested.

We hiked down this drainage from the pass between Bilk Basin and Navajo Basin, leaving a car at both ends of the trip: one at the ranch ruins on 623, the other at the trailhead north of Dunton, on the southern slope of the San Miguel Mountains.

Bilk Creek Falls★★★★
(See San Miguel River group map, page 188.)

Access: Hike
Rating: ★ to ★★★
Type: 1 block and 3 horsetails (one not seen)
USGS Topographic Quad: Mount Wilson (37107 G8)
Trail Miles: 1 to 6
Altitude: 10,600 feet, 10,370 feet, 10,550 feet, 10,720 feet
Elevation Change: From 10,080 feet at trailhead to first falls, +520 feet; from
    trailhead to second falls, +290 feet; to third falls, +80 feet; to fourth
    falls, +170 feet

The first falls is 600 feet and .2-mile above the road just before it ends at
the wilderness boundary. We crossed this drainage at the end of our hike, and
were so tired that we not only didn't see the falls but we didn't even notice
the stream running beneath the road.

The second falls, visible from the trail, is a strong, broad leap of 20 feet with
a white slide of water above it. The second falls is a few hundred yards below
and east of the trail after a .5-mile hike from the trailhead.

The third falls is about 70 feet high with a strong upper leap that spreads
on the rocks below, stark against the enclosing cliff wall and creating an isolated, cloistered feeling. It is on Bilk Creek, visible from the trail 200 yards
beyond the second falls.

The trail now goes all the way to within 50 yards of the third falls, where
you get a decent, though not completely clear view of the third and fourth
falls up the creek.

A faint trail parallels the creek and leads into the small amphitheater holding
the third falls. The fourth falls cannot be seen at all from within this amphitheater.

The fourth falls is 100 feet high with beautiful spreading braids and splashes
and is located 200 yards upstream from the third falls, just above the confluence of Bilk Creek and the unnamed creek whose source is Gladstone Lake.
From a distance the two separate waterfalls seem to be one continuous fall
of water, but they are separated by extremely dense brush and cliffs.

The trail is easy going from the trailhead to its view upstream of the third
falls. Then it starts a series of long switchbacks to climb above the falls on its
way higher into the basin, and provides several different views of the waterfalls.

The Mount Wilson quad shows the switchbacks beginning much nearer the
trailhead than is actually the case—presumably to provide better views of the
falls, or maybe to reclaim the slope.

The trail crosses the long slope above and west of the falls and finally meets the old trail indicated on the quad. Bushwhacking down to the base of the fourth falls is steep but fairly easy if you can maintain your sense of direction (take compass headings). We hit the old trail on our way out, not knowing that's what it was, and got rather confused when it suddenly ended in the middle of nowhere on the slope.

Beyond the waterfalls, trail 623 meets another one coming from the direction of Lizard Head Pass, then climbs up into the glacial basin encircled by Gladstone and Wilson peaks.

Gladstone Lake Falls *
(See San Miguel River group map, page 188.)

Access: Hike and bushwhack
Rating: ★ ★
Type: Horsetail
USGS Topographic Quad: Mount Wilson (37107 G8)
Trail Miles: 3.2 to lake; .3-mile easy bushwhack to base of falls
Altitude: 12,100 feet
Elevation Change: From 10,080 feet at trailhead, +2,020 feet

This is a 100-foot horsetail spilling noisily down sheer rock from a glacier below Gladstone Peak. Glacial melting means a variable flow from early morning to late in the day. There are many steep cascades and small leaps on the stream all the way down to Bilk Creek. This falls is not marked on the topo but makes an enchanting accompaniment to the unnamed lake below Gladstone Peak.

This lake, which we call Gladstone Lake, is at 12,000 feet on the approach to Wilson Peak. The trail climbs up out of the lush vegetation of Bilk Basin (see Bilk Creek access drainage information above) onto stony tundra, passing between rock formations that are reminiscent of collapsed castles. At the lake, the view of the upper basin opens up, and you can see the falls on the cliffs below Gladstone Peak, beyond the southwest end of the lake.

Anticipate meeting other hikers along the trail.

The Telluride Vicinity

Telluride is mostly noted these days for its star quality, and for the series of summer festivals that it hosts, including the film and bluegrass festivals. The

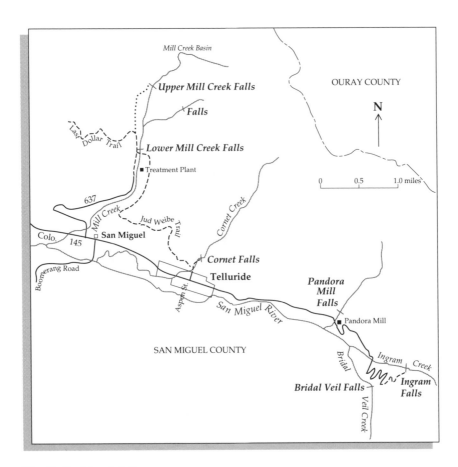

The Telluride vicinity group
(**#41** on Gunnison, San Miguel, and Uncompahgre rivers drainages map,
page 184):

Bridal Veil Falls
Ingram Falls
Cornet Falls
Mill Creek Falls, Upper and Lower
Pandora Mill Falls

valley of the San Miguel is narrow, so any increase in population, however temporary, can threaten to wipe away the very things that attract people to the mountains in the first place—like the solitude and sense of isolation.

Fortunately for the resorts and ski areas, all people do not want the same things we do when we head for the hills. But even if you enjoy the crowds and the mountains at the same time, there may be moments when you'd like to ditch everyone—*todos del mundo,* "all of the world," as they say in Mexico—and there are places close to town where this is possible.

There are six waterfalls we know of in the immediate vicinity of Telluride. All are reached by driving on the dead-end spur of Colorado 145 that leads directly into town whether you come from Dolores to the south, or from Ridgway (or Ouray) via Placerville down the San Miguel to the west.

You reach Bridal Veil Falls and Ingram Falls by driving 3 miles beyond Telluride into the head of the valley, past the Pandora Mill, then uphill on a dirt road that switchbacks to Bridal Veil in .6-mile, then another .5-mile to a trail that climbs .4-mile to the top of Ingram Falls.

Bridal Veil Falls

(See Telluride Vicinity group map, page 195.)

Access: Roadside
Rating: ★ ★ ★ ★
Type: Horsetail
USGS Topographic Quad: Telluride (37107 H7)
Trail Miles: 0
Altitude: 10,000 feet
Elevation Change: None

Bridal Veil Falls is the highest falls in Colorado, 365 feet by some accounts, but the wooden sign at the falls indicates a height of 431 feet, presumably including the cascades downstream. The falls does not really qualify as a plunge, because there is no pool at the bottom, just an enormous pile of eroded rock. When water flow is low, as in late fall before it has frozen completely, the water leaves the rock for relatively short distances until it breaks up into a rainlike mist. At times of higher flow, as in late June, the torrent is so strong that it falls freely several hundreds of feet, and the apparent slow motion of the leap is hypnotic when seen from any distance.

Bridal Veil Falls is the result of a hanging valley carved by the Wisconsin glaciation. The volcanoes of the Silverton series laid down the lava, which

Bridal Veil Falls

stream flow eroded into a plain that the glaciers carved into. Because the glacier of the central valley carved deeper into the valley of the San Miguel than into the smaller basins above, the deeper gorge of the San Miguel glacier left a sheer cliff 400 feet high, over which Bridal Creek now tumbles to create the falls.

The picturesque powerhouse above the falls operated from 1904 to 1954. You can no longer drive up to the powerhouse, but you can drive right to the falls. A truck with good tires could make it, but we recommend four-wheel-drive.

We've visited Bridal Veil several times: at the height of summer and in early autumn, when it begins to freeze and the spreading rime of ice is already forming.

In late October some water is still coming over the edge, but more flows over the rock east of the powerhouse buildings, making a second falls about two-thirds the height of Bridal Veil.

The road to Bridal Veil, and to a trailhead to Ingram above it, was snow-packed in October. Its steep hairpin turns made it prudent to get down off the cliffside before evening froze it into a toboggan run. Ingram Falls was already frozen at the top and showed little sign of flowing water.

In late March, the frozen falls spreads all over the mountain in a gigantic lacework pattern. The road to the falls is plowed barely to the end of the road in front of the Pandora Mill, and a hike up to Bridal Veil through the knee-deep snow had me begging for snowshoes.

This Bridal Veil Falls, incidentally, is one of five sharing the name in the state. But once you've seen it, you won't confuse it with any of the others.

Ingram Falls
(See Telluride Vicinity group map, page 195.)

Access: Roadside
Rating: ★ ★
Type: Horsetail
USGS Topographic Quad: Telluride (37107 H7)
Trail Miles: 1 from Bridal Veil, .6-mile from end of road
Altitude: 11,000 feet
Elevation Change: From 10,300 feet, +700 feet

Ingram Falls is a horsetail cascade, steepest over a stretch of perhaps 80 to 90 feet. It stands out brilliantly in the sunlight at the head of the San Miguel valley but is eclipsed by Bridal Veil the moment you see it. At the top of Ingram Falls is the base of an abandoned tramway and the Black Bear Mine. The entrance of the Meldrum Tunnel is located at the base of the steep cliffs north of the waterfall. It connects with the Treasury Tunnel, whose entrance is a few miles south of Ouray at Ironton Park.

Cornet Falls
(See Telluride Vicinity group map, page 195.)

Access: Walk in
Rating: ★ ★
Type: Plunge
USGS Topographic Quad: Telluride (37107 H7)
Trail Miles: .25-mile
Altitude: 9,200 feet
Elevation Change: From 8,880 feet, +320 feet

Cornet Falls

Cornet Falls is a 50-foot plunge off an eroded sandstone escarpment not a quarter of a mile north of Telluride. Cornet Creek was flowing nicely when we visited in late March, and there wasn't too much snow to cross. The falls had built up a cone of ice 30 to 40 feet high, and as spring encroached the stream of the fall had cut right into the center of the cone, leaving a shape very like a huge cornet.

Many people were hiking to the falls when we were there, and I'm sure in the summer it must be zoolike.

Colorado Avenue is Telluride's main street. It intersects Aspen Street in the center of town, immediately west of the New Sheraton Hotel and the court-house. Three short blocks uphill (north) on Aspen take you to the Jud Weibe trailhead and a small parking area. The quarter-mile trail to Cornet Falls heads directly up the Cornet Creek drainage; alternatively, the Jud Weibe trail cuts across the slope to the west, providing views of the town and the valley.

Mill Creek Falls* *
(See Telluride Vicinity group map, page 195.)

Access: Hike
Rating: ★ ★
Type: Plunge and horsetail
USGS Topographic Quad: Telluride (37107 H7)
Trail Miles: 1, 2
Altitude: 10,400 feet
Elevation Change: From about 9,700 feet at end of dirt road, + 700 feet

The Mill Creek waterfalls are not indicated on the 15-foot quadrangle, but the upper falls is marked on the Uncompahgre National Forest map, and on the USGS 1:100,000 series.

Drive about a mile west of Telluride, to the cluster of buildings called San Miguel on the quad. There's a Texaco station to mark the location of the com-munity, which is fairly scattered. A cattle-guard gate and dirt road to the north cross private property but are the national forest access to the Deep Creek trail. This road (Forest Road 637) winds northwest uphill, then hairpins back to the east, giving great views of the San Miguel valley instantly. Drive to the fence guarding the Telluride water treatment facility. The Deep Creek trailhead is just below a parking area at the fence.

The Deep Creek trail (418) skirts the facility, then parallels Mill Creek for about a mile before turning sharply west. Twenty minutes from the trailhead there's

Lower Mill Creek Falls

a fork in the trail with a sign prominently marking the Deep Creek trail and mileage to the Lost Dollar trail, to the left. If you hike a few yards farther on the main trail you came up on, it will soon cross the creek on a bridge and head back across the slope east toward Telluride. Stay on a faint trail scrambling up and down over deadwood and rocks on the west side of Mill Creek, and within two to three minutes it turns to reveal a beautiful 30-foot leap down the walls that are making Mill Creek so difficult to follow. This is Lower Mill Creek Falls.

If you want to make your way on up Mill Creek, you can scramble up the loose slopes to cross the trail several hundred feet above, or you can backtrack to the better trail you left below the bridge (where the sign to Last Dollar is), which climbs uphill through the woods and into a clearing in .4-mile. From here you get an open view into the upper valley, and you can make out the tiny white splinter of Upper Mill Creek Falls over half a mile away.

The view includes Mill Creek Tributary Falls, which is high in the cliffs to the northeast.

Upper Mill Creek Falls is a 100-foot horsetail that can be seen on and off as one climbs through the dense aspen and fir to the cliff it breaches. This is more of an accent falls than a main event, because the surrounding peaks are so impressive. There are only game trails through the woods and some bushwhacking—the climb becomes fairly steep near the base of the falls, and when you get to the level of the falls on the surrounding cliffs only its top can be seen.

Pandora Mill Falls

(See Telluride Vicinity group map, page 195.)

Access: Roadside
Rating: ★
Type: Plunge
USGS Topographic Quad: Telluride (37107 H7)
Trail Miles: 0
Altitude: 9,200 feet
Elevation Change: None

Pandora Mill Falls is a 15-foot leap on an unnamed creek flowing through the Pandora Mill property to the San Miguel below. Every view of the falls is obscured by mill equipment. There is a road to a trail above the falls, but it's marked as private. The mill is past the cemetery, 3 miles east of Telluride on Highway 145. You probably won't notice this falls, since you'll be gawking at Bridal Veil and Ingram and the enormity of the cliffs all around and above you.

The Ouray Vicinity

Ouray is an ideal place from which to explore the surrounding mountains and see a few of the dozen waterfalls within an hour of town.

At an elevation of 7,800 feet, Ouray was founded as a silver- and gold-mining town and named in 1876 after a famous Ute chief. The townsite was part of the Ute Reservation at the time. The Utes were forced to relocate to another, less desirable location only five years later, in 1881.

In any case, the highway now provides access to three waterfalls on the north side of Red Mountain Pass. There are two more within easy walking distance of the town. A handful of falls up the Camp Bird road toward Telluride completes our Ouray survey. The hot springs, at several hotels or at the swimming pool at the north end of town, are a wonderful place to ease the soreness of a day's hike or jeep ride.

Cascade Falls
(See Ouray Vicinity group map, page 204.)

Access: Walk in
Rating: ★ ★
Type: Plunge
USGS Topographic Quad: Ouray (38107 A6)
Altitude: 8,360 feet
Elevation Change: From 8,310 feet, + 50 feet

Cascade Falls is on the cliffs east of Ouray and is visible from many points in and around town. Walk up Eighth Avenue from Main Street to the beginning of a short ten-minute hike to the base of the falls. Cascade Creek tumbles 80 feet over the lip of rock to a winding cascade, then is channeled into a concrete culvert through town.

The 80-foot leap visible from the trail is not the entire stretch of the falls, however. There are tracks people have made climbing or attempting to climb higher on the extremely steep dirt and wooded slopes around the falls, but there is another way to see the upper falls. Drive south through town on Main

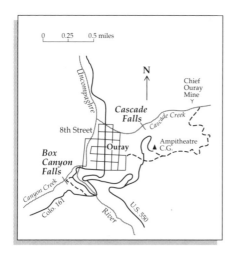

Street (U.S. 550), which makes a hairpin right outside of town. Then there's a left turn off the highway to Amphitheater campground. The Upper Cascade trail begins at the campground and climbs to the top of the cliffs east of town. Several waterfalls are visible as it approaches Cascade Creek. The trail ends at the Chief Ouray Mine across the creek. Total hiking distance is 2.5 miles, with an elevation gain of 1,500 feet.

Cascade Falls freezes in winter to provide good ice-climbing.

The Ouray vicinity group
(**#43** on Gunnison, San Miguel, and Uncompahgre rivers drainages map, page 184):

Cascade Falls
Box Canyon Falls

Box Canyon Falls

(See Ouray Vicinity group map, this page.)

Access: Walk in
Rating: ★ ★ ★
Type: Plunge
USGS Topographic Quad:
Ouray (38107 A6)
Trail Miles: .2-mile
Altitude: 8,000 feet
Elevation Change: From 7,900 feet, + 100 feet

Box Canyon Falls is the centerpiece of a park at the southwest end of Ouray. The cliffs that enclose Canyon Creek are so steep that it is difficult, if not impossible, to see the whole of the falls from any one viewpoint. Its total height is reputed by the town's vacation guidebook to be 285 feet.

There are two viewpoints of the falls provided by the park. Walkways with handrails lead to the inner chasm of the falls. Although the canyon is open to the sky, inside the falls' chasm you feel like you've entered a cave. The final leap pounds onto a slab of rock inside the chasm. There's also a trail that climbs to a footbridge built at the top of the canyon, directly above the falls. From this trail you have great views of Ouray and the surrounding mountains, including Cascade Falls across the valley.

There is a modest fee for entering the park. To reach the park, take Third Avenue across Canyon Creek, or stay on 550 to the end of the first hairpin, where a road bridges the canyon and a sign directs tourists to the falls.

The Million Dollar Highway

Ouray is the terminus of the "Million Dollar Highway," the 12-mile stretch of U.S. 550 extending through the San Juans from Ouray toward Silverton. The highway took its name officially in 1924, when it was dedicated, from the approximate cost of repairs to the original mining road to make it suitable for auto traffic. A more appropriate name might adjust the number to record what the miners in the area got from selling out the Utes.

There are three waterfalls to see along this road, two from the roadside.

Bear Creek Falls

(See Ouray Vicinity group map, page 206.)

Access: Wheelchair
Rating: ★ ★
Type: Plunge
USGS Topographic Quad: Ironton (37107 H6)
Trail Miles: 0
Altitude: 8,550 feet
Elevation Change: None

Bear Creek runs right under U.S. Highway 550 only 2.6 miles south of Ouray. There's a parking area just before the highway crosses the top of the falls several hundred feet above the Uncompahgre River. Bear Creek Falls plunges at least a hundred feet of this long drop, but it is very difficult to see it except from directly above, on the bridge. The slopes surrounding the falls are loose and steep and not recommended for two-footed creatures. The view from the parking area up the canyon of the Uncompahgre is worth the stop.

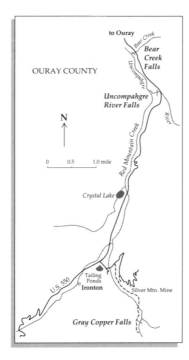

The Ouray vicinity group
(**#44** on Gunnison, San Miguel, and Uncompahgre rivers drainages map, page 184):

Bear Creek Falls
Uncompahgre River Falls
Gray Copper Falls

Uncompahgre River Falls*
(See Ouray Vicinity group map, this page.)

Access: Roadside
Rating: ★ ★
Type: Horsetail
USGS Topographic Quad: Ironton (37107 H6)
Trail Miles: 0
Altitude: 8,800 feet
Elevation Change: None

Uncompahgre River Falls is a steep cascade of 200 feet down rolling rock into the canyon of Red Mountain Creek. The Uncompahgre River originates 5 miles north of here at Como Lake. Below the confluence, the stream flow and canyon are named for the Uncompahgre.

Pull off the road near the top of the falls at a curve opposite the turn up the four-wheel-drive road to Engineer Pass, 3 miles north of Ouray and .75-mile south of Bear Creek Falls. A short scramble over some rocks and down from the road rewards you with expansive views up and down the canyon, which dwarfs the falls, the road, and just about everything else.

Gray Copper Falls

(See Ouray Vicinity group map, page 206.)

Access: Hike
Rating: ★
Type: Plunge
USGS Topographic Quad: Ironton (37107 H6)
Trail Miles: 1.3
Altitude: 10,800 feet
Elevation Change: From 10,230 feet, -150 feet, +720 feet

Gray Copper Falls is in a 100-foot cliff of red rock chipped by nature and rock miners. The hike takes half an hour along a fairly clear trail and is interesting because of the variety of terrain and vegetation. The falls, unfortunately, was barely a streak of water and a little mist down the rocks when we visited in late August.

To reach the falls, take U.S. 550 north of Ouray. After 5 miles of switchbacks the road straightens out, paralleling the brightly colored Red Mountain creekbed. About 7.7 miles from Ouray there's the high restraining slope of a tailings pond, colored bright orange, on the east side of the highway. A dirt road goes east from the highway. Turn left again .2-mile up the dirt road, the access to the Brown Mountain trail. The Silver Mountain Mine is at the 9-mile mark from Ouray, 2.3 miles from the tailings pond. But before you reach the mine, there's a dirt four-wheel-drive road that heads sharply down toward Gray Copper Creek to the north.

Take the four-wheel-drive road down, but instead of going to the bottom, take a spur (marked as a jeep road on the topo) and follow it to the end, where it will meet up again with the road from below. Keep to a contour; when the road peters out, park and head on foot down the dirt track in the grass to the right, then turn to the left across a stand of willows to pick up the trail slightly downhill from the road.

We had some trouble finding the trail at this point and climbed uselessly up the north slope trying to find it. The trail is actually fairly clear on the other side of the willows, and we had no trouble on the way back.

From the end of the road, the trail drops gradually to the drainage, crosses it, and climbs to within sight of the mineral-stained wall creating the falls. To get close for a clear view requires working through some scrub pine on a hill between the trail and the falls. Gray Copper Falls wasn't much to look at, since most of the water in the creek comes from a drainage to the east and from a nearby spring—but it might be better in June.

Camp Bird/Yankee Boy Basin Road

Ouray is surrounded by some of the most beautiful and precipitous terrain in the San Juans, and for better or worse, much of it is accessible by four-wheel-drive. Several of the most popular four-wheel-drive tours, including the Imogene Pass and Governor's Basin roads, take you into the valley of Canyon Creek, south and west of Ouray on Colorado 361. There's no arguing with the spectacular views and the thrill of driving up the canyon—especially if, choking on the dust of three or four vehicles ahead of you, you can't even see the road. The glacier-carved upper canyons sparkle with waterfalls, and there are a couple hidden deep in the crevices as well.

The road up the canyon is easily reached from U.S. 550 at the end of the first hairpin curve south of town. The waterfalls along Colorado 361 are listed here in order as you drive away from Ouray.

Senator Gulch Falls

(See Ouray Vicinity group map, page 209.)

Access: Roadside
Rating: ★ ★
Type: Tiered
USGS Topographic Quad: Ironton (37107 H6)
Trail Miles: 0
Altitude: 9,200 feet
Elevation Change: None

On the road to Yankee Boy Basin, Senator Gulch Falls is easy to overlook as you go around the twists and turns above the canyon on the narrow road. The water falls in a couple of sequential leaps; the highest is up in the rocks, partly hidden, but it probably drops 80 feet in a single plunge.

Easily seen from the road, the falls is difficult to get close to. There may be a trail up the hill to the left of the drainage, although we didn't seek a better vantage than could be had from the road.

Senator Gulch is on the north side of the road, 3.2 miles from the intersection of 361 with U.S. 550 outside of Ouray. Look for the falls from a turnout at the lower loop of the longest, tightest double switchback in the road.

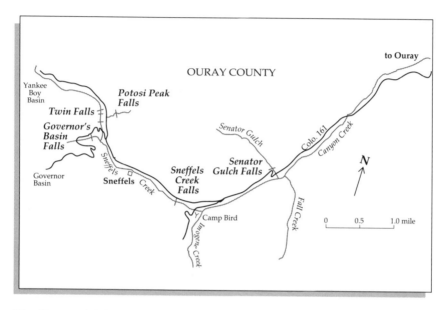

The Ouray vicinity group
(**#42** on Gunnison, San Miguel, and Uncompahgre rivers drainages map, page 184):

Senator Gulch Falls
Sneffels Creek Falls
Governor's Basin Falls
Twin Falls
Potosi Peak Falls

Sneffels Creek Falls

(See Ouray Vicinity group map, page 209.)

Access: Roadside
Rating: ★ ★
Type: Plunge
USGS Topographic Quad: Ironton (37107 H6)
Trail Miles: 0
Altitude: 10,000 feet
Elevation Change: None

Colorado 361 up Canyon Creek is occasionally rough and steep, though not requiring four-wheel-drive except when the road is wet or the weather questionable. We tried it once in a passenger vehicle in the fog and didn't get very far.

Canyon Creek becomes Sneffels Creek past the confluence of Sneffels Creek and Imogene Creek, 4.5 miles from Ouray.

Sneffels Creek Falls is on Sneffels Creek, deep in the chasm just beyond where the road actually drives under a spectacular overhang carved out of the native rock. You can't stop the car, there is a lot of traffic, and the 100-foot-high falls are hidden deep in shadow just when you have to keep your eyes on the road every minute.

The waterfall is visible below the edge of the road beyond the overhang at about 4.75 miles from Ouray, .25-mile past the overlook at Camp Bird Mine. We could not take any decent photographs because of the depth of shadow in the canyon.

Governor's Basin Falls

(See Ouray Vicinity group map, page 209.)

Access: Roadside
Rating: ★
Type: Horsetail
USGS Topographic Quad: Ironton (37107 H6)
Trail Miles: .1-mile
Altitude: 10,900 feet
Elevation Change: None

This waterfall is visible across the valley of Sneffels Creek from the four-wheel-drive road heading into Yankee Boy Basin from Colorado 361 just

Twin Falls

beyond the turn to Twin Falls. We didn't get close enough to see if there was a trail, but the four-wheel-drive road up Governor's Basin goes to within an eighth of a mile of the falls' drainage. The falls looked to us like a long, steep cascade, perhaps 150 feet long, burning white even in the shadow, a jewel in the emerald setting of the basin.

Twin Falls
(See Ouray Vicinity group map, page 209.)

Access: Roadside (four-wheel-drive)
Rating: ★ ★ ★
Type: Segmented and tiered horsetails
USGS Topographic Quad: Telluride (37107 H7)
Trail Miles: 0 to .2-mile
Altitude: 10,920 feet to 11,200 feet
Elevation Change: From 10,870 feet, +50 feet, -100 feet

About 7 miles from Ouray on Colorado 361 and .5-mile beyond the old ruin of Sneffels (marked by a sign), a four-wheel-drive road starts up into Yankee Boy Basin proper. You can see the four-wheel-drive road to Governor's Basin starting on the left fork down closer to Sneffels Creek. In another quarter of a mile you come up on a rise with a view of the basin and get your first glimpse of Twin Falls.

It is tempting to think it is called Twin Falls because you see two waterfalls side by side. But if you continue up the road another few hundred yards, you will see *another* double leap. There is also another waterfall in between the two sets of twins, so you could justifiably call this a quintet of waterfalls. Yet none of them is marked on any map.

Two horsetails about 60 to 70 feet in length make up the lower limb of Twin Falls; the huge black rock between them dominates the view. You can drive an eighth of a mile down a side road to the lower limb and the old mine building right next to it. The flowers on the surrounding hills gently reflect the August sunlight.

Drive another .1-mile beyond the lower leap on the Yankee Boy Basin road. You can reach the middle limb of Twin Falls by hiking a trail from the road for less than an eighth of a mile. The middle limb is one leap of 20 feet split into a steep horsetail and a fan over a boulder the height of the falls.

The upper limb or set of waterfalls is very similar to the lower. The upper falls are perhaps prettier, though not as high, being only 40 to 50 feet. The two sets of double leaps can be seen together at one point from the road. We recommend four-wheel-drive, although we saw one hardy passenger car, bless his drive axle.

Potosi Peak Falls *
(See Ouray Vicinity group map, page 209.)

Access: Roadside (four-wheel-drive)
Rating: ★
Type: Horsetail
USGS Topographic Quad: Telluride (37107 H7)
Trail Miles: .1-mile
Altitude: 11,120 feet
Elevation Change: None

Potosi Peak Falls is a 60- to 70-foot horsetail, a glimmering in the cliffs at the base of Potosi Peak if you look northeast from the four-wheel-drive road near the top of Twin Falls (see above). The waterfall looks very small in relation to the mountain and the vast encirclement of Yankee Boy Basin. We did not try to cross the talus to get any closer to the falls.

The Big Blue Wilderness, North

The Big Blue Wilderness, 98,585 acres set aside within Uncompahgre National Forest, takes its name from Big Blue Creek, which flows into the Gunnison River at the eastern end of the Black Canyon. Also tributary to the Gunnison from within Big Blue Wilderness are, from east to west, the Little Cimmaron River and the East, Middle, and West forks of the Cimmaron. Cow Creek flows into the Uncompahgre.

Big Blue is bounded on the east by the Lake Fork of the Gunnison, on the west by the Cimmaron Ridge east of Ouray. It contains twelve peaks over 13,000 feet, including Wetterhorn Peak (14,015 feet), Uncompahgre Peak (14,309 feet), Matterhorn Peak (13,509 feet), Wildhorse Peak (13,266 feet), and Silver Mountain (13,714 feet). All the streams of Big Blue flow north to the Gunnison, and the rugged glacial topography of the wilderness has created a concentration of waterfalls rivaled only by Rocky Mountain National Park.

We begin our survey with the waterfalls reached most easily from the south side of the wilderness.

Wildhorse Basin and Upper Cow Creek

Wildhorse Basin Falls * * * * * * (*)
(See Big Blue Wilderness group map, page 214.)

Access: Overnight, bushwhack
Rating: ★ ★ to ★ ★ ★
Type: All types
USGS Topographic Quad: Wetterhorn Peak
Trail Miles: 4, 5, 6, 6.25
Altitude: 12,000 feet, 11,520 feet, 11,120 feet from Engineer Pass at 12,800 feet
Elevation Change: From 12,800 feet, -800 feet, -1,680 feet

There are five waterfalls indicated on the Wetterhorn quadrangle either on Cow Creek or its tributary, Wildhorse Creek. Cow Creek is a tributary to the Uncompahgre north of Ridgway. Access is not up the drainage from the north,

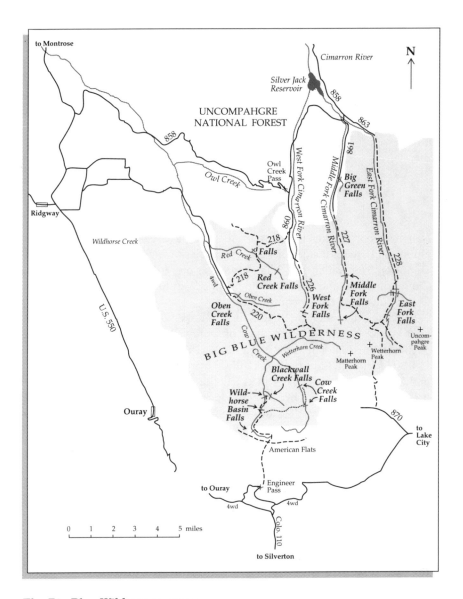

The Big Blue Wilderness group

(**#45** on Gunnison, San Miguel, and Uncompahgre rivers drainages map, page 184):

Wildhorse Basin Falls
Blackwall Creek Falls
Cow Creek Falls
Oben Creek Falls
Red Creek Falls

West Fork of the Cimarron Falls
Big Green Falls
Middle Fork of the Cimarron Falls
East Fork of the Cimarron Falls

however, but from either Lake City, Silverton, or Ouray by the Engineer Pass road, which requires four-wheel-drive. A 12-mile hike from Ouray to American Flats is also possible.

To get to Wildhorse Basin from Engineer Pass, hike northwest from the sign marking the pass at 12,800 feet to get around the base of the ridge that rims the headwaters of Henson Creek. Stay high on the rolling hills of American Flats, following the route of a dirt road indicated on the quad, or following the line-of-sight stock-driveway posts. The junction of trails at a cairn and post at the top of American Flats is about 2 miles from the pass. Stay off the Horsethief and Bear Creek trails. There is no clear trail into Wildhorse Basin, but there is an intermittent stock driveway close to the streamcourse on the eastern slope, which becomes a good trail at about 11,500 feet. Just hike north into the head of Wildhorse Basin from American Flats and stick close to the water. Wildhorse Peak looms magnificently above you to the right.

A mile into the basin, you will come to Wildhorse 1, at 12,000 feet one of the highest-elevation waterfalls we've seen. The trail is gradual and steady, but the falls is not visible from it. However, the shelf of rock that creates the falls is a very obvious drop-off from far up the valley, so finding the falls is no problem. Two steep horsetails, the highest 15 feet, the second 12 feet, plus several fans and cascades, create a beautiful sheltered environment for flowers and lush vegetation, in contrast to the many tiny tundra flowers out of the creek's ravine. Columbines, harebells, asters, paintbrush, and rose crown thrive in the shelter of the falls.

As you hike into the basin another mile, the trail on the eastern slope is clearer and drops 500 feet to another ring of cliffs across Wildhorse Creek. There are good camping sites at the top of the ridge on the east side of the creek.

If you cross Wildhorse Creek to the west side at the top of these cliffs, you cross above the first 10-foot leap of Wildhorse 2. Work your way down a grassy slope and into the valley a little way, then look back for a wonderful view of the lower leap of Wildhorse 2. The creek plunges 65 feet into a pool in a water-blackened cut in the volcanic rock. The falls is tucked into a narrow defile perhaps a hundred feet deep, with flowers and moss all over, and a stunning moss wall like a waterfall of green sprinkled with tiny yellow flowers. Downstream from this point there is a trail for about half a mile, which then disappears into the grass. Cross where you can back to the east side of the creek.

From Wildhorse 2 it's an easy mile (and 400 feet in elevation loss) down the valley to Wildhorse 3, the third falls down the Wildhorse Creek drainage from American Flats. Wildhorse 3 is actually a string of leaps and cascades: two braided fans (of 12 and 30 feet) and an interrupted leap, one side of which arcs into the plunge pool. Then, another eighth of a mile downstream there's another leap of about 15 feet, and below that another plunge of 60 feet. This last plunge cannot be seen from above, so it's necessary to cross to the west side of the creek, walk over a hill to circle left around the top of the falls, and then cut down a game trail 200 feet or more into the mossy amphitheater created by the falls. The cumulative drop of Wildhorse 3, including the run of water between the leaps, is about 150 feet.

Blackwall Creek Falls*
(See Big Blue Wilderness group map, page 214.)

Access: Overnight, bushwhack
Rating: ★ ★
Type: Horsetail
USGS Topographic Quad: Wetterhorn Peak (38107 A5)
Trail Miles: 6.25
Altitude: 11,200 feet
Elevation Change: From Engineer Pass at 12,800 feet, -1,600 feet

Blackwall Creek flows into Wildhorse Creek .2-mile below Wildhorse 3. If you head northwest from Wildhorse 3 and climb a little, in .1-mile you intersect the Blackwall Creek drainage. Climb up the rim of the drainage near the edge of the woods and you'll see Blackwall Creek Falls across the canyon, a sinuous thread of silver making its way 100 feet down the wall opposite. The edge of the chasm is sheer enough to make friends with children nervous. Note: There are no trails in this part of the basin. Take your map and compass, and be prepared for bad weather at all times!

Cow Creek Falls*
(See Big Blue Wilderness group map, page 214.)

Access: Overnight, bushwhack
Rating: ★ ★ ★
Type: Fan
USGS Topographic Quad: Wetterhorn Peak (38107 A5)
Trail Miles: 5 to 6
Altitude: 10,500 feet
Elevation Change: From Engineer Pass at 12,800 feet, -2,300 feet

Hidden deep in the canyon of Cow Creek, Cow Creek Falls is a spectacular 150-foot fan with a 30-foot leap at the top and a classic, spreading 120-foot fan to its base. Precipitous viewpoints from the top of the falls are reachable on both sides of the creek, but this is not a falls for the acrophobic. Twenty yards above this fan is another 10-foot leap and a long series of cascades all the way up the Cow Creek drainage.

You could conceivably reach Cow Creek Falls from below, up the drainage, but climbing the cliffs doesn't seem appealing. We got to the falls from Wildhorse Basin by climbing over a pass between Wildhorse Peak and Blackwall Peak. There are intermittent game trails, but mostly you find your way by dead reckoning. The pass is at 12,600 feet, the falls at 10,500 feet, so some real elevation gain and loss are involved. It's .8-mile from Wildhorse 2 to the pass, then another 2 miles down to the falls. A mile down from the pass brings you to Cow Creek, where it's easy to cross above a noticeable falls not marked on the quad. You can pick up a stock driveway on the east side of the creek that has been pounded into muck in many places. This trail stays high above the creek most of the way, and splits and ravels as stock trails will. I went down into the drainage to rock-hop, then crossed to a viewpoint on the west side. A more prudent companion stayed high on the east side and came out on the knob indicated on the quad, north of the falls, for a good view. The canyon of Cow Creek below the falls is eroded into shapes reminiscent of Bryce Canyon.

The falls was definitely worth the hike, and there are many lovely cascades above it. We arrived in camp just after sunset thoroughly chilled—in mid-August. Take gloves, gaiters, raingear, and boots. Don't count just on your luck.

The Big Blue Wilderness, South

The northern slopes of the Big Blue Wilderness are virtually littered with waterfalls. Every major drainage contains at least one, and the East Fork of the Cimarron displays so many we were not sure what to count and what to merely admire.

Virtually all of the falls in the Cimarron area are horsetails; their watercourses cut deeply into breccias that erode in strange gray lancelike shapes reminiscent of Bryce Canyon. They tower hundreds of feet in ramparts above the valley. Water cuts deep gorges at a very steep slope, not like the flat canyons of the Colorado. *Cimarron*, incidentally, means "wild, untamed" in Spanish. The area lives up to the name.

Oben Creek Falls *
(See Big Blue Wilderness group map, page 214.)

Access: Hike, bushwhack
Rating: ★
Type: Horsetail
USGS Topographic Quad: Wetterhorn Peak (38107 A5)
Trail Miles: .5-mile
Altitude: 8,800 feet
Elevation Change: From 8,320 to 9,000 feet to falls, + 680 feet, -200 feet

Oben Creek Falls consists of two leaps, 10 feet above, 60 feet below, hidden in a canyon shrouded in deep brush and sheltered by deep forest.

The falls is on Oben Creek, a small drainage tributary to Cow Creek, which flows ultimately to the Uncompahgre and eventually the Gunnison. Drive east from Ridgway 5 miles on 858, then turn south (before reaching Owl Creek Pass) up a four-wheel-drive road that penetrates 5 miles into the fastness of the Big Blue Wilderness.

The road crosses two streams, Cow Creek and Red Creek, requiring some careful driving for 30 to 40 feet directly up Red Creek's streambed.

From the end of the road, near a miner's explosives shed, trail 220 goes up the hill north of the Oben Creek drainage, climbing steeply for 600 feet. When the trail turns directly east (by compass heading) at the top of the switchbacks, go about 100 yards and drop off the trail down onto a bench that follows the course of the drainage onto the top of some cliffs that lead to views of the falls from relatively precarious perches among the trees at the edge. We first tried to come down on the falls from above, but they can't be seen that way, and the slope of the drainage is very steep.

A view of the falls is only ten minutes northeast of the trail, but there is no sign or marker for where to drop off, except that it's about 20 yards past half of a sign saying that the wilderness is closed to motorized traffic. The hike requires about half an hour from the trailhead. The most exciting part of the trip is the drive up Red Creek, to be avoided at high water.

Cimarron River Waterfalls

All the forks of the Cimarron River are approached either from the north at Silver Jack Reservoir, or from the west at Ridgway by way of Owl Creek Pass. To get to Silver Jack, drive 2 miles west of Cimarron on U.S. 50. Turn south on Forest Road 858, which is clearly marked for access to the national forest and Silver Jack Reservoir. Silver Jack is 22 miles from U.S. 50 on 858.

From Ridgway, take the Owl Creek Pass road .6-mile south of Dallas. Owl Creek Pass is 25 miles from Highway 550.

Our descriptions begin with the West Fork of the Cimarron River, which is nearest Owl Creek Pass.

Red Creek Falls
(See Big Blue Wilderness group map, page 214.)

Access: Hike, bushwhack
Rating: ★ ★
Type: Plunge
USGS Topographic Quad: Wetterhorn Peak (38107 A5)
Trail Miles: 2, 4, 4.5
Altitude: 10,200 feet
Elevation Change: From 8,320 feet to 10,600 feet, +2,280 feet; to 10,000 feet, -600 feet; to 10,200 feet, +200 feet

We saw a waterfall on Red Creek, but I don't believe we reached the upper falls marked on the Wetterhorn Peak quad. We thought we started our hike to Red Creek early enough in the day, but the hike became quite a harrowing adventure.

The Courthouse Mountain trailhead is 1.5 miles south on 860 from its junction with the Owl Creek Pass road, .4-mile south of the pass. The trail climbs steeply out of the valley of the West Fork, climbs about 700 feet to a ridge south of Courthouse Mountain, then starts down on its way to cross Red Creek. Then the trail fades into a densely vegetated meadow where we groped around for a way down the steep hillside along game trails that led in the right direction, and eventually we hooked up with the trail again. The trail from the ridge down, and the trail from the bottom up, are not what I would call well spliced.

After following a very clear trail for a mile, we left the Courthouse Creek trail and took a left fork down toward Red Creek into another meadow, where we lost the trail a second time.

On the way back, we found that you need to simply proceed 15 to 20 yards down the meadow and pick up the trail crossing uphill from the south; but we headed on down the drainage instead and wound up at a surprise waterfall, Red Creek Tributary Falls, a 20-foot leap on one of the tributaries to Red Creek. We climbed around it, walked down the drainage until we could cross to Red

Creek, then came back up the Red Creek drainage in the streambed. I noted where the trail we'd lost comes down the hill from the left and clambers up the other side. This is how we climbed out on the way back to camp.

Working our way up Red Creek, at the 4-mile mark from our trailhead we came to a solid 20- to 25-foot cliff of dark red rock. It was our main falls for the day, and it streams over the center of the wall and splatters on the stream gravels below.

Although it was time to head back, I sent my son Natt to the top of the falls to reconnoiter, and while Nancy and I tried to follow him, we climbed too high, realized the slope was too steep and loose, and decided to go back down to the base of the falls. Meanwhile, Natt had decided to climb to meet us and got too high! I shouted at him to climb up and out, not to cross the slope we were on or to try to get back down the way he'd gone up.

He took a couple of long slides on his stomach down that slope and concluded the same thing. He eventually climbed to a ridge and worked down it to meet us in the drainage, where I applied iodine-water to his scrapes and we all heaved a sigh of relief. We'd taken too long to reach our turnaround point, and I had been afraid we'd be spending the night in the canyon with him stuck up on the slope God only knew where. At one point I had him in my binoculars and watched him suddenly disappear from view. I didn't realize he'd stepped on a loose rock and had started a 40-foot slide toward the edge of a precipice.

It was 4:30 P.M. when we started back, and things went better until we lost the trail again climbing back up the steep game-trail-scarred hillside on the southwest side of the Courthouse and had to scramble by dead reckoning to reach the ridge and then used a compass to relocate the trail before nightfall. Natt led us out in the dark.

The safety lesson here: Set a turnaround time at the beginning of the trip to make sure you can get back to your camp while it's still light out. Your turnaround time should be no later than the midpoint of the total time allowable for the hike. And in case the worst happens, always be prepared to spend the night on the trail in an emergency. *Always!*

West Fork of the Cimarron

At least three waterfalls can be reached by driving up the West Fork from Owl Creek Pass. Forest Road 860 is only .4-mile south of the pass. You can drive a passenger car comfortably 2 miles south on 860, then it turns into a four-wheel-drive road that crosses the West Fork and deposits you at a trailhead at the 3-mile mark.

West Fork of the Cimarron Falls*
(See Big Blue Wilderness group map, page 214.)

Access: Four-wheel-drive, hike
Rating: ★
Type: Horsetail
USGS Topographic Quad: Wetterhorn Peak (38107 A5)
Trail Miles: .75-mile (with four-wheel-drive)
Altitude: 11,480 feet
Elevation Change: From trailhead at 10,760 feet, +720 feet

West Fork of the Cimarron Falls is an easy .75-mile hike up the West Fork valley from a trailhead at the end of road 860, requiring about a mile of four-wheel-drive travel to get to.

The waterfall is not particularly inspiring, sliding as it does 50 to 60 feet down a narrow defile, although the overall setting—near-tundra surrounded by high cliffs and peaks—is very appealing. In late August the flowers made their last colorful effort before autumn's bite. It sprinkled a little while we hiked, but then we rested above the falls and sunbathed before the hail began in earnest.

When you come to the head of the valley there are three separate drainages coming together. A new trail switchbacks to the east, but the old trail goes straight up the central drainage past the top of the falls, which is more a steep cascade and slide. The valley is worth the hike, and we were tempted to climb up the pass for a look at Wetterhorn Basin, but not tempted enough to actually do it.

The Middle and East Forks of the Cimarron

The Middle Fork road provides access to three waterfalls on the Middle Fork of the Cimarron, as well as to the many waterfalls on the East Fork drainage. You can also hike directly up the long valley of the East Fork, traveling about 6.5 miles to reach the lower falls. However, we combined a trip up the Middle Fork with a hike over a pass into the East Fork drainage, which not only got us to the falls and minimized backtracking, but also showed us wonderful views of Wetterhorn, Matterhorn, and Uncompahgre peaks from the head of the East Fork.

The Middle Fork road (Forest Road 861) is 6 miles from Owl Creek Pass, only 1 mile from the southern end of Silver Jack Reservoir, and 24 miles from the junction of Forest Road 858 and U.S. 50. The road up the East Fork (863) is .2-mile closer to Silver Jack than the Middle Fork road, but only goes 1.5 miles up the valley.

The trailhead for the Middle Fork trail (227) is 4.6 miles south on 861 from its junction with 858. On your way in or out, you can stop along the road for a mercifully short hike to what we call Big Green Falls.

Big Green Falls
(See Big Blue Wilderness group map, page 214.)

Access: Walk in (.25-mile on established trail)
Rating: ★ ★ ★
Type: Horsetail
USGS Topographic Quad: Courthouse Mountain (38107 B5)
Trail Miles: .5-mile
Altitude: 9,900 feet
Elevation Change: From 9,750 feet, + 150 feet

About 3.1 miles south of the Owl Creek Pass road (858) on the Middle Fork road (861), and 1.5 miles north of the Middle Fork campground and trailhead, a sign on the east side of the road says simply "waterfall" with an arrow pointing up a trail that leads within 100 yards to a sheer rock amphitheater and a lively 60- to 70-foot segmented falls plunging brightly amidst a fabulous display of moss. The brightness of the water makes the rock seem very black. The trail is well used, but signs of abuse are minimal. We decided to call this one Big Green Falls because the drainage is unnamed and the display of moss is our last memory of the Big Blue Wilderness.

Middle Fork of the Cimarron Falls * * *
(See Big Blue Wilderness group map, page 214.)

Access: Overnight, bushwhack to upper falls
Rating: ★ ★
Type: Tiered, horsetail, and plunge
USGS Topographic Quad: Wetterhorn Peak (38107 A5)
Trail Miles: 2.6, 4.6
Altitude: 11,900 feet, 12,400 feet
Elevation Change: From 10,000 feet, + 1,900 feet, + 2,400 feet

The Middle Fork road (861) is passable by passenger cars to the end of the road, where there's a large camping area and turnaround. The campground is in the woods at the edge of a long meadow with an extended view of the valley and its organ-pipe western ridge. The trail follows but never enters the broad, washed-out drainage of the Middle Fork. It winds gently up through tall stands of lodgepole, then climbs gruelingly to the 11,000-foot level, where it passes, at about the 2.6-mile point, the Lower Middle Fork Falls, which is a series of leaps not more than 10 feet each through a deeply cut canyon with steep cliff walls about 100 feet in height. Views of the falls are accessible but somewhat precarious.

Intermittent Tributary Falls is another .25-mile above Lower Middle Fork Falls, on an intermittent stream that comes down to the Middle Fork from the east side of the valley. This falls, not marked on the quad, is a sinuous 65-foot horsetail and is near a copse of trees that has been used for camping. The trail climbs more gradually from here into a long meadow with a view of Upper Middle Fork Falls, 2 miles up the valley, which is set like a tiny jewel among the enclosing peaks.

To get to the upper falls, we hiked up the valley on the trail another 1.25 miles. When the trail veers left to climb to the east, leave it and go uphill through the woods half a mile for a nice view of the falls directly above.

In between gusts of hail, we climbed up the ridge, grassy on one side and eroded gravel on the other, directly to the base of the falls. This route is not for hikers with vertigo. A somewhat less nerve-wracking approach is possible up through the rocks and grass a little to the east.

Upper Middle Fork Falls is a sheer drop of 80 feet from the cliff wall—and at 12,400 feet, the top of the falls is the highest I can recall having visited. The flow of water was not impressive in late August; this falls is most striking as an accent in its magnificent setting, giving scale to the whole embrace of the mountains.

East Fork of the Cimarron Falls

(See Big Blue Wilderness group map, page 214.)

Access: Overnight
Rating: ★ ★ to ★ ★ ★ ★
Type: 1 segmented, 3 horsetails, 1 punchbowl, and 1 plunge
USGS Topographic Quad: Uncompahgre Peak (38107 A4)
Trail Miles: 10 to 12 from Middle Fork trailhead
Altitude: 11,440 feet, 11,320 feet, 12,004 feet, 2 at 11,200 feet, 11,000 feet
Elevation Change: From 10,100 feet to pass, + 2,500 feet; to uppermost falls, -1,160 feet; to lowermost falls, -440 feet

Lower East Fork of the Cimarron Falls

About 3.5 miles up the Middle Fork valley the trail turns uphill to the east and climbs on a well-worn trail over a pass into the valley of the East Fork of the Cimarron. The pass is at 12,600 feet; follow the posts set in the grass, because the trail is often faint in the deep grass and flowers. There is a good trail switchbacking up the last few hundred feet of elevation. From the pass you can see all the way down the Middle Fork to the hills of the lower Cimarron valley, as well as have views of Wetterhorn and Matterhorn peaks, and of Uncompahgre Peak to the east.

The trail down into the East Fork is also marked by posts, but the ones on the higher slopes are misleading because they are used for grazing stock, not for directing waterfall hunters. However, one trail marked by posts drops straight into the head of the valley right to the base of Matterhorn Peak. Then the trail crosses to the south side of the East Fork. There is a good trail on the north side as well, on the inner curve of the valley; it is therefore shorter, although it loses elevation gradually to meet the river beyond the upper falls. (This is the route we used to return to our camp on the Middle Fork.)

We took the trail on the south side, lost it in the trees, but came out of the woods below a waterfall on an unnamed tributary to the East Fork not marked on the maps. This is a segmented step cascade coming out of a deeply cut arroyo and dropping 30 to 40 feet in a gorgeous tumble a few hundred yards before flowing into the East Fork. We call it Surprise Falls. This confluence is about 2 miles down from the pass and can be seen from the trail on the west side of the river. The confluence is quite unmistakable, with a good flow of water.

Another eighth of a mile downstream the East Fork begins cutting deeply into the breccias in the middle of the grassland and willows at the valley bottom, and this culminates in a series of leaps over a stretch of several hundred yards. The rock is purple, but minerals in the water turn them golden or ocher. Near the falls another deposit of white mineral turns the rocks white at the water line all the way downriver to the lower falls and beyond.

Upper East Fork Falls is a twisting, tumbling series of 5- to 6-foot leaps hidden deep in flower-bedecked rocks. The river flattens out into gravel where the trail on the southeast side crosses the stream as indicated on the maps. The falls is right above the ford.

Another .75-mile of easy, fast hiking takes you past falls in the cliffs on the east side of the river, just north of Uncompahgre Peak. The upper falls is at a heading of 100 degrees relative to Uncompahgre Peak.

The lower falls are at 140 degrees to Uncompahgre Peak. They are not visible from the main trail. You know you're getting close when the trail feeds into the remains of a long-unused four-wheel-drive road. Then it crosses a slope of talus, splitting to allow hikers to bypass the talus through a grassy meadow. The distance from the pass at this point is about 3 miles (6.5 miles from the East Fork trailhead, downriver).

It is easy to hear the falls, which are about 200 yards off the trail across marshy grass and through the woods. Lower East Fork Falls consists of two separate waterfalls surrounded by hundred-foot cliffs. The main body of the East Fork takes four or five leaps, from aquamarine pool to aquamarine pool, and a pure bridal-veil leap of 30 feet joins the dance from the small tributary the trail dropped into and crossed about an eighth of a mile above where you leave the trail.

The purple volcanic rock turns gold where wet but is white from the mineral deposits where dry. The blue-green plunge pools, the surrounding spruce forest, the mosses, the black rock of the tributary falls, and the gold and purple of the main falls create a real color feast.

There are also small horsetail waterfalls visible on both sides of the canyon from a knoll near the trail less than an eighth of a mile above Lower East Fork Falls. Two drainages enter the East Fork from opposite sides, making winglike falls in the cliffs.

The hike out was slow and exhausting but with only a little rain and hail, and there was actual sunshine in the valley as we headed down to camp.

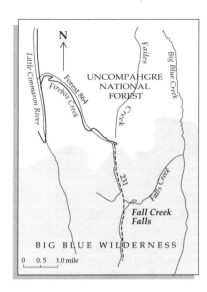

The Big Blue Wilderness group (**#47** on Gunnison, San Miguel, and Uncompahgre rivers drainages map, page 184):

Fall Creek Falls

Fall Creek Falls *
(See accompanying map.)

Access: Hike, bushwhack
Rating: ★ ★ ★
Type: Segmented plunge
USGS Topographic Quad:
Sheep Mountain (38107 B4)
Trail Miles: 2.4 inside Big Blue
Wilderness
Altitude: 11,100 feet
Elevation Change: From 9,800 feet
to 11,200 feet on trail, + 1,400 feet;
bushwhack -100 feet

Take County Road 864 south from U.S. 50, 3 miles east of Cimarron. This is the Little Cimarron road—don't confuse it with 858 to Silver Jack Reservoir. Follow the road up the Little Cimarron River 19.9 miles, all the way to the trailhead at the end. Trail 231 starts here at 10,960 feet, gaining only 2,200 feet in 2 miles to climb out of the Firebox Creek drainage through a long, wide meadow into the Fall Creek drainage.

Trail 231 continues on to meet and cross Fall Creek, but as soon as you're down off the tree-covered rise that separates the Firebox Creek and Fall Creek drainages, turn left and skirt the meadow below the edge of the woods an eighth of a mile east to the cut, which is visible from the trail in the breccia created by Fall Creek. You can hear the falls if the wind is right.

Fall Creek cuts 150 feet into the cliffs before it leaps down another 80 to 100 feet to create the main falls. The cliff rock is eroded into knobs and ridges and is loose. You cannot obtain a view of the falls from above, except for the first few preliminary cascades. To view the falls' main leap, it's necessary to hike into the woods to the north and find a negotiable dirt chute that cuts steeply down from the cliffs. Then it's possible to work across to the falls. This is a route for experienced climbers only. It takes about half an hour to get to the bottom of the falls, a drop of 300 feet. There is no trail. If you don't climb down to see the falls, the views to the northeast of the Big Blue valley are sublime.

The Lake City Vicinity

There are four waterfalls in the immediate vicinity of Lake City. Each embodies a slightly different conception of the "wise use" philosophy, which embraces the idea that nature exists for mankind's benefit and exploitation.

Treasure Falls
(See Lake City Vicinity group map, page 228.)

Access: Hike
Rating: ★
Type: Washed-out
USGS Topographic Quad: Lake City (38107 A3)
Trail Miles: 0
Altitude: 9,000 feet
Elevation Change: None

Where Treasure Falls used to be, 2.5 miles west of Lake City, now stand the ruins of a dam that once tamed the canyon of Henson Creek. Whatever the treasure was, the falls has been reduced to a cascade. A similar snaggle-toothed dam encroaches upon the stream near the mine workings a couple of miles up the road toward Engineer Pass.

The dams were built a century ago to capitalize on the kinetic energy of the falling water. When the dam washed out, so did the waterfall. This scenario was confirmed by conversation with a knowledgeable old-timer manning the information center in town.

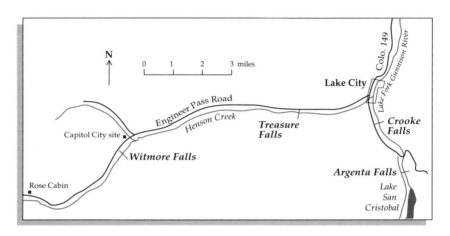

The Lake City vicinity group
(**#46** on Gunnison, San Miguel, and Uncompahgre rivers drainages map, page 184):

Treasure Falls
Witmore Falls
Crooke Falls
Argenta Falls

Witmore Falls
(See Lake City Vicinity group map, this page.)

Access: Walk in
Rating: ★ ★ ★
Type: Punchbowl
USGS Topographic Quad: Red Cloud Peak (37107 H4)
Trail Miles: 50 yards
Altitude: 9,800 feet
Elevation Change: From 9,850 feet, -50 feet

Witmore Falls is on Henson Creek just beyond Capitol City, 9 miles west of Lake City on the Engineer Pass road. A sign marks the trailhead on the south side of the road. A trail leads steeply down to the falls in less than

Witmore Falls

200 yards, and the falls is visible from an observation point 50 yards from the road. Witmore is a clear leap of about 30 feet into a deep pool encircled by cliff walls 70 feet high. The stream has cut a narrow gorge 40 feet deep into the rock at the head of the falls. Witmore is not on any map I have.

Four miles farther on, there is the remains of a log stable at Rose Cabin. Apparently this was a booming little supply depot and stage stop from when a man named Rose built his first cabin in 1874 until the resulting twenty-two-room inn closed in 1900. Miners from up and down Henson Creek resupplied there, and the daily stages to Ouray and Silverton from Lake City stopped there overnight.

Crooke Falls

(See Lake City Vicinity group map, page 228.)

Access: Walk in
Rating: ★ ★
Type: Segmented
USGS Topographic Quad: Lake City (38107 A3)
Trail Miles: 150 yards
Altitude: 8,720 feet
Elevation Change: None

Crooke Falls is .8-mile south of Lake City on the property of a lodge called The Texan. It can't be seen from Highway 149. There is a diversion structure and bridge just above the falls on the Lake Fork of the Gunnison. To get to Crooke Falls requires driving on a frontage road through and onto land being developed by the resort. The bridge can be crossed on foot: Follow the rim of the canyon a hundred yards upstream, double back downstream, and climb down to a view of the falls. The crashing water is impressive, but the concrete diversion above it lessens the impact.

Argenta Falls

(See Lake City Vicinity group map, page 228.)

Access: Walk in
Rating: ★
Type: Plunge
USGS Topographic Quad: Lake San Cristobal
Trail Miles: 40 yards
Altitude: 9,000 feet
Elevation Change: None

Argenta Falls is .4-mile north of Lake San Cristobal, on the Lake Fork of the Gunnison River. A man named Simmons owned the land immediately adjacent to Highway 149 at the time of our visit, and the head of the falls is probably 100 to 125 feet from the highway straight across his driveway. No one was home, so we couldn't ask permission to view the falls.

There's another view of Argenta from the woods below it, which are posted but unfenced. The hills along the drainage are steep, but a climb to the foot of the plunge should not be too difficult.

Argenta Falls is about 50 feet high with a lot of white water plunging down through the trees pressing closely on both sides, and therefore difficult to photograph.

Waterfalls North and West of the Gunnison River

Ten waterfalls are on tributaries to the Gunnison that do not originate in the San Juans. Seven are on streams flowing into the Gunnison from the north, out of the Sawatch, Elk, and West Elk mountains. One is on the Gunnison itself, at the bottom of the Black Canyon. Deep, arid canyons west of Delta hide two intermittent falls. The easternmost is near Tincup. The westernmost hangs on the edge of Grand Mesa, 92 miles from Tincup by air.

West Soap Creek Falls *
(See map on page 232.)

Access: Hike, bushwhack
Rating and Type: Not visited
USGS Topographic Quad: Big Soap Park (38107 F3)
Trail Miles: 3.3 to 4
Altitude: 9,820 feet
Elevation Change: From end of road at 8,360 feet, +2,040 feet to 10,400 feet on trail; bushwhack -580 feet

Access to West Soap Creek Falls is from U.S. 50 about 30 miles west of Gunnison. After the highway crosses the branch of Blue Mesa Reservoir created by the Lake Fork drainage, go 1 mile to the intersection of Colorado 92, then 1.2 miles north and west on 92 across the Gunnison. Highway 92 continues west, but take the sharp right turn to Sapinero. Follow this road past the Ponderosa, Soap Creek, and Commissary campgrounds 17 miles on Forest Road 721 to the trailhead for trail 456, .3-mile south of the Waterman Ranch. Trail 456 starts at 8,360 feet at Big Soap Creek, but after .6-mile forks upward to the northeast and climbs out of Big Soap Park. The trail goes uphill another 3.3 miles (total 3.9 miles); this is the trail's closest approach to the falls, which is .4-mile east, on an unnamed tributary to Big Soap Creek. We haven't visited this falls yet

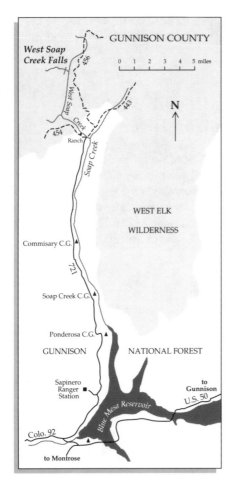

Waterfalls north and west of the Gunnison River

(**#48** on Gunnison, San Miguel, and Uncompahgre rivers drainages map, page 184):

West Soap Creek Falls

so will not hazard a guess about the best route for bushwhacking to it, or even if it's worth the trip.

West Beaver Creek Falls *

(See map on page 233.)

Access: Hike
Rating: ★ ★
Type: Punchbowl
USGS Topographic Quad: Squirrel Creek (38107 F1)
Trail Miles: 2.8
Altitude: 9,200 feet
Elevation Change: Trailhead is marked on topo at 10,132 feet; drop to 8,760 feet, -1,372 feet; then climb to 9,200 feet, +440 feet

West Beaver Creek Falls is a classic 36-foot leap into a deep plunge pool with a secondary leap forming behind it. The surrounding cliffs are about 50 feet high, but the creek has gouged its course deeply into the rock.

Closer access to the falls is down a steep grassy slope through fallen timber. The courageous and careful can get right up to the plunge pool, and even in it, if you can stand the temperature.

Fallen logs thrust in every direction on the creek bottom, and the water winds its way through the moss-covered walls.

We couldn't gauge the depth of the symmetrical plunge pool, which is 20 to 25 feet across. The plunge transforms the amphitheater into a Shangri-la in miniature. Nancy saw a bear track in the trail that was still moist from rains the day before.

To reach West Beaver Creek Falls, take U.S. 50 west of the Gunnison city limits 5 miles, .7-mile past milepost 160. Turn right onto a dirt road going uphill and follow it 1.7 miles to a junction. Take the right fork, BLM Route 3113, and drive another 9.7 miles on Forest Road 726 (2.5 miles past the national forest boundary). The drive to the falls first rolls over sage-covered hills (in yellow bloom in August), then winds up through long stands of aspen interspersed with areas where logging has taken place farther up the road from the trailhead.

At 11.4 miles from Highway 50, there's a turnout on the left where a four-wheel-drive road goes down the

Waterfalls north and west of the Gunnison River
(**#49** on Gunnison, San Miguel, and Uncompahgre rivers drainages map, page 184):

West Beaver Creek Falls

hill. This road is suitable only for serious four-wheel-drive enthusiasts, and possibly not even for them (there's a vehicle carcass down the way). This "road" ends at Beaver Creek. Cross the creek to the trail on the other side and follow it north about .75-mile to a cabin; go around the north end of its fence, where a sign identifies Route 447. West Beaver Creek Falls is below the trail in about a mile and is visible from the trail through the trees if you don't hear it first.

Old and new maps are misleading. Other routes to the trailhead may be just as good, but because of the volume of recent logging traffic, this seems the best route. Four-wheel-drive is required only if rains have been heavy.

West Beaver Creek Falls

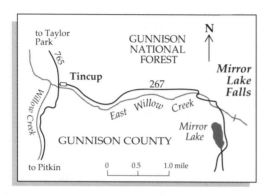

Waterfalls north and west of the Gunnison River (**#50** on Gunnison, San Miguel, and Uncompahgre rivers drainages map, page 184):

Mirror Lake Falls

Mirror Lake Falls

(See map, this page.)

Access: Roadside
Rating: ★
Type: Block
USGS Topographic Quad: Cumberland Pass (38106 F4)
Trail Miles: .1-mile bushwhack
Altitude: 11,300 feet
Elevation Change: From 11,000 feet, +300 feet

Visible from Mirror Lake campground and road, Mirror Lake Falls was barely a trickle of water in late September. There are two leaps, 10 feet each, about 50 yards and 100 feet of elevation apart. But it was so dry that the rocks were barely wet. It could be inspiring in June.

To get to the falls, drive east through Tincup on Forest Road 267 to Mirror Lake, about 3 miles. The Willow Creek drainage is visible from the campground at the north end of the lake. To climb up the drainage directly requires a .2-mile bushwhack 300 feet uphill through willows. A better approach is up the slope at an angle from the lake, where the vegetation is less formidable.

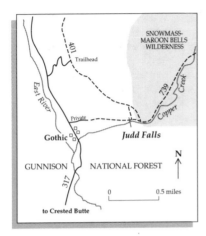

SNOWMASS-
MAROON BELLS
WILDERNESS

401
Trailhead

East River

739

Copper Creek

Private

Gothic

Judd Falls

N

GUNNISON   NATIONAL FOREST

317

0   0.5 miles

to Crested Butte

**Waterfalls north and west of
the Gunnison River**
(**#51** on Gunnison, San Miguel,
and Uncompahgre rivers drainages
map, page 184):

Judd Falls

Judd Falls
(See map, this page.)

Access: Hike
Rating: ★ ★
Type: Twisted horsetail
USGS Topographic Quad: Gothic
    (38106 H8)
Trail Miles: .5-mile
Altitude: 9,800 feet
Elevation Change: 9,920 feet to
    10,040 feet to 9,800 feet;
    + 120 feet, - 160 feet

Drive north from Crested Butte on
Forest Road 317 (through the ski area)
7 miles to Gothic. The Rocky Mountain
Biological Laboratory has taken over
Gothic, and the most direct trail to the
falls is now private. But a sign by the
road in town directs you a mile north
to a trailhead where a sign says "Judd
Falls 2 miles." A good dirt road uphill
from here leads to a parking area and
second trailhead where another sign
indicates that it's 1 mile to the falls
(although a sign at Judd Falls says it's
.5-mile to trailhead—which is about right). Keep on the trail. It climbs over
a hill and then drops through aspen woods to the old private road (no longer
accessible because of the wilderness area upstream from the falls) to Conun-
drum Pass and Copper Lake. Go down (not up) this road to a barricade erected
to keep you out of biological laboratory property. Judd Falls is just off the trail,
below the wilderness boundary sign.
    Judd Falls leaps 20 feet, then twists into a broad 30-foot slide. Its upper
leap is visible from a seat carved in memory of Garwood Hall Judd, "the man
who stayed," March 14, 1852-May 15, 1930.
    Copper Creek ran red with mud when we were there because of mud slides
upstream. The area is very popular with hikers, bikers, and outfitters, and there
were many people, horses, and false trails.
    There is no clear indication of where the falls is where the trail meets the

old road, and the current road of access is marked neither on the national forest map nor on the Gothic quadrangle. We hiked in a drizzle probably half a mile up the road until it was clear that by heading up the valley we had missed the falls. Then I started searching along the steep banks of Copper Creek and down false trails other people have made looking for the falls and almost fell down the hill into the creek. Once you know where the falls is, it's an easy fifteen-minute hike from and to the trailhead. Falling into the creek is not obligatory.

Cliff Creek Falls *
(See map on page 238.)

Access: Hike
Rating and Type: Not visited
USGS Topographic Quad: West Beckwith Mountain (38107 G3)
Trail Miles: 1.6 + .2-mile bushwhack
Altitude: 7,800 feet
Elevation Change: Road is at 7,360 feet, ranch property line extends to 7,600 feet

Cliff Creek Falls has been rendered inaccessible by the presence of Davenport Ranch. According to a ranch hand who refused us permission to cross ranch property, the owner lives in North Carolina, his son-in-law at Crystal Meadows Resort, and access is denied even to employees of the ranch. Even though the falls is inside West Elk Wilderness, the only public access requires a climb over Mosley Ridge south of the ranch property, then by trail upstream beyond the ranch property. The climb looks formidable but possible. Maybe we'll see you there.

Turn off Highway 133 south along Coal Creek from the southern end of Paonia State Recreation Area to a turnaround at Davenport Ranch; the falls is 1.5 miles up Cliff Creek, .25-mile up the unnamed drainage to the northeast. The stream is marked as intermittent.

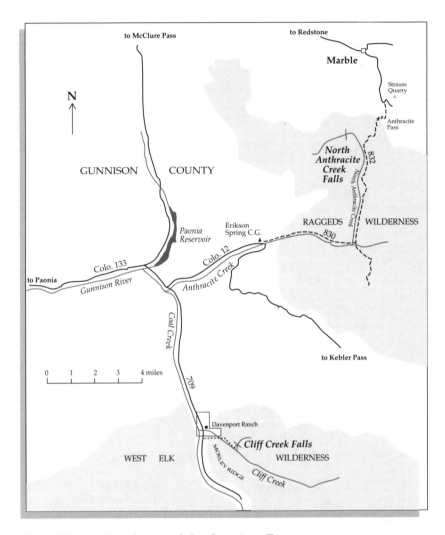

Waterfalls north and west of the Gunnison River
(**#52** on Gunnison, San Miguel, and Uncompahgre rivers drainages map,
page 184):

Cliff Creek Falls
North Anthracite Creek Falls

North Anthracite Creek Falls*
(See map on page 238.)

Access: Overnight
Rating: ★
Type: Horsetail
USGS Topographic Quad: Marble (39107 A2)
Trail Miles: 6 to 7
Altitude: 9,200 feet
Elevation Change: From 9,150 feet to pass, +2,220 feet; to North
  Anthracite Creek, -2,200 feet; to falls, +50 feet

North Anthracite Creek is a tributary of the Gunnison River, and access is possible from the Keebler Pass road between Crested Butte and Paonia Reservoir. However, hiking distance is shorter from the road to the Yule Marble Quarry southeast of Marble. The four-wheel-drive road across the bridge south of town takes you toward the quarry. Four miles up the road, at 9,025 feet, trail 832 starts for Anthracite Pass (11,345 feet). Once you are over the pass and down into the North Anthracite Creek valley, go north around the pond at the head of the drainage and head up the trail another .5-mile to the falls. The falls is a narrow 30-foot slide in a slick-rocked, mossy environment, and can be seen from the pond.

The Escalante Canyon Vicinity

Waterfalls in dry environments can be wonderfully refreshing, as we've learned from hiking in the desert, so we were pleased to discover three waterfalls in the canyon lands west of Delta, on the gulches tributary to the Gunnison as it makes its way through Escalante Canyon (Escalante never got up here).

However, if you hope to see any water flowing in this arid environment, the time of year of your visit is critical. From a viewpoint opposite the "confluence" of Palmer Gulch and the Gunnison, on the cliffs of Escalante Canyon, there appeared to be water in the upper reaches of the gulch, but it was bone dry at the outlet in August. We decided to go back sometime when things were wetter.

The hike is over dry vegetation and sunburnt rock, but still it's very peaceful and interesting. Bring your own water.

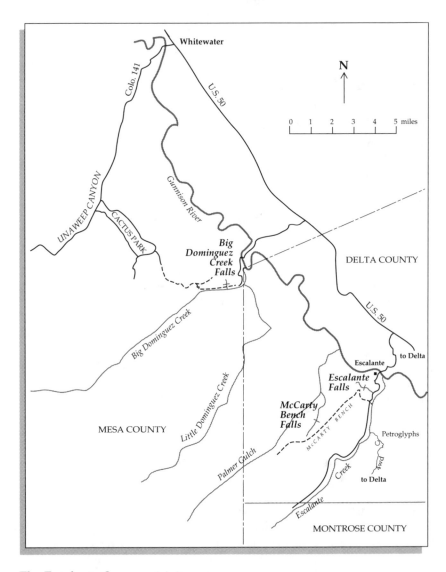

The Escalante Canyon vicinity group

(**#53** on Gunnison, San Miguel, and Uncompahgre rivers drainages map, page 184):

Escalante Creek Falls
McCarty Bench Falls
Big Dominguez Creek Falls

Escalante Creek Falls* (on unnamed tributary to Escalante Creek)
(See Escalante Canyon Vicinity group map, page 240.)

Access: Hike
Rating: ★
Type: Block
USGS Topographic Quad: Good Point (38108 F3)
Trail Miles: 1 to lower, 3+ to Palmer Gulch Falls
Altitude: 5,200 feet
Elevation Change: From 5,000 feet, +200 feet

McCarty Bench Falls* (on unnamed tributary to Palmer Gulch)
(See Escalante Canyon Vicinity group map, page 240.)

Access: Hike
Rating and Type: Not visited
USGS Topographic Quad: Good Point (38108 F3)
Trail Miles: 3.5
Altitude: 6,000 feet
Elevation Change: From 5,500 feet, +1,000 feet

Eleven miles west of Delta on U.S. 50 there's a historical marker at an intersection on the south side of the highway. From here, a dirt road goes south toward Escalante Forks. Via this road, it's 2.4 miles to the bridge crossing the Gunnison, then another 2.3 miles along Escalante Creek to the trailhead.

The trail to both of these falls begins across the road from a farmhouse. The contrast between the irrigated green fields on one side and the hard-baked rock on the other amused us. The trail starts as a rocky road going up a wash, then rapidly deteriorates, but it can be followed as indicated on the quad. A trail taking a direct route onto McCarty Bench forks off to the south at about .5-mile.

To see the lower falls, follow this track across the hillside to the north, then cut uphill northwest over the rocks to the crest of the hill, with its clear view of the bridge over the Gunnison at Escalante Canyon. The lower falls steps down bare rock into the wash, with a possible leap of 10 to 12 feet and several pools below. Go only in spring or fall, or you'll see more rock than water, as we did.

The trail, if you can find it, cuts back up onto the McCarty Bench from the northeast, avoiding the cliffs on the east end.

The upper falls is on an unnamed tributary to Palmer Gulch. At 3.75 miles (from the trailhead) along the McCarty trail, go cross-country about a quarter of a mile west to the rim of the bench. If any water is running, the falls should be visible 200 feet below.

Petroglyphs farther south on the Escalante Creek road indicate that Indians made their homes in this harsh environment hundreds of years ago. Now fences protect the petroglyphs, but the condition of the petroglyphs suggests the effort was too late.

Big Dominguez Creek Falls *
(See Escalante Canyon Vicinity group map, page 240.)

Access: Hike
Rating and Type: Not visited
USGS Topographic Quad: Triangle Mesa
Trail Miles: 4 to 5
Altitude: 5,200 feet
Elevation Change: From 6,250 feet to 5,200 feet, -1,050 feet

According to the book *Colorado BLM Wildlands,* 9 miles south of White-water on Highway 141 take the Cactus Park turnoff to the southeast. It's 7 miles of initially good road, then 2 miles (requiring high clearance) to a trailhead. The quad shows a trail to Triangle Mesa; but when you reach the ridge south of Triangle Mesa, drop downhill 400 feet into the Big Dominguez drainage. Another mile and a half downstream you come to the falls about a mile above the confluence of Big Dominguez and Little Dominguez creeks. Pearson says there are also large boulders with petroglyphs. Fielder's photo shows a 30-foot horsetail sliding down red slickrock into the Big Dominguez streambed from an unnamed tributary, with red-rock mesas providing a backdrop. I am guessing Fielder's photo looks to the northeast, placing the falls on the western side of the canyon, but the light in the photo is not direct enough for me to be sure.

The book also says that access to Big Dominguez is possible by crossing the Gunnison from Bridgeport. Supposedly, the bridge there is now closed to the public, but it is possible to cross the river by boat or canoe and hike up the Big Dominguez a mile to the confluence with the Little Dominguez, then another mile to the falls.

The Escalante Canyon vicinity group
(**#54** on Gunnison, San Miguel, and
Uncompahgre rivers drainages map,
page 184):

Black Canyon Falls

Black Canyon Falls*
(See map, this page.)

Access: Bushwhack, parachute
useful
Rating: ★ ★
Type: Cascade and block
USGS Topographic Quad:
Grizzly Ridge (38107 E6)
Trail Miles: 1.5
Altitude: 5,900 feet
Elevation Change: From 7,700
feet, -1,800 feet

As the Gunnison River cuts
through Black Canyon National
Monument, it drops an average of
95 feet per mile. From Pulpit Rock
to Chasm View it plunges 180 feet
in a half-mile! In a canyon with rock
this hard, you'd expect a falls or
perhaps a hundred. And one
waterfall *is* marked on the Grizzly
Ridge quad, opposite Chasm
View.

This falls is accessible from the
North Rim via SOB Draw, which
is steep enough to cause vertigo
and requires 1.5 to 3 hours to
reach the bottom. The trail into the draw begins from the road between the
ranger station and the campground, about 30 yards east of the turnaround
at the registration kiosk. The trail goes north from this road, immediately passing
through a barbed-wire fence. (When we were there, the monument literature
said to look for a cattle guard, but this had been taken out and a planned
turnstile was not yet installed.) The trail crosses chaparral through junipers
to skirt the rim of the draw. As you head down into SOB Draw, stay to the
right side; there are several different routes but only occasionally a clear trail
marked by cairns or ribbons. Beware of poison ivy. There is no water in the
draw, and the rangers recommend that visitors carry two quarts of water per
person and that any water collected from the Gunnison be purified by an

The author in the Black Canyon

established method. You can see the river clearly from many places in the draw, and there are striking views up and down the canyon.

The falls opposite Chasm View consists of several violent cascades, a few deep pools, and a 6- to 10-foot-high Niagara-shaped block falls. Both sides of the river are clogged with huge boulders up and down the canyon, and it is possible to move upstream only 50 or 60 yards beyond the falls. There is one tiny beach downstream a hundred yards. This is a stark and demanding environment, and you will feel about as significant as a spider in a pile of base-balls. Downstream from the falls you can see The Painted Wall, at 2,800 feet the highest cliff in Colorado.

In addition, a descent from Tomichi Point on the South Rim, according to the monument literature, leads to a series of "cascades" (marked neither on the USGS quad nor on any of the other maps I obtained) along a mile of river accessible on the bottom, but with no beaches. This trip would take 1.5 to 3 hours one way.

All the primitive routes into the canyon are difficult, and a permit from the monument ranger station is required before hikers set out. Camping is limited.

To reach the South Rim of the Black Canyon, turn north off U.S. 50 7 miles east of Montrose. Colorado 347 leads up onto the plateau of the canyon rim, the campground, and the visitor's center. The viewpoints are well marked along the road.

To reach the North Rim, drive south on Colorado 92 from Hotchkiss for 10 miles, to Crawford. Take Colorado 347 west from Crawford: You will cross the Smith Fork in 1.3 miles and the road will turn south. In 2 more miles you will come to an intersection with Black Canyon Road, which is clearly identified by a series of signs. Turn right (west), go .75-mile, and turn south again. It's about 7.5 more miles to the campground.

Established in 1933 to protect the 22-mile heart of the 53-mile canyon, the Black Canyon of the Gunnison National Monument sees 300,000 visitors each year.

Coal Creek Falls *
(See map on page 246.)

Access: Bushwhack
Rating: ★
Type: Plunge
USGS Topographic Quad: Land's End (39108 A2)
Trail Miles: 0
Altitude: 9,950 feet
Elevation Change: From 10,000 feet, -50 feet

To see Coal Creek Falls and experience firsthand the vastness of Colorado's mesa country, drive up Colorado 65 through Mesa and Skyway to the road (26 miles from the Colorado River) to Land's End in Grand Mesa National Forest.

It's 12 miles to the information center at Land's End (which was closed in late November) and breath-giving views of the La Salles to the west, the San Juans to the south, and the Grand Valley in its broad splendor.

We found the waterfall in this unlikely place, where Coal Creek (about 10 miles from Colorado 65) leaves the mesa top to plummet toward the plains.

When we visited in November, Coal Creek Falls was a frozen column of 50-foot-long icicles and a mass of icy lace draped 70 to 80 feet down basalts that keep Grand Mesa aloof from the maelstrom seas of erosion.

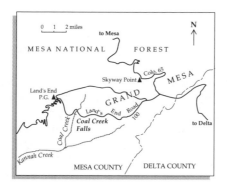

The Escalante Canyon vicinity group
(**#55** on Gunnison, San Miguel, and
Uncompahgre rivers drainages map,
page 184):

Coal Creek Falls

I don't know how much
water flows in spring, but
the drive is worth it just for
the views. The falls can be
seen most easily by ap-
proaching the Coal Creek
drainage from the road 125
yards to the west. This road
crosses the Coal Creek
drainage, which is marked
by a wooden sign.

Land's End can be ac-
cessed either from Mesa or
from Whitewater on U.S.
50. I was tempted to in-
clude this falls in the Colorado River chapter, but actually Coal Creek is tributary
to Kannah Creek, which
drains into the Gunnison a
few miles south of Grand
Junction.

Coal Creek Falls

The Colorado River
Drainage Map

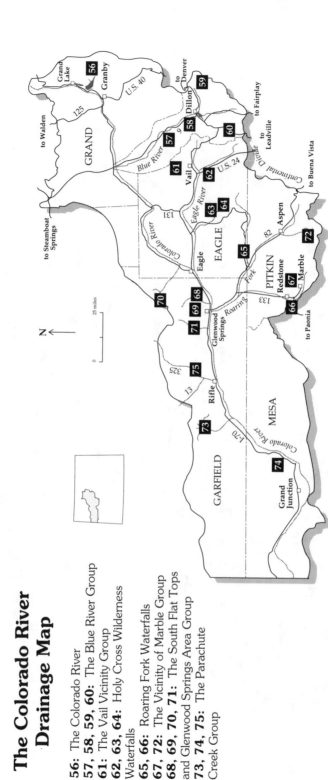

56: The Colorado River

57, 58, 59, 60: The Blue River Group

61: The Vail Vicinity Group

62, 63, 64: Holy Cross Wilderness Waterfalls

65, 66: Roaring Fork Waterfalls

67, 72: The Vicinity of Marble Group

68, 69, 70, 71: The South Flat Tops and Glenwood Springs Area Group

73, 74, 75: The Parachute Creek Group

7

The Colorado River

The Colorado River, near the Colorado-Utah state line, drains an area of 17,843 square miles. This is only seven percent of the total area of the Colorado Basin (244,000 square miles), which is the area drained by the Colorado River and made up of Wyoming, Utah, New Mexico, Arizona, Nevada, and an itty-bitty piece of California.

Fifteen percent—225 miles—of the Colorado River's total 1,450-mile length is in Colorado. So the acreage per mile donating water to the river is half that of the rest of the basin. But the river collects sixty percent of the state's precipitation, and this amounts to one-third of the Colorado River's total annual flow of 14 million acre-feet.

Of course, the other states contribute their share. The Colorado's longest tributary, the Green River, which flows through just 40 miles of Colorado's northwest corner, carried nearly 2 million acre-feet (627 billion gallons) to the Colorado River in Utah in 1990—and that was a drought year!

There is something about the Colorado that inspires superlatives, even negative ones. It's one of the saltiest, siltiest rivers in North America, and it has the greatest elevation drop of any river on the continent, from nearly 14,000 feet

249

in the Never Summer Range to 4,300 feet at the Colorado-Utah border. It has been called "the most legislated, litigated, and debated" river in the world because of the legal and monetary battles fought over the rights to its waters.

The Colorado Territory took its name from the river in 1861, because the river rises in the Colorado mountains. At the time, there was no river actually named "Colorado" within the state's present boundaries. Surviving maps from two hundred years of exploration gave it nine different names, including "El Rio de Buena Guia," and "Firebrand River." Until seventy years ago it was called the Grand River from its headwaters to its confluence with the Green, where the "Colorado River" moniker took over.

On July 25, 1921, a bill was approved that changed the river's name to Colorado all the way to its headwaters in the Never Summer Mountains, on the western border of Rocky Mountain National Park. There are still some old-timers who refer to it as the Grand.

The San Juan, Gunnison, Yampa, Roaring Fork, Dolores, Eagle, Navajo, Piedra, Animas, White, Green, and Blue rivers all flow eventually into the Colorado. Officially, the Colorado Basin includes all of the state west of the Continental Divide. However, this chapter describes waterfalls only in the drainages tributary to the main stem of "The Grand" before it crosses the Utah border, excepting the Gunnison Basin, which has its own chapter.

We list forty-nine waterfalls ranging from wild-horse territory near Grand Junction to the forested hills above Granby; from a famous marble quarry to one of the world's most famous ski resorts; from the stalking grounds of treacherous snow bunnies to the back door of the Mount of the Holy Cross.

Roaring Fork Falls *
(See Colorado River map, page 251.)

Access: Bushwhack
Rating: ★
Type: Cascade
USGS Topographic Quad: Shadow Mountain (40105 B7)
Trail Miles: .25-mile
Altitude: 8,600 feet
Elevation Change: From 8,200 feet, +400 feet

This is a small waterfall in the upper reaches of the Colorado River drainage. It is at the southwest end of Lake Granby and is the only waterfall in this area that is not inside Rocky Mountain National Park.

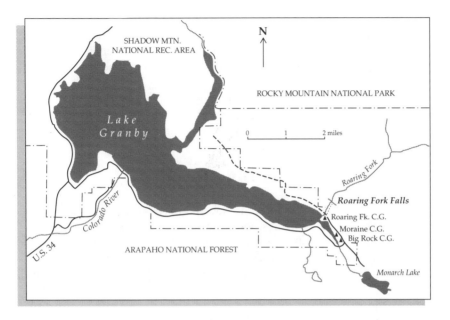

The Colorado River
(**#56** on Colorado River drainage map, page 248):

Roaring Fork Falls

   Roaring Fork Falls is a 100-foot series of cascades down the steep wooded slope enclosing the northern edge of Arapaho Bay, at the extreme southeast end of Lake Granby. Before crossing the drainage on the trail from the Roaring Fork ranger station, there is a sort of trail leading up the south side of the drainage. Try to stay out of the brush close down to the stream. The cut is very steep and the dirt does not provide good footing. You have to climb 600 feet in .3-mile of bushwhacking.
   The Roosevelt National Forest map shows a trail up the north side of Roaring Fork that is not indicated on the 15-foot quad or the 1:100,000 USGS map. We did not know about this trail when we were searching for the waterfall one night at dusk.

Take U.S. 34 north of Granby. There are turnoffs to the western end of the lake 4 and 5 miles from the intersection of 34 and 40. Moraine campground is another 8 miles. Drive around the end of the lake to the Roaring Fork campground and ranger station. Roaring Fork is about a hundred yards beyond the ranger station.

Filled in 1952, Lake Granby is a man-made catchment for diversion of water pumped uphill to Grand Lake and then through the 13-mile Adams Tunnel under the Continental Divide to Eastern Slope farms and towns.

The Blue River

The Blue River flows north from its source in the Tenmile Range 15 miles to Dillon Reservoir. It continues north, through Green Mountain Reservoir, another 35 miles to its confluence with the Colorado. Green Mountain Reservoir collects water for the farmers and ranchers of the Western Slope. Dillon sheds water under the Continental Divide into the North Fork of the South Platte at the rate of nearly 83,000 acre-feet per year for the municipal use of several Front Range cities.

In the 1800s, the Blue River valley was a spot favored by mountain men. It had a good supply of beaver and was in a neutral zone between the Osage tribe to the north and other hostile tribes farther south.

The river's name is from "L'Eau Bleu," the name used by French mine workers when the water was still tinged with minerals from heavy placer-mining on its headwaters.

The Blue River North of Dillon

This small group of waterfalls is in the Gore Range, off State Highway 9. Take the Silverthorne exit (#205) off I-70 near Dillon Reservoir.

Cataract Creek Falls*

(See map, this page.)

Access: Hike
Rating: ★ ★ ★
Type: Segmented horsetail
USGS Topographic Quad:
  Mount Powell (39106 G3)
Trail Miles: 1
Altitude: 9,100 feet
Elevation Change: From
  8,640 feet, +360 feet

Map labels: Kremmling 16 mi.; Heeney; Green Mountain Reservoir; Colo. 9; SUMMIT COUNTY; Cataract Creek; ARAPAHO NATIONAL FOREST; Cataract C.G.; N; Lower Cataract Lake; Wilderness Boundary; Cataract Creek Falls; 0 0.5 1.0 miles; Tipperary Lake; EAGLES NEST WILDERNESS

The Blue River group
(**#57** on Colorado River drainage map,
page 248):

Cataract Creek Falls

Cataract Falls is the jewel of the valley of Lower Cataract Lake, which is really saying something. The falls is high on a cliff side, visible from clear across Lower Cataract Lake and beyond almost as soon as you're past the campground, which is .5-mile below the lake.

The area was very popular the weekend before July 4, and Nancy and I were not alone at the top of the falls. Trails encircle the lake, but the one on the south side of the loop is prettier. The north side of the loop (the one we took on the way up) is less traveled.

On the north side of the footbridge crossing Cataract Creek, trails lead upward steeply but irregularly through the trees and rocks to the top of the falls, and every stage along the way is worth the effort.

The main leap is no more than 20 feet, but the total length of the falls probably exceeds 300 feet or more of white water, and what a beautiful noise it makes. It's also potentially deadly, as it has apparently demonstrated in the past. According to Dan Burnett, who works with the county rescue service, it took twenty people to figure out how to retrieve the body of a man who had fallen over the top of the falls.

Take the road to Heeney on the west side of Green Mountain Reservoir 4 miles to the campground and bear left to a parking area in another .25-mile. The lake is an additional .25-mile.

Cataract Creek Falls is not indicated on the quad. There are additional falls rumored above this on Cataract Creek. The hike up one side of the lake is roughly a mile; the hike uphill from the footbridge is a steep .25-mile.

Boulder Creek Falls***
(See Blue River group map, page 255.)

Access: Hike
Rating: ★ ★
Type: Cascade and horsetail
USGS Topographic Quad: Willow Lakes (39106 F2)
Trail Miles: 3 to lowermost falls, 5.75 to uppermost falls
Altitude: 10,350 feet, 10,800 feet, 10,980 feet
Elevation Change: From 9,400 feet to lowest falls, +950 feet; to uppermost falls, +1,580 feet

There are three waterfalls on Boulder Creek in the Gore Range. Only the upper two are marked on the Willow Lakes quadrangle.

Take Rock Creek Road directly across from Blue River campground, which is about 7.4 miles north of Silverthorne on Colorado 9. After 1.4 miles, take the left turn to the Rock Creek trailhead and drive another 3 miles to the end of the road and a turnaround.

The trail here follows an old road for a third of a mile to where the Gore Range trail intersects the road.

The Gore Range trail climbs through aspen woods and crosses a ridge at 10,100 feet, then drops to meet the trail coming up Boulder Creek at a point 2 miles from the trailhead. Take the merged trails to the left (west) .25-mile farther to Boulder Lake. Cross Boulder Creek by a log bridge at the east end of the lake and proceed on up the Boulder Creek drainage around the lake and upstream another 1.75 miles. The trail comes very close to the creek, then crosses over two well-placed logs to the south side of the creek and follows its course on that side as it climbs over several alternating meanders and moss-covered shelves of rock, and sometimes through cuts in the rock 40 to 50 vertical feet at a time.

Tim Kelley's *Fishing Guide* says the trail ends at the falls 1 mile from Boulder Lake. Lower Boulder Creek Falls is actually around the bend .25-mile after

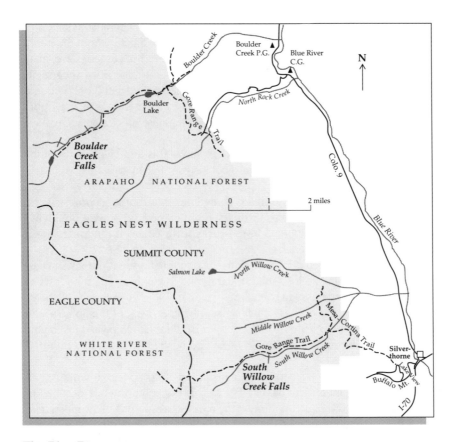

The Blue River group
(**#58** on Colorado River drainage map, page 248):

Boulder Creek Falls
South Willow Creek Falls

the trail crosses the creek and just as it starts into the rock where Boulder Creek tumbles down through the boulders and meets a smaller tributary from the north. This tributary leaps twice to meet Boulder Creek, and the cascades are steep and rocky up Boulder Creek. I decided to call this a falls, since it certainly amounts to one as much as do those upstream that are indicated on the quad.

Tim Kelley also says that there are cutthroat in the ponds in the upper reaches, and brookies below. The cutthroat are a native species and may have been there before the falls.

The trail heads right up a cut in the rock above this and gives views of the water—probably very dramatic at times of high runoff. The stream cut is green, picturesque, and memorable.

Continuing on upstream the trail is sometimes thin, but it becomes clearer as it twists through the Douglas fir until extending around a large bouldered talus slope, where it disappears in the rocks for a while. It reappears again at the lower end of a meander.

The glaciers of the Boulder Creek drainage deposited a series of rock shelves. The creek flows from shelf to shelf, meandering through serene meadows of yellow grass, making passage sometimes a little marshy, even in mid-October.

The trail climbs one of these shelf series, finally arriving at the lip of a lake at 10,900 feet at the 5.75-mile mark. Upper Boulder Creek Falls is just below the lip. To find it requires leaving the trail and bushwhacking a few hundred yards north.

The falls is more like a steep cascade dropping 60 to 70 feet down the shelf to the first of the meanders below. The falls is not a worthwhile destination by itself, although the climb up through the rocks, the autumn yellow meanders, and a flawlessly blue-skyed October day make for a rewarding hike.

It turned out to be a bit much for one day, because I included a side trip to find a second falls marked on a tributary to Boulder Creek north of Upper Boulder Creek Falls. To find it, drop with Boulder Creek from the upper falls about a hundred yards, then cut north to meet the tributary drainage. The second falls is in the woods just above a set of meanders, on the same shelf as the main falls. It's possible to reach this second falls coming upstream, but the water leaps only 5 to 6 feet, and it's not worth the effort to get to—unless you just want to be alone, which you will be.

Boulder Lake is worth seeing. The valley is deep and long. On an October day between hunting seasons I had it entirely to myself, although I didn't see a single deer or even a sign of one all day. Either the weather had been so warm that they hadn't come down yet or the hunters scared them all back up. The waterfalls on Boulder Creek are not worth the trip from Boulder Lake in themselves.

South Willow Creek Falls *
(See Blue River group map, page 255.)

Access: Hike, bushwhack
Rating: Not visited
Type: Segmented
USGS Topographic Quad: Willow Lakes (39106 F2)
Trail Miles: 4
Altitude: 10,200 feet
Elevation Change: From 9,200 feet, + 1,000 feet

This is a 15- to 20-foot segmented falls on South Willow Creek. Exit I-70 at Silverthorne. Almost immediately after getting off the interstate, head north on Colorado 9 and turn left (west) at the first stoplight. In .25-mile turn right onto Buffalo Mountain Road, head around a left-hand curve, and bear to the right up Gore Range (or Lake View) to the trailhead for the Mesa-Cortina and Gore Range trails.

This combined trail, popular and well beaten, crosses northwest to the Willow Creek drainage in about 2.5 miles. The Mesa-Cortina continues north; turn left on the trail to head upstream to the falls for a total hiking distance of about 4 miles. We've been told that there are other waterfalls on Willow Creek in this general area, but they are not visible from the trail.

The Blue River South of Dillon

We know of two waterfalls south of Dillon Reservoir in the Blue River drainage. One is on the North Fork of the Snake River, near the Arapahoe Basin ski resort. The other is on Spruce Creek, a tributary to the Blue south of Breckenridge.

Snake River Falls
(See map on page 258.)

Access: Walk in
Rating: ★ ★
Type: Segmented
USGS Topographic Quad: Loveland Pass (39105 F8)
Trail Miles: .2-mile
Altitude: 10,400 feet
Elevation Change: From 10,560 feet, -160 feet

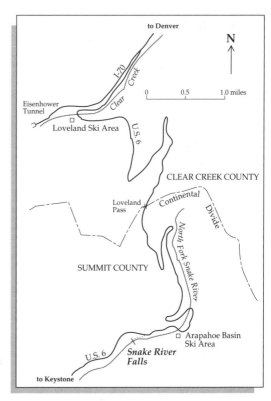

The Blue River group
(**#59** on Colorado River
drainage map, page 248):

Snake River Falls

Snake River Falls is a ten-minute hike from U.S. 6 at an unmarked turnout just down the highway from the entrance to the Arapahoe Basin ski area, itself 3.5 miles south of Loveland Pass. A usable trail heads down into the woods toward the river, then angles downstream. Where the cliffs become more clearly defined above the riverbed there is a trail down into the gorge, right to the falls.

Snake River Falls runs out of what seems to be a crack in the rock wall but is actually a sharp cleft carved by the water; it is very sheer and hangs over the falls. The falls plunges and sprays several levels for a total of 20 feet. The wet rocks are beautifully striated—red, yellow, and black—and the water has brought out the best in their colors.

Snake River Falls

Some trash below the falls indicates frequency of visitation, but there was no one there on the cool, wet day in September that we visited. Some of the trash may actually be from the ski area and lodge a few hundred yards above the falls.

Continental Falls
(See map on page 261.)

Access: Hike
Rating: ★ ★
Type: Tiered cascade
USGS Topographic Quad: Breckenridge
Trail Miles: .5-mile
Altitude: 11,600 feet
Elevation Change: From 10,940 feet, +660 feet

Continental Falls is a long series of cascades down a slope of hard metamorphic marble cake. Its single leap, of less than 10 feet, makes that awesome "falls thunder" sound as it plunges into a pool on its way through the rocks. Out of the cut it seemed as though the moisture in the air, in the form of gently falling snow, was muffling the sound of the water somehow.

Get to the falls by driving south out of Breckenridge 1.5 miles on Colorado 9. On the west side of the highway, opposite Goose Pasture Tarn, a dirt road climbs through a small group of residential cabins. Stay on this road to its end, about 3.1 miles, where a trail goes up an old four-wheel-drive road. Then the trail climbs rapidly to tree line past the abandoned cabins of mining operations that took place along Spruce Creek near the falls.

The steepest part of the lower cascade is visible from the east side of the creek, less than half a mile from the parking area. To get to the main leap, you have to approach around the rocks above the water on the west side. We crossed by clambering over trees fallen across the creek. The leap and plunge are very near the bottom.

The total hiking distance to the bottom of the falls is about a half-mile. You can see the waterfall from a distance, and it is possible to make your way up the rocks containing the falls to see other cascades, which were covered for us by late spring snow. There are more remains of the mining operation, including cables and an old mining cart. It snowed lightly on June 4 as we picnicked below the falls.

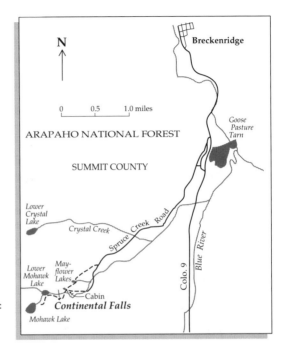

N

0   0.5   1.0 miles

ARAPAHO NATIONAL FOREST

SUMMIT COUNTY

Breckenridge

Goose
Pasture
Tarn

Lower
Crystal
Lake

Crystal Creek

Spruce Creek Road

Colo. 9

Blue River

Lower
Mohawk
Lake

May-
flower
Lakes

Cabin
Continental Falls

Mohawk Lake

The Blue River group
(**#60** on Colorado River
drainage map, page 248):

Continental Falls

The Vail Vicinity

Gore Creek, flowing north and east from Vail Pass, carved the magnificent valley that is now renowned as the location of the Vail ski area. Golf courses, condominiums, and upscale social amenities abound. To some, Vail is a sort of vacationer's paradise. But there are times when the appeal of crowds and parties fades, and we're pleased to report that a little way upstream and across I-70 from the glitter there are several trailheads that provide hikes into the Eagles Nest Wilderness. Two of these have waterfalls on them. And there's even a small waterfall that glimmers at you as you whiz by on the highway.

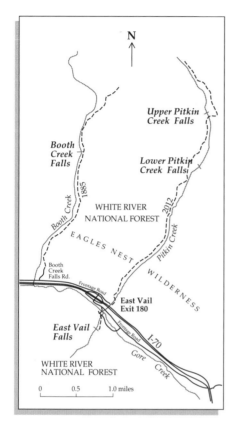

The Vail vicinity group
(**#61** on Colorado River drainage map, page 248):

East Vail Falls
Pitkin Creek Falls
Booth Creek Falls

East Vail Falls *
(See Vail Vicinity group map, this page.)

Access: Roadside
Rating: ★ ★
Type: Tiered
USGS Topographic Quad: Vail East (39106 F3)
Trail Miles: .25-mile
Altitude: 8,680 feet
Elevation Change: From 8,400 feet, + 280 feet

Dwarfed by the purple cliffs on the south side of the Vail valley, a sliverlike waterfall hangs above East Vail, sometimes barely seeming to wet the rock.

To reach it, take the East Vail exit, #180, from I-70. Take the road under the overpass, drive back southeast into East Vail, then take the first turn off the frontage road toward the homes along the base of the cliff. Not very far from the underpass there's a sheer black rock face visible amidst the dense vegetation. A thin falls drops straight down the face in one leap of 15 to 20 feet, and then a shower drops another 15 to 20 feet to a steep cascade below it.

The trail to the falls begins at a small unmarked turnoff just to the west of the creek. The slope grows very steep toward the top, but tree roots and fallen branches provide a way to pull yourself up. Then the trail winds through dense vegetation and actually goes behind the second leap. I lost the trail coming down, swinging, as Nancy said, from tree branch to tree root like a monkey.

When we visited in September, there was very little water. One of the nice things about this waterfall is that you can check out how much water is flowing over it as you drive by on I-70.

Pitkin Creek Falls* *
(See Vail Vicinity group map, page 262.)

Access: Hike
Rating: ★
Type: Cascade
USGS Topographic Quad: Vail East (39106 F3)
Trail Miles: 3
Altitude: 9,960 feet, 10,520 feet
Elevation Change: From 8,400 feet to lower falls, + 1,560 feet; to upper falls, + 560 feet

During the course of researching this book, I was often compelled to do unreasonable things—such as look for waterfalls in November. I drove to exit 180 on I-70 at East Vail, then backtracked .2-mile on the frontage road on the north side of the highway. The Pitkin Creek trail (#2012) starts near a cluster of condominiums here. It was under snow from about 9,500 feet onward. Ice had already formed a shell over the creek in its upper reaches.

Lower Pitkin Creek Falls is 2 miles from the trailhead, and Upper Pitkin Creek Falls is 3 miles. Both are off the trail and seem to be steep cascades twisting up shelves of rock.

The steepness of the climb out of the valley and away from the highway made me feel, at one point, as though the world was tilting slightly sideways and I had to stand at an angle to it to keep from falling down. The sound of the highway fades, then disappears in the wind at half a mile.

Eventually, where the trail crosses the creek, the footsteps of others before me ended in the snow and turned back. Sometimes I followed the paths of rabbits or deer, or catlike prints, deeper and deeper into the woods as the sun threatened to sink below the horizon.

My reward was not the upper falls but its sound in a tumble of rocks half-concealed by snow and the sterling silence of the woods at the beginning of winter.

As the light was striking the tops of the Gore, I found my way back to the lower falls, which was visible in a cleft rising in the rock 200 yards east of the trail, about 2 miles from the trailhead. There was a little leap still left open at the bottom of the falls, and I glimpsed the water at the top splashing into the air before it plunged down under icy lacework.

Pitkin Creek valley is wide open beyond the rise above the highway and scattered with aspen woods. It is very popular in summer but totally solitary in November. I'd bet on the flowers at the lower falls being really stupendous in July.

Booth Creek Falls *
(See Vail Vicinity group map, page 262.)

Access: Hike
Rating: ★ ★
Type: Horsetail
USGS Topographic Quad: Vail East (39106 F3)
Trail Miles: 2
Altitude: 9,800 feet
Elevation Change: From 8,400 feet, + 1,400 feet

Booth Creek Falls is a 60-foot braided horsetail 1.8 miles from the trailhead. It cuts deeply into the rock and twists into a nice little pool at the bottom. The steepest drop is hidden in a twisting cut in the cliffs.

Views are possible opposite the top of the falls, and we climbed down to a platform inside the cut about halfway down the falls, right across the cut from the water. This closer view is not recommended for those with children, vertigo, or both.

The trailhead to Booth Creek Falls is at the end of Booth Falls Road, which is a right-hand turn up the hill 1 mile west of the East Vail exit (#180) via the frontage road on the north side of I-70. There's a prominent trailhead sign with a map. The trail climbs steeply out of the valley, rapidly entering a long, pretty stretch of aspen. The Booth Creek trail (#1885) is the fourth most popular in the region and well used.

The Booth Creek valley was lush with flowers and the high green of August when we visited. The waterfall is not visible from down the valley, but the trail reaches close enough that the sound will tell you when you're there.

Four miles up the trail is Booth Lake and views of the Gore.

Booth Creek Falls

Holy Cross Wilderness Waterfalls

Holy Cross Wilderness lies at the north end of the Sawatch Range, spans 126,000 acres, including five major glaciated valleys, and contains twenty-five peaks over 13,000 feet in altitude. Its centerpiece, the Mount of the Holy Cross (14,005 feet), was once designated a national monument, and pilgrimages were made to view its slopes.

Most visitors to Holy Cross Wilderness still go to climb the famous mountain or to see it from the shelter atop Notch Mountain. But it is only one of countless wilderness attractions, including wetlands, wildlife, and waterfalls.

In 1962, Aurora and Colorado Springs obtained rights to upper Eagle River water, and in 1967 Homestake Reservoir Dam was completed, diverting water from Homestake, French, Fancy, Missouri, and Sopris creeks. This was called Homestake Phase I. The hike we describe up Fancy Creek begins at one of Homestake I's intrusive 6-foot-diameter diversion pipes.

Homestake Phase II would place diversion dams on Cross, West Cross, East Cross, and Fall creeks. Engineering reports state that Homestake II would affect 240 acres of wetlands below the diversion sites, altering the ecosystem forever.

In the meantime, Holy Cross Wilderness is available for viewing in a relatively pristine condition, and there are waterfalls scattered all through the wilderness. We describe nine of them.

Reach Holy Cross Wilderness on the east side by driving south from I-70 on U.S. 24, and take exit 171, Dowd's Junction, toward Minturn and Leadville. There are many possible points of entry. The most used are on Forest Road 707, 1 mile south of Minturn, to Half Moon campground and the climb up Notch Mountain; or up Homestake Creek on Forest Road 703, 2.5 miles south of Redcliff, which is the route to the waterfalls we describe on French and Cross creeks.

The west side of the wilderness can be reached either from Basalt, past Ruedi Reservoir on Forest Road 105, or by driving south on Forest Road 400 from Eagle. Or, for that matter, by four-wheel-drive from Leadville over Hagerman Pass. The west side of the wilderness is more isolated, less visited, and contains most of the falls we'll describe, near Fulford and up Lime Creek.

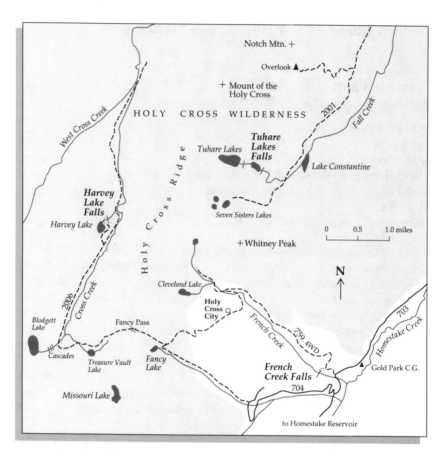

Holy Cross Wilderness waterfalls
(**#62** on Colorado River drainage map, page 248):

French Creek Falls
Harvey Lake Falls
Tuhare Lakes Falls

Eastern Slope of the Holy Cross Wilderness

French Creek Falls*
(See Holy Cross Wilderness Waterfalls map, page 267.)

Access: Hike, bushwhack
Rating: ★ ★
Type: Plunge
USGS Topographic Quad: Mount of the Holy Cross (39106 D4)
Trail Miles: .25-mile + .1-mile bushwhack
Altitude: 9,560 feet
Elevation Change: From 9,340 feet, + 220 feet

French Creek Falls is two simultaneous leaps of about 15 feet in an intimate amphitheater of square-cracked gneiss, hung generously with moss and lined with small aspen trees. This amphitheater offers secluded, calming, and wonderfully cool relief from the peskiness of flies and mosquitoes.

Turn onto Forest Road 703 13.5 miles south of Minturn on Colorado 24. Gold Park campground is 6.7 miles from the turn. One-quarter mile south of the Gold Park campground is the jeep road to Holy Cross City. This is the access to the falls.

Within an eighth of a mile up this jeep road there are two deeply eroded spots filled with head-size rocks. We turned around and parked at the bottom. A sprightlier four-wheel-drive got over this barrier; another had to winch itself out.

Just under .25-mile up the road (.1-mile beyond the second washed-out place), there's an old dirt road into the woods on the south. Take a line directly perpendicular to the road down this old track into the woods until you hit French Creek, which will be near the top of the falls. Work down the hill through the small stand of aspen and then back upstream to the falls amphitheater.

There were other people there but no signs of human erosion or trash, which is remarkable considering the proximity of the road and the campground. The old track toward the falls is fenced and posted. This is a nice little falls near a popular four-wheel-drive road and campground with high traffic volume.

French Creek Falls

Harvey Lake Falls *
(See Holy Cross Wilderness Waterfalls map, page 267.)

Access: Overnight
Rating: ★
Type: Cascade
USGS Topographic Quad: Mount Jackson (39106 D5)
Trail Miles: 6.5
Altitude: 11,000 feet
Elevation Change: From 10,100 feet, +2,300 feet, -1,400 feet from the pass

Harvey Lake Falls barely qualifies as a falls, although the forest service troubled itself to mark it on a map. Its steepest drop is a sheer 15-foot horsetail with no distinguishing leap, just part of the steady flow of water out of Harvey Lake dropping 250 feet through a woods lush with fern and paintbrush. The falls isn't much of a goal, but the hike down Cross Creek, with its many lakes, meadows, and old cabins, kept us from regretting the trip.

It's possible to hike directly up Cross Creek, although this way Harvey Lake is over 9 miles from the trailhead, a mile south of Minturn. The quickest way to the falls is up Fancy Creek to Fancy Lake and over Fancy Pass. To get to the trailhead, drive a mile past the Gold Park campground on Forest Road 703 and take a right turn up 704. After 2 miles the Missouri Lakes trailhead is at a sharp curve in the road. The Fancy Creek trailhead is another .4-mile farther on.

The Fancy Creek trail (#2006) follows an old road (now blocked) .2-mile past a diversion dam, then 2.3 miles directly up the drainage, which is lush with paintbrush of orange, crimson, and fuchsia. The trail is easy to follow, including a well-hiked but very steep quarter-mile section below the lake, which is not indicated on the quad.

Once at Fancy Lake, hike a hundred yards northeast to meet the trail coming up from Holy Cross City. Then follow the trail up to the northwest, climbing immediately to fabulous views over Fancy Lake.

Fancy Pass is at 12,400 feet, 1,000 feet but only .4-mile above the lake. Even in late July there were patches of snow burying the trail on the upper end of the climb to the pass, and the rock is treacherous.

It was raining when we crossed the pass with its far-ranging view of the upper end of the Cross Creek valley and the forbidding ridges of the wilderness displayed for miles. The rolling tundra on the west side of the pass is in striking contrast to the steep, rocky profile of the west side, which drops very swiftly to spruce forest.

The trail passes near Treasure Vault Lake at 11,500 feet, crosses a cascade below the lake, then goes around the end of the valley down past the old mill and "hotel," 2.5 miles below the pass. In another half-mile there's a sign at a fork in the trail that says it's an eighth of a mile to Harvey Lake.

The easiest way to the falls is to go to the lake and work down the drainage, although frankly the lake is much more impressive than the falls. The lake has been camped heavily but not trashed.

You can see the back of the Mount of the Holy Cross and Holy Cross ridge from the valley. Incidentally, there are a couple of small waterfalls right above Fancy Lake, and nice runs of water down from Treasure Vault and Blodgett lakes in the Cross Creek drainage.

Tuhare Lakes Falls * *
(See Holy Cross Wilderness Waterfalls map, page 267.)

Access: Overnight
Rating and Type: Not visited
USGS Topographic Quad: Mount Jackson (39106 D5)
Trail Miles: 4.8, 5.1
Altitude: 12,000 feet, 12,200 feet
Elevation Change: From 10,600 feet, + 1,400 feet, + 1,600 feet

As we were completing this book for publication, our sons, Zach and Natt, came back from a backpack into the Holy Cross Wilderness raving about 40- to 50-foot waterfalls below the spillways of both Tuhare lakes. They said each plunge was preceded by a long cascade.

To reach the lakes, drive 2 miles south of Minturn on U.S. 24 and take Forest Road 707 to Half Moon campground. Take trail 2001, which goes south. In 2 miles trail 2001 climbs to a view of the Mount of the Holy Cross, and forks to the west. Stay on 2001 itself another 2 miles to Lake Constantine. Go another half-mile before leaving the trail to climb the Tuhare Lakes drainage. You'll leave the trail at about 11,500 feet. It's .3-mile of bushwhacking up to the lower lake, then another .3-mile to the upper.

Western Slope of the Holy Cross Wilderness

The waterfalls on Nolan Creek and Lime Creek are reached by taking the Eagle exit off I-70. Drive directly through town on Main Street and bear left to the Sylvan Lake road, which is White River National Forest Road 400.

Nolan Creek Waterfalls

Drive south of Eagle on Forest Road 400 about 10 miles to its intersection with 415. Turn left on 415 and continue about 8 miles. One-quarter of a mile past the turn to Yeoman Park campground take a left on 418, which switchbacks up the hill 3.5 miles to the left turn to the new summer community of Fulford, a motley but charming collection of old and new homes and cabins. The Nolan Creek trailhead begins in the ruins of old Fulford, across the road.

Nolan Lake Access Stepped Falls*
(See Holy Cross Wilderness Waterfalls map, page 273.)

Access: Hike
Rating: ★
Type: Horsetail
USGS Topographic Quad: Fulford (39106 D6)
Trail Miles: 2
Altitude: 11,040 feet
Elevation Change: From 10,080 feet, +960 feet

Just to the right of the trail to Nolan Lake, at about the 2-mile mark, a stepped horsetail cascading down sharply planed rock is visible from the trail. There are other cascades and slides of water all along the trail between here, where the trail climbs steeply out of the Nolan Creek drainage, and where the trail turns back toward Nolan Lake.

Nolan Lake Falls*
(See Holy Cross Wilderness Waterfalls map, page 273.)

Access: Hike
Rating: ★ ★
Type: Cascade
USGS Topographic Quad: Fulford (39106 D6)
Trail Miles: 3
Altitude: 11,200 feet
Elevation Change: From 10,080 feet to lake at 11,300 feet, +1,120 feet; -100 feet to falls

As you hike up the Nolan Creek trail, a waterfall below the rim of Nolan Lake is visible in the cliffs when there's enough water. When we visited there

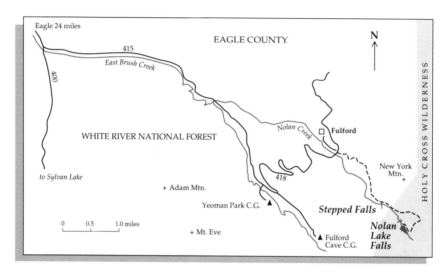

Holy Cross Wilderness waterfalls
(**#63** on Colorado River drainage map, page 248):

Nolan Lake Access Stepped Falls
Nolan Lake Falls

was a steady flow out of the lake, but not enough to matter. When there is a waterfall, it's a sudden cascading drop of 40 to 50 feet directly below the outlet. You can't see the falls from the lake. The easiest way to get down for a close-up view is on the north side.

Nolan Lake is surrounded by marbled granite cliffs and tundra, but the most remarkable thing about the place should be the wildflowers near the first of August and the aspen all around Fulford in late September.

We both got giardiasis from drinking the water entering the lake, and that was *after* we disinfected the water with an iodine tablet. Beware, especially when flow is sparse!

Lime Creek Waterfalls
Take Forest Road 400 south of Eagle (see Nolan Creek access, above) 5 miles

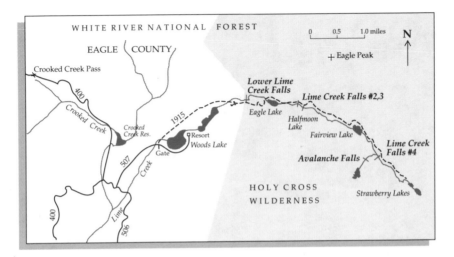

Holy Cross Wilderness waterfalls

(**#64** on Colorado River drainage map, page 248):

Lower Lime Creek Falls
Lime Creek Falls 2 and 3
Avalanche Falls
Lime Creek 4

past Sylvan Lake to Crooked Creek Pass, 20 miles from Eagle. Then drive 3.5 miles to the left-hand turn up 507 and another 2 miles to the Lime Creek trailhead, where there's a parking area and a gate to prevent you from entering Woods Lake Resort.

The badly designed narrow trail climbs gradually through aspen and high grass north around Woods Lake, gaining 160 feet, then drops 70 feet to Lime Creek (at 9,450 feet) beyond the property line, 1.75 miles from the trailhead. In .1-mile, cross the creek on a bridge near a powerhouse, then climb steadily up the cliffs to meet the creek again and enter the Holy Cross Wilderness.

Lower Lime Creek Falls*
(See Holy Cross Wilderness Waterfalls map, page 274.)

Access: Hike
Rating: ★★
Type: Fan
USGS Topographic Quad: Mount Jackson (39106 D5)
Trail Miles: 2
Altitude: 9,800 feet
Elevation Change: +350 feet from powerhouse

Lower Lime Creek Falls is below the trail .25-mile beyond the powerhouse. The noise of the falls will compel you to step off the trail for a look. It's a powerful 25-foot braided fan set in a 50-foot-high granite cliff that is difficult to get any closer to but that may be viewed with delight from trailside.

Continue on up the trail, climbing steeply through moss-covered moraine shelves, to reach Eagle Lake, 2.5 miles from the trailhead.

Eagle Lake is in a gorgeous valley below Eagle Peak. Campsites around the lake have been posted for revegetation.

Lime Creek Falls 2 and 3**
(See Holy Cross Wilderness Waterfalls map, page 274.)

Access: Hike
Rating: ★★
Type: Punchbowl and cascade
USGS Topographic Quad: Mount Jackson (39106 D5)
Trail Miles: 3.2, 3.3
Altitude: 10,120 feet, 10,240 feet
Elevation Change: +650 feet, +790 feet from powerhouse

The trail up Lime Creek comes to Eagle Lake at its southwest corner. Cross the Lime Creek drainage at the west end of the lake, then follow the trail around the lake right along the edge of the water through the rocks on its north side. Beyond the lake the trail is relatively clear; stay always down out of the rocks except when it's necessary to climb to get up over the tarn shelves created by glaciation.

The first falls on Lime Creek above Eagle Lake, Lime Creek 2 is encountered just after skirting the marsh at the east end of Eagle Lake, at the 3.2-mile mark.

Lime Creek Falls 2

Go past the lake and then beyond the meadows, which are a serpentine shape on the topo. You enter the woods at about 3 miles from the trailhead, or .5-mile beyond Eagle Lake. The trail enters the woods and turns sharply to the north to avoid the confluence of Lime Creek with one of its tributaries. This sharp turn is where Lime Creek 2 is, a clean 10-foot leap against a beautiful mossy rock wall—almost a tableau of woodsy wilderness.

Then the trail begins its climb of the shelf below Half Moon Lake, and along the way in another .1-mile passes a steep cascade, Lime Creek 3, which, although it's admittedly marginal, makes enough noisy white water and drops far enough to be called a "falls."

Avalanche Falls *

(See Holy Cross Wilderness Waterfalls map, page 274.)

Access: Overnight
Rating: ★ ★
Type: Tiered
USGS Topographic Quad: Mount Jackson (39106 D5)
Trail Miles: 4.75
Altitude: 11,400 feet
Elevation Change: + 1,950 feet from powerhouse

Avalanche Falls, on the cliffs on the southwest side of Avalanche Peak, is visible from the valley of Lime Creek 5 miles from the trailhead. It's the only falls in the upper end of the Lime Creek valley that's on any map. You don't actually see the falls, which is east of Avalanche Peak, until you're past Fairview Lake.

You first see Fairview Lake from above, after climbing over its retaining glacial shelf. It's deep blue and surrounded by the head wall above Strawberry Lakes, which is an unbroken talus-strewn ridge that undulates at the 12,800- to 13,000-foot level southeast from Avalanche Peak (12,803 feet) all the way around to Eagle Peak (13,043 feet) across the valley. The sheltered lake and the grandeur of the ridge make a very peaceful and inviting place—exceptionally calm in late September, just as the aspen are beginning to turn. You can see the trout through the crystal-clear water along the shore of the lake.

Avalanche Falls is a thin, 80- to 120-foot, two-leaped fall out of an unnamed lake hundreds of feet above the trail, and its sound can barely be heard above the lively gurgle of Lime Creek.

Lime Creek 4*

(See Holy Cross Wilderness Waterfalls map, page 274.)

Access: Overnight
Rating: ★ ★
Type: Plunge
USGS Topographic Quad: Mount Jackson (39106 D5)
Trail Miles: 5.5
Altitude: 11,000 feet
Elevation Change: + 1,550 feet from powerhouse

Lime Creek 4 is roughly .75-mile beyond Fairview Lake, 5.5 miles from the trailhead. Visible from the trail by its movement, it is easily reached within 20 to 30 yards after leaving the trail and following the creek.

Lime Creek 4 comes over a 12-foot wall of metamorphic schist, probably uplifted by faulting. The creek comes over in one broad leap and a thinner auxiliary leap, then turns sharply northwest to run along the foot of the rock face.

This is a burly though modest falls, very white and noisy, and surrounded by wooded, rocky hills and moss. The approach takes you on stepping stones up the creek to the face of the falls, where boulders provide several viewpoints in and out of the mist. Very refreshing.

Camping along Lime Creek at the best, most logical sites is discouraged by a wilderness rehabilitation project that began in the 1980s. But there are plenty of not-so-obvious campsites, and the trout basking lazily in the quiet of Half Moon and Fairview lakes should tempt even the lazy angler.

The falls are not singularly striking destinations, but they punctuate gracefully the beauty of the hike from the powerhouse all the way to Strawberry Lakes.

Once you've returned to the trailhead, you could try to return to civilization via Hagerman Pass and Leadville instead of backtracking to Eagle. Four-wheel-drive is recommended. The pass is above tree line, and the views are spectacular in all directions. This is not the quick way out, however.

Roaring Fork Waterfalls

The Roaring Fork enters the Colorado River at Glenwood Springs. Ten miles upstream, the Crystal River enters from the Elk Mountains to the south. Another 10 miles toward Aspen the Frying Pan River enters from the Sawatch Range to the east. The Roaring Fork originates below the Continental Divide between

Castle Peak and Independence Pass. The Maroon Bells-Snowmass Wilderness is embraced by the arms of the Crystal River on the west and the main stem of the Roaring Fork on the east.

Unfortunately, the waterfalls of the region are not much more than accents in the stunning beauty of the landscape. Whether or not you like what Aspen represents for the future of the state, there's good reason the rich and status-motivated have settled here. A drive up the Redstone valley in late September is best made by inches, with frequent stops to catch one's breath and recover from wonder.

The Pennsylvanian and Mississippian metamorphic rock of the Elk Mountains is too vulnerable to erosion to present a strong cliff front for falling water. But there are a few scattered falls.

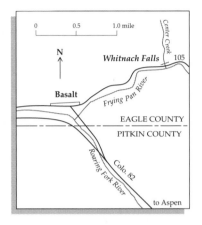

Roaring Fork waterfalls
(**#65** on Colorado River drainage map, page 248):

Whitnach Falls

Whitnach Falls
(See map, this page.)

Access: Roadside
Rating: ★
Type: Cascade
USGS Topographic Quad: Leon (39107 D1)
Trail Miles: 0
Altitude: 6,800 feet
Elevation Change: None

Whitnach Falls is a narrow 20-foot-long cascade, 1.8 miles toward Ruedi Reservoir from Basalt on Forest Road 105. Even though it had been raining off and on for hours before our visit, there was not a great deal of water flowing down the falls, which is visible from the road. We drove past it in both directions before Nancy finally picked it out.

It does create a pretty little mossy environment in the red cliffs on the way

Roaring Fork waterfalls
(**#66** on Colorado River drainage
map, page 248):

Hayes Creek Falls
Crystal Falls

to Ruedi Reservoir. The presence of
a trail indicates usage by people seek-
ing some goal in the cliffs above. It's
sort of a "mystery" falls: It makes you
wonder why and when it was named,
and by whom.

Hayes Creek Falls
(See Roaring Fork Waterfalls map,
    this page.)

Access: Roadside
Rating: ★ ★
Type: Cascade
USGS Topographic Quad: Placita
    (39107 B3)
Trail Miles: 0
Altitude: 7,600 feet
Elevation Change: None

Hayes Creek Falls is on the west
side of Colorado 133 1.8 miles south
of Redstone. It's a steep cascade cutting down a deep angular defile in the
beautiful red rock that gives the town
its name. It has no major leaps, but
its strong, deep cut in the rock is very
picturesque and probably continues
similarly on up the cliffs. Only about
25 feet of the falls is visible from the
base.

Crystal Falls *
(See Roaring Fork Waterfalls map, page 280.)

Access: Roadside
Rating: ★
Type: Horsetail
USGS Topographic Quad: Placita (39107 B3)
Trail Miles: 0
Altitude: 7,400 feet
Elevation Change: None

This is a 30-foot horsetail that slides down the red Paleozoic rock right into the Crystal River. It is next to Highway 133 about 2.5 miles south of Redstone. Its drainage is not named.

The Vicinity of Marble

The old quarry town of Marble is in a cul-de-sac as far as civilized passenger-car traffic is concerned. It's hemmed in by the Elk Mountains to the north and east, the Raggeds Wilderness and West Elk Mountains to the south. We were told by local residents that there is an Indian curse on the valley, that no white man's enterprise should ever succeed there. Which seems okay to us. We list the waterfalls of the area as they're encountered as you move closer to the headwaters of the Crystal River.

Milton Creek Falls
(See Vicinity of Marble group map, page 282.)

Access: Walk in
Rating: ★ ★
Type: Plunge
USGS Topographic Quad: Marble (39107 A2)
Trail Miles: .25-mile
Altitude: 7,920 feet
Elevation Change: + 120 feet

Milton Creek Falls is 65 feet high and consists of one beautiful, slow main leap and several sprays over rock into pools, then it splits again into three

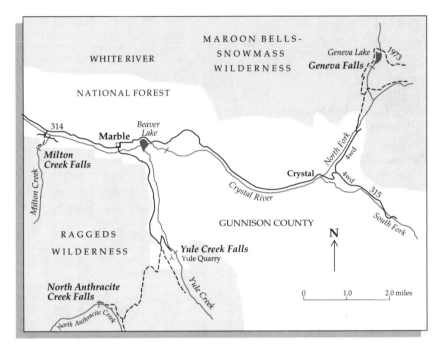

The Vicinity of Marble group
(**#67** on Colorado River drainage map, page 248):

Milton Creek Falls
Yule Creek Falls
Geneva Falls

streams down into a cascade. Fallen logs and loose rock litter the steep hillside near the falls. The trail is easily lost as you admire the moss and abundant ferns, but just follow the creek.

Drive 2.5 miles past Bogan Flats campground on County 314 to about 1 mile west of Marble. Milton Creek Falls is visible in cliffs to the south. Cross the bridge over the Crystal River half a mile east of the cemetery, just west of the airstrip. Go straight past the first left about .1-mile to a dirt track heading straight uphill. All of this is private property, although the falls itself is just within the Raggeds Wilderness boundary. Do not park on private property without permission. It's best to park on the north side of the bridge and walk in.

From the end of the dirt track, near a private home, there is a faint trail upstream along Milton Creek through the woods. Follow it until you come to a big log across the creek, then hike another eighth of a mile to within sight of the falls. The total hike takes twenty minutes and is .25-mile. We were told by people who live nearby that this falls was used as a backdrop by the Coors people for a commercial for their beer, but we didn't recognize it.

Yule Creek Falls
(See Vicinity of Marble group map, page 282.)

Access: Four-wheel-drive, walk in
Rating: ★ ★
Type: Horsetail
USGS Topographic Quad: Marble (39107 A2)
Trail Miles: .5-mile
Altitude: 9,350 feet
Elevation Change: From 9,200 feet, + 150 feet

The Yule Quarry (9,350 feet) is 5 miles on a four-wheel-drive road south of Marble (7,956 feet). Drive into the center of town, turn down the few blocks to the quarry-mill parking area. Take a turn on the footpaths among the discarded marble monoliths through the mill site. It feels like someone intended to build a pure marble Stonehenge somewhere nearby, or perhaps an Olympian god planned a palace to rival Zeus's, with predictable results.

The quarry ceased operation in the late 1940s, and the company stripped all salvageable materials, leaving a ruin that seems much older than fifty years. There used to be a great deal more to the town of Marble, but mud slides have had their way with it over the years. You can still find pieces of ruined houses poking out of slides close to the river.

From the parking area near the top of the quarry road it's an easy half-mile up Yule Creek to the quarry site. As recently as 1990, these huge man-made caverns, which produced the marble for the Lincoln Monument and the old Denver Post Office, were silent and dripping with water. The quarry reopened in 1990, and its operators have limited access on occasion, despite agreements to the contrary with the town.

Milton Creek Falls

Yule Creek Falls is a 6- to 8-foot horsetail, broader than it is high, where Yule Creek tumbles out of its natural course across a shallow streambed now paved with marble chips. It's a nice place to rest after clambering over the tons of discarded marble at the base of the hill below the quarries.

Geneva Falls *
(See Vicinity of Marble group map, page 282.)

Access: Hike
Rating and Type: Not visited
USGS Topographic Quad: Snowmass Mountain (39107 A1)
Trail Miles: 2.8
Altitude: 10,400 feet
Elevation Change: From Crystal at 8,880 feet, + 1,520 feet

Drive east of Marble on Forest Road 314 for 2 miles, to a right turn down the Crystal River. The site of Crystal is another 5 miles on a road that's a little rough for some passenger cars.

Beyond the town site, Crystal River Road (315) is definitely four-wheel-drive only, and I'm told by the locals it gets worse (and more popular) every year. There's also a four-wheel-drive road turning northeast out of Crystal, 2 miles and 700 feet in elevation gain, up the road to Lead King Basin.

It's about 2 miles to the end of the four-wheel-drive road in Lead King Basin, then another mile and a half to the falls. We've heard there are others in the area.

Castle Creek Falls *
(See map on page 286.)

Access: Hike
Rating and Type: Not visited
USGS Topographic Quad: Hayden Peak (39106 A7)
Trail Miles: 0
Altitude: 11,200 feet
Elevation Change: From 9,728 feet, + 1,472 feet

Castle Creek Falls is a 30-foot falls below the summit of Castle Peak (14,265 feet) on the road to the Montezuma Mine. Take Forest Road 102 south of

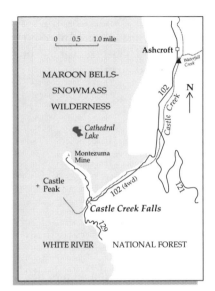

The Vicinity of Marble group
(**#72** on Colorado River drainage
map, page 248):

Castle Creek Falls

Aspen through Ashcroft. At 13.2 miles
it becomes a four-wheel-drive road
starting up Castle Creek, which it
crosses in 2 miles. The waterfall is above
the road at this crossing, from which
you can either continue to the Montezuma Mine at 12,700 feet or take a
sharp left on a jeep trail and wind your
way to Pearl Pass (12,705 feet).

The Southern
Flat Tops and
Glenwood Springs Area

The White River Plateau north of
Glenwood Springs is one of four large
island plateaus in Colorado's western
quarter etched out of flat-lying sedimentary rock. The plateaus were not
bent into mountains by the Laramide
Orogeny but have nevertheless been
elevated 2 miles above sea level. Consequently, the plateau's stream gradient
is very steep, and the rivers of the Colorado Basin have carved canyons as
much as 2,000 feet deep. Heavy faulting, caused by the raising of the Elk
Mountains to the south of Glenwood,
has further disturbed the gorges of the
plateau, completing the sudden steep drops necessary for waterfalls.

A 30-mile stretch of the Colorado, from Rifle to Sweetwater, receives five
tributaries sustaining thirteen waterfalls from the southern White River Plateau.
Two are easy to get to.

We'll describe the falls in order, moving down the Colorado and starting
near Sweetwater.

Sweetwater Creek Waterfalls

The road to Sweetwater Lake provides access to eight waterfalls, two inside the Flat Tops Wilderness. Take County Road 301 north from Dotsero up the Colorado River 7 miles to a left turn toward Sweetwater Lake, which is a total of 15.5 miles from Dotsero.

Turretito Falls *
(See Southern Flat Tops and Glenwood Springs Area group map, page 288.)

Access: Roadside
Rating: ★
Type: Plunge
USGS Topographic Quad: Sweetwater Lake (39107 G2)
Trail Miles: 0
Altitude: 8,100 feet
Elevation Change: From 8,150 feet, +50 feet

This is a thin leap of 70 feet in the cliffs above Turret Creek on private property to the northeast, just before the road beyond Sweetwater Lake steepens to climb to Hilltop Ranch and the trailhead for trails 1854 and 1832. The falls is most easily seen from the road near the ranch on the cliffs opposite.

Turret Creek Falls, Lower *
(See Southern Flat Tops and Glenwood Springs Area group map, page 288.)

Access: Hike
Rating: ⌡
Type: Cascade
USGS Topographic Quad: Sweetwater Lake (39107 G2)
Trail Miles: 1
Altitude: 8,100 feet
Elevation Change: From 7,800 feet to 8,180 feet on trail, +300 feet; to falls, -80 feet

Lower Turret Creek Falls is indicated at a sharp twist in the creek about .5-mile on trail 1832 from Hilltop Ranch. You can clearly hear the falls from the trail and even see the white water, although the falls only amounts to a broad

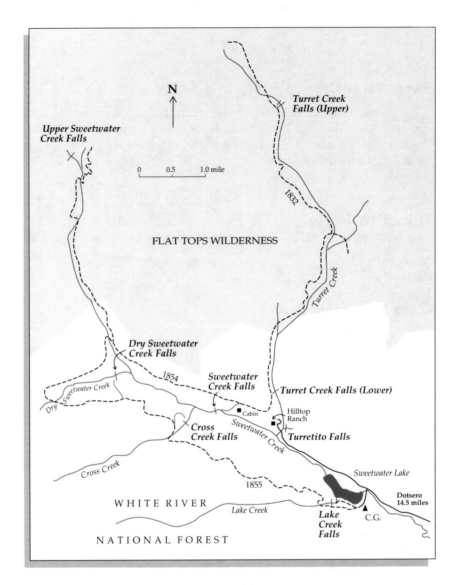

The southern Flat Tops and Glenwood Springs area group

(**#70** on Colorado River drainage map, page 248):

Turretito Falls
Turret Creek Falls, Lower
Turret Creek Falls, Upper
Sweetwater Creek Falls

Lake Creek Falls
Cross Creek Falls
Dry Sweetwater Creek Falls
Upper Sweetwater Creek Falls

5-foot horsetail and fast-moving cascades cutting through a volcanic cliff. It seems as though the stream has shifted course above the falls, leaving another fall of rock smooth and exposed. I suspect that there was a higher leap or slide at the same spot but that the steady erosive power of the water has done most of its job. It would be interesting to know how long it's taken.

The falls is about 80 feet below the trail. The Turret Creek drainage looks very promising—the Flat Tops stand up above the thick, smooth, brushy-looking aspen forests, trunks pale yellow in the afternoon light of winter.

Turret Creek Falls, Upper*
(See Southern Flat Tops and Glenwood Springs Area group map, page 288.)

Access: Overnight
Rating and Type: Not visited
USGS Topographic Quad: Trappers Lake
Trail Miles: 6.5
Altitude: 10,500 feet
Elevation Change: From 7,800 feet, +2,700 feet

Start at the Hilltop Ranch trailhead at the end of the road about 1.25 miles beyond Sweetwater Lake. Less than .25-mile beyond the ranch, the trail forks. The trail north (#1832) enters the Flat Tops Wilderness in about 1 mile and climbs into Turret Creek Meadows in another 2 miles. The falls is indicated on the Trappers Lake quadrangle as 6.5 miles from Hilltop Ranch.

In another 2.5 miles this trail passes south of Shingle Peak (12,001 feet) and meets trail 1856 coming up Sweetwater Creek. This suggests an interesting backcountry loop up Turret Creek and down Sweetwater Creek, or vice versa, visiting most of the waterfalls in the area. We have not attempted this and cannot testify one way or the other to its difficulty.

Sweetwater Creek Falls*
(See Southern Flat Tops and Glenwood Springs Area group map, page 288.)

Access: Hike, bushwhack
Rating and Type: Not visited
USGS Topographic Quad: Sweetwater Lake (39107 G2)
Trail Miles: 1.25
Altitude: 8,800 feet
Elevation Change: From 7,800 feet to start of bushwhack, +800 feet; to falls, -600 feet

This waterfall is hidden in a wooded draw at the bottom of Sweetwater Creek canyon, 2 miles upstream from Sweetwater Lake. The bottom of the valley is very marshy.

We've reconnoitered this falls by taking the trail from Hilltop Ranch, then taking the west fork (trail 1854) .25-mile from the ranch. In another half-mile we dropped below the trail, across the rocks, to seek a glimpse of Sweetwater Creek Falls or the one indicated on the quad on the cliffs across the valley. There's an old cabin in the woods, and beyond it a draw down toward the creek bottom, which could provide access to the streamcourse and the falls a little upstream. This would be an elevation loss of 600 feet. We have not attempted this, however, and cannot testify one way or another to its difficulty.

Lake Creek Falls*
(See Southern Flat Tops and Glenwood Springs Area group map, page 288.)

Access: Hike
Rating: ★
Type: Cascade
USGS Topographic Quad: Sweetwater Lake (39107 G2)
Trail Miles: .3-mile
Altitude: 7,800 feet
Elevation Change: From 7,750 feet, +50 feet

Lake Creek Falls is on the south side of Sweetwater Lake. Drive to the lake and turn south to the parking area and campground. A trail begins at the upper end of the camping area to cross the hillside several hundred feet above the lake. The trail skirts the woods, providing a view of the lake and its surrounding hills. After about 500 yards there is an official viewing area with a fence immediately above the Lake Creek drainage.

The falls is on around and down into the cut of Lake Creek. It's necessary to find your way down a steep slope, across shale talus, and through some dense brush to get to the falls.

Sweetwater Lake Falls is a series of small leaps cascading down a black, steplike rock face 20 to 30 feet wide, with a total drop of perhaps 40 feet. It's in a moist, very lush environment, and the layers of moss are beautiful. It's probably well visited later in the year, but we saw no one there in early May. Vegetation could make a visit difficult later in summer. There is a cave in the cliffs above.

Cross Creek Falls*

(See Southern Flat Tops and Glenwood Springs Area group map, page 288.)

Access: Hike, bushwhack
Rating and Type: Not visited
USGS Topographic Quad: Sweetwater Lake (39107 G2)
Trail Miles: 3.5
Altitude: 8,600 feet
Elevation Change: From 7,750 feet to 8,900 feet on trail, +1,150 feet; drop to falls, -300 feet

Drive to Sweetwater Lake, turn left, and drive to the campground parking area. Trail 1855 begins at the south end of the campground, climbs up through the woods to cross Lake Creek, and continues 3.25 miles to the Cross Creek drainage. Cross Creek Falls is 400 feet below the trail, .5-mile down the creek. It looks from the quad that it might be possible to work down through the woods on the north side of the creek for a look at the waterfall, but we haven't tried it yet.

Dry Sweetwater Creek Falls*

(See Southern Flat Tops and Glenwood Springs Area group map, page 288.)

Access: Hike, bushwhack
Rating and Type: Not visited
USGS Topographic Quad: Sweetwater Lake (39107 G2)
Trail Miles: 3.5
Altitude: 8,600 feet
Elevation Change: From 7,750 feet to 9,000 feet on trail, +1,250 feet; down to falls, -400 feet

If you take a heading northwest off trail 1855 1 mile beyond Cross Creek (see above), a half-mile bushwhack should take you to the Dry Sweetwater Creek drainage, where a falls is indicated at 8,100 feet.

Upper Sweetwater Creek Falls*
(See Southern Flat Tops and Glenwood Springs Area group map, page 288.)

Access: Overnight
Rating and Type: Not visited
USGS Topographic Quad: Sweetwater Lake (39107 G2)
Trail Miles: 6.75
Altitude: 10,200 feet
Elevation Change: From 7,800 feet, +2,400 feet

This waterfall is indicated on Sweetwater Creek nearly 7 miles up trail 1854 from Hilltop Ranch. Drive as nearly as your vehicle will allow to the end of the road, beyond Sweetwater Lake, to the parking area near Hilltop Ranch. The trail forks in .2-mile. Take the west fork. The trail (#1854) crosses Sweetwater Creek for the second time at about 6 miles; the falls is in the cliffs to the northwest, a thousand feet above the creekbed. This is about 2 miles into the Flat Tops Wilderness.

Three miles along the trail from Hilltop Ranch trail 1854 intersects 1855 coming up from the creek. Returning to Sweetwater Lake campground via 1855 might complete an interesting loop, but it would add 3 miles of additional hiking, more if you didn't have a second car stationed either at Hilltop Ranch or the campground. We have not attempted this and so cannot testify one way or another to its difficulty.

Bridal Veil Falls (Colorado River drainage)
(See map on page 293.)

Access: Hike
Rating: ★ ★ ★
Type: Plunge
USGS Topographic Quad: Shoshone (39107 E2)
Trail Miles: 1
Altitude: 7,200 feet
Elevation Change: From 6,200 feet, +1,000 feet

Bridal Veil Falls is an extremely popular destination for families driving through Glenwood Canyon on I-70. The East Fork of Dead Horse Creek pools below travertine cliffs to create Hanging Lake. The creek comes over the moss-hung cliffs in two 20- to 25-foot leaps, one of them dividing further into a triplet of "veils" falling directly into the lake.

The trailhead to Hanging Lake is 10 miles east of Glenwood Springs, in the heart of Glenwood Canyon. Take exit 125 from I-70 and drive half a mile east to the Hanging Lake Rest Area. A trail from the rest area continues upriver .4-mile to the old picnic area, then turns up Dead Horse Creek 1 mile and 1,000 feet in elevation gain to the lake.

Despite the frequent presence of giddy teenagers, Hanging Lake is a worthy destination. Boardwalks take you close to the falls, and the trail continues above to Spouting Rock.

This is one of five waterfalls with the same name in Colorado.

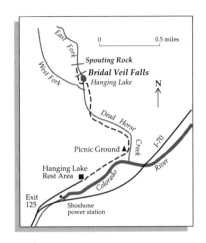

The southern Flat Tops and Glenwood Springs area group (**#68** on Colorado River drainage map, page 248):

Bridal Veil Falls

Grizzly Creek Falls * *

(See Southern Flat Tops and Glenwood Springs Area group map, page 294.)

Access: Overnight
Rating: ★
Type: Cascades
USGS Topographic Quad: Broken Rib Creek (39107 F2)
Trail Miles: 5.4, 5.7
Altitude: 8,600 feet, 8,500 feet
Elevation Change: From trailhead at 10,150 feet to upper falls, -1,550 feet; to lower falls, -100 feet

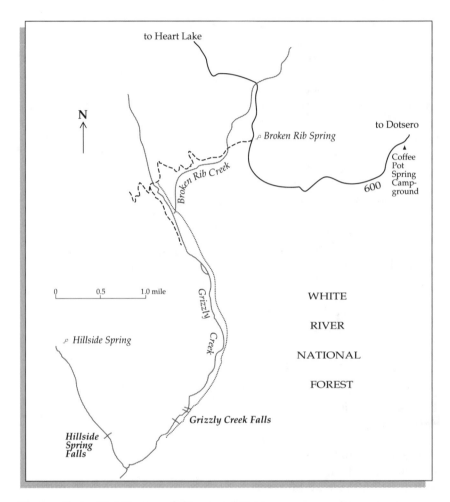

The southern Flat Tops and Glenwood Springs area group
(**#69** on Colorado River drainage map, page 248):

Grizzly Creek Falls
Hillside Spring Falls

Hillside Spring Falls *

(See Southern Flat Tops and Glenwood Springs Area group map, page 294.)

Access: Overnight
Rating and Type: Not visited
USGS Topographic Quad: Carbonate (39107 F3)
Trail Miles: 5.5 from I-70; 6.7 alternate
Altitude: 9,400 feet
Elevation Change: From 10,150 feet to stream opposite falls on cliff, -1,950 feet (falls is on cliffs 1,200 feet above stream)

If you're up to a strenuous hike and bushwhack through trackless wilderness, take the Dotsero exit off I-70, go .7-mile on County 301, then turn left on Forest Road 600. This good dirt road passes through the bottom of Deep Creek Canyon, then climbs swiftly in a series of switchbacks to spectacular views of the Colorado and Eagle river valleys. At 13.4 miles from the turn onto 600, you will pass the Coffee Pot Springs campground. Another 2.3 miles farther is the start of trail 1849 across the road from Deep Creek Spring, where there is a pipe gushing forth clear, cold (and clean, I hope) water. The trail starts down the drainage 10 to 20 yards south of the spring and follows it 2 miles nearly to its confluence with Grizzly Creek.

The USGS quadrangle shows the trail crossing the creek right above the confluence, but it seemed to us to cross on the east side of the creek. Where it drops into the marsh at the edge of the meadow, 2.5 miles from the trailhead, we stayed on the east side through the meadow, skirted the marshes, and followed game trails, good and bad, on and off, all the way to the falls, about 5.5 miles from the trailhead.

At the end of the meadow, skirt the rock slide as much as possible near the water, although some rock-hopping may be necessary. Game trails weave through the aspen on the cliffs above the creek, then there's more bushwhacking through high, succulent ground cover and another grassy meadow beneath spruce and fir. The game trails are fairly consistent, though hard to follow at times through the dense underbrush. Just move slowly and you'll get through.

The first waterfall occurs where Grizzly Creek cuts through a knob of quartz-marbled metamorphic rock and is seen from on top of a knob—about 75 feet high—still on the east side of the creek. It's a large cascade (or a small waterfall) made up of a series of short but wide and foamy leaps that wind steeply around the foot of the knob.

There's a small second falls marked on the quad .3-mile downstream. It sounds a lot bigger than it is, which is an unremarkable 4- to 6-foot cascade.

Hillside Spring Falls is marked on an unnamed drainage on the western cliffs
another .7-mile downstream, but the slopes in that part of the canyon are as
wild as they come. Perhaps we can see the lower falls someday by hiking
5.5 miles up the trail from I-70. Grizzly Creek enters the Colorado where there
is now a well-developed boating and rafting facility below the trusses and spans
of the new improved I-70.

Canyon Creek Falls *
(See map on page 297.)

Access: Bushwhack
Rating: ★ ★
Type: Fan
USGS Topographic Quad: Adams Lake (39107 F4)
Trail Miles: .5-mile
Altitude: 9,900 feet
Elevation Change: From 10,200 feet, −300 feet

Canyon Creek Falls is a precipitous stair-stepped cascade that fans out like
a silver fall of permed hair 70 feet high. It's viewed from a rocky perch on
the steep hillsides of a tributary to Canyon Creek at the southern edge of the
White River Plateau.

Unfortunately, to get to it you have to endure an interminable 5.6 miles
(the sign says 9, and it feels like it) on excruciatingly bad four-wheel-drive roads
to Adams Lake.

Exit I-70 at Dotsero, drive north .7-mile on County Highway 301, and take
the left turn up Deep Creek on Forest Road 600, climbing 13.4 miles to Coffee
Pot Springs campground. Pass Broken Rib Spring and the trailhead to Grizzly
Creek at 15.7 miles. Continue on Forest Road 600 across the glaciated peneplain toward the Flat Tops.

At 23.9 miles, bear left toward Heart Lake. Just south of the lake, turn left
toward Bison Lake. In another .7-mile turn left again toward Supply Basin.
In another mile bear right onto Forest Road 601. From here on the road gets
steadily worse, becoming impassable to anything but four-wheel-drive vehicles.
The familiar washboard pattern here is scaled for giants. Sheer sharp-rocked
stretches eventually lead you into the valley below Adams Lake.

At the bottom of the steep .7-mile final climb to the lake, the road to Johnson
Creek has been blocked. This is where the 2-mile stroll to the falls begins. We
saw some ATVs beyond this barrier; they crossed moatlike ditches dug by the
forest service to prevent motorized traffic.

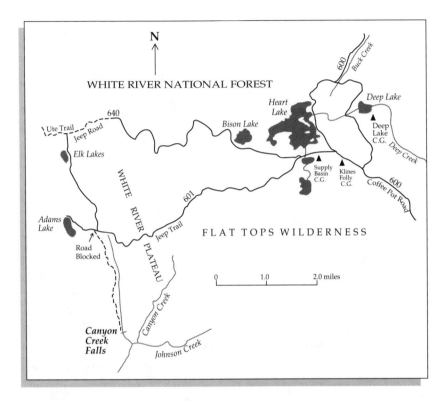

The southern Flat Tops and Glenwood Springs area group
(**#71** on Colorado River drainage map, page 248):

Canyon Creek Falls

The old road winds straight south below the timber but out of the marsh, past a small falls in the rocks above to the east. The road leads deeper and deeper into Canyon Creek's drainage. Even the ATV tracks peter out eventually, where fallen trees have made the road totally impassable to wheeled vehicles of any sort. There is no trail from here, but just follow the unnamed stream downhill .1-mile to the rock outcrop that provides a view of the waterfall.

Canyon Creek Falls

Parachute Creek

There are four waterfalls on the tributaries to Parachute Creek. Unfortunately, all of them are on land owned by Unocal or Exxon, and permission is required to get through the gate in order to drive or hike to them.

Drive 16 miles west of Rifle on I-70 and take the Parachute exit. This used to be called Grand Valley but was renamed after the massive oil-shale research effort initiated in the 1970s by Unocal and Exxon on Parachute Creek. As of this writing, the plant has shut down. Save your gas unless you're connected with someone in the oil business and have made arrangements in advance. Or perhaps you're better at ingratiating yourself with security types than I am. The supervisor of security and safety may be reached at 285-7600 in Parachute.

Drive north out of Parachute 10.5 miles to the oil-shale plant security gate. The road providing access to the waterfalls on Light Gulch, West Fork, and East Middle Fork turns off the main road half a mile south of the plant gate. The road up the East Fork turns east just before it reaches the plant.

Light Gulch Falls *
(See Parachute Creek group map, page 300.)

Access: Bushwhack, or roadside visible by jeep
Rating and Type: Not visited
USGS Topographic Quad: Circle Dot Gulch (39108 E2)
Trail Miles: 1.5
Altitude: 7,500 feet
Elevation Change: From 6,150 feet, +1,350 feet

West Fork Falls
(See Parachute Creek group map, page 300.)

Access: Hike
Rating and Type: Not visited
USGS Topographic Quad: Cutoff Gulch (39108 F2)
Trail Miles: .5-mile or 4
Altitude: 7,200 feet
Elevation Change: From 6,600 feet at end of jeep road, +600 feet;
    from 6,100 feet at main road, +1,100 feet

Drive to .5-mile south of the plant and turn left onto a dirt road heading up the West Fork of Parachute Creek. The Cutoff Gulch quadrangle indicates

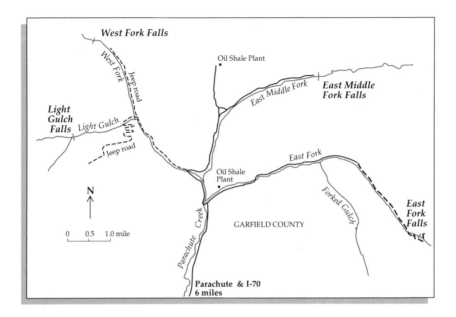

The Parachute Creek group

(**#73** on Colorado River drainage map, page 248):

Light Gulch Falls
West Fork Falls
East Middle Fork Falls
East Fork Falls

a jeep trail starting up the West Fork 1 mile from the main road. At 1.5 miles up this road you will pass the Light Gulch drainage.

Light Gulch Falls is 1.5 miles up the drainage. The security guard said that there is a four-wheel-drive road up a ridge to Red Point. From the point there is a view of the falls, which he said rivals Rifle Falls, and which was the only falls still running in the Parachute Creek valley when we tried to visit in November.

The jeep trail following the West Fork drainage appears to go another 1.5 miles, to within half a mile of West Fork Falls, 120 feet higher than the end of the jeep road.

East Middle Fork Falls

(See Parachute Creek group map, page 300.)

Access: Dirt road
Rating and Type: Not visited
USGS Topographic Quad: Forked Gulch (39108 E1)
Trail Miles: Unknown
Altitude: 6,650 feet
Elevation Change: None

There are three separate waterfalls at the end of the East Middle Fork. The upper falls, coming off the edge of the Roan Plateau, is a plunge of a hundred feet. This falls flows year-round but can be a mere trickle in dry years. The middle falls is a hundred-foot horsetail, and the upper and middle falls can be seen together from certain points on the road. The lower falls is reputedly more spectacular than the upper but is not described specifically in our source of information, a study of the Parachute Creek environment made before the Colony Shale project was begun.

To get to East Middle Fork Falls, drive up the Middle Fork 1.7 miles past the West Fork drainage (described above), then bear right onto a dirt road going up the East Middle Fork drainage. The falls is at the end of the road. According to the security guard, it was dry in November.

East Fork Falls*

(See Parachute Creek group map, page 300.)

Access: Hike
Rating and Type: Not visited
USGS Topographic Quad: Forked Gulch (39108 E1)
Trail Miles: 2.3
Altitude: 7,480 feet
Elevation Change: From 6,390 feet, + 1,080 feet

Take the dirt road heading up the East Fork drainage almost 4 miles. A trail climbs up the drainage and then above the falls in about 2.5 miles. This waterfall is beyond the boundary of the Unocal/Exxon property and on the Naval Oil Shale Reserve.

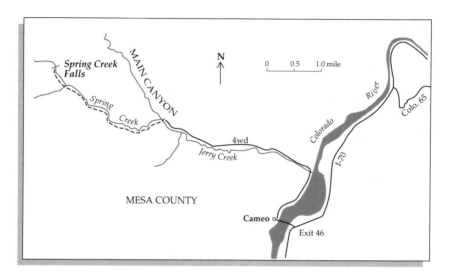

The Parachute Creek group
(**#74** on Colorado River drainage map, page 248):

Spring Creek Falls

Spring Creek Falls*
(See map, this page.)

Access: Hike
Rating: ★ ★
Type: Punchbowl
USGS Topographic Quad: Round Mountain (39108 B4)
Trail Miles: 5.5
Altitude: 6,000 feet
Elevation Change: From 4,770 feet, + 1,230 feet

Spring Creek Falls includes several deeply water-worn plunge pools encircled by polished limestone and consists of two main leaps 50 or 60 yards apart. The upper leap falls about 9 feet into a broad arenalike bowl, the lower leap falls 10 to 12 feet and twists through a crack, or perhaps slips around a huge boulder, or perhaps does both.

Take exit 46 from I-70 at Cameo, which is about 10 miles west of Grand Junction. Drive across a bridge to Cameo on the other side of the Colorado River. Take the dirt road north along the canal about a mile to the Jerry Creek drainage. This used to be wild horse country but was so dry in 1989 that the BLM moved the horses to Debeque Canyon, where they joined another herd of one hundred.

The Round Mountain quad shows no road or trails, but there is a clear four-wheel-drive road all the way up Jerry Creek, so you can drive easily the 3 miles to the junction of Spring Creek and hike the remaining 2.5 miles to the falls. There was water running in Jerry Creek, but Spring Creek was dry except for faint remnants of recent snows and curtains of icicles in the cliffs above the falls. The canyon is narrow, and I wondered where you could hike when the riverbed was actually filled with spring runoff. It's dry most of the time, but the erosion clearly testifies to the violence of the water when it does run.

Rifle Falls
(See map on page 304.)

Access: Wheelchair
Rating: ★ ★ ★ ★
Type: Segmented
USGS Topographic Quad: Rifle Falls
Trail Miles: 100 yards
Altitude: 6,580 feet
Elevation Change: None

Rifle Falls is actually three leaps. Rifle Creek divides in three as it comes over the edge of a limestone cliff and plunges 60 to 70 feet, splattering into cascades of white water and shimmering green moss.

There are well-trodden paths below and above the falls; there's even a little platform above the falls on the cliff to give a good view of it.

One of the leaps was once harnessed by a power company in 1910 that left a wooden structure and a pipe that is still the mouth of the easternmost leap.

There is a trail along the cliff on the west side of the creek that provides easy access to a series of interesting caves on the way to the falls. Unfortunately, many pieces of crystallized travertine have been broken off inside the caves for souvenirs, spoiling the effect.

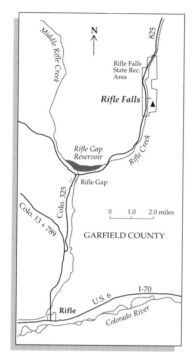

The Parachute Creek group
(**#75** on Colorado River drainage
map, page 248):

Rifle Falls

The falls is very impressive. It's possible
to walk right behind the westernmost leap,
and there is moss all over the place ranging
in color from deep green to ocher and
making the falls seem almost tropical. The
softness of the rock and the lushness of the
vegetation create an otherworldly feel, in
contrast to the dark granites of so many
of the other falls we've seen. It almost
seems as if you've entered Central America rather than the Colorado Rockies.

To reach the falls, take Colorado State
Highway 325 north out of Rifle toward
Meeker. A sign directing you to the Rifle
Falls Recreation Area is very clear on the
right about 6 to 7 miles out of town.

Follow the road 18 miles through Rifle
Gap to the reservoir, and bear right around
the reservoir. The recreation area and falls
are 5 miles beyond the reservoir.

The Rifle Falls State Recreation Area
campground is well situated along Rifle
Creek, with open pads for RVs and a walk-
in camping area for people with tents.
Campsites are on a reservation system run
by the state. There is a daily entrance fee
of three dollars per vehicle, plus six dollars per night to camp.

Beyond the campground there's a well-
kept picnic area that stretches all the way
to the falls.

Rifle Falls

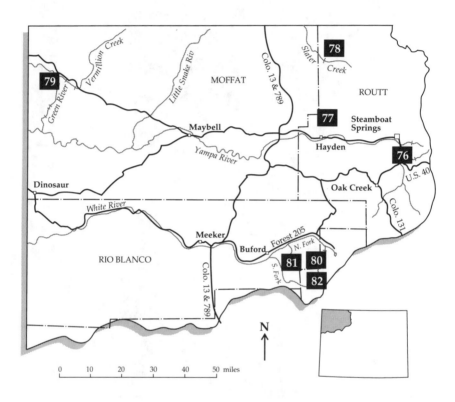

The Yampa, Green, and White Rivers
Drainages Map

76, 77, 78: The Yampa River Drainage Group
79: Green River Waterfalls
80, 81, 82: The White River Group

8

The Yampa, Green, and
White Rivers Drainages

There are several handfuls of waterfalls on the tributaries to these northern Colorado Basin rivers. Three of them play an exciting part in the history not only of the area but also of the development and exploration of the entire American West.

The White River is tributary to the Yampa. The canyons and confluence of the Yampa and Green now lie tamely within the boundaries of Dinosaur National Park, where 700,000 pounds of fossilized dinosaur bones have been painstakingly unearthed since 1909.

The Green meets the Colorado inside Canyonlands National Park, in Utah, 150 miles south. The combined annual flow of the Green, Yampa, and White rivers is about 1,925 million acre-feet, fourteen percent of the Colorado's average annual flow—an amount of water roughly equal to that lost from the entire Colorado River system *by evaporation*.

In this chapter, we list thirteen waterfalls in four groups, starting on the Yampa near Steamboat Springs, then moving northeast into the Elkhead Mountains on the Wyoming border. Next we describe the waterfalls of the Green River and finish on the northern White River Plateau.

307

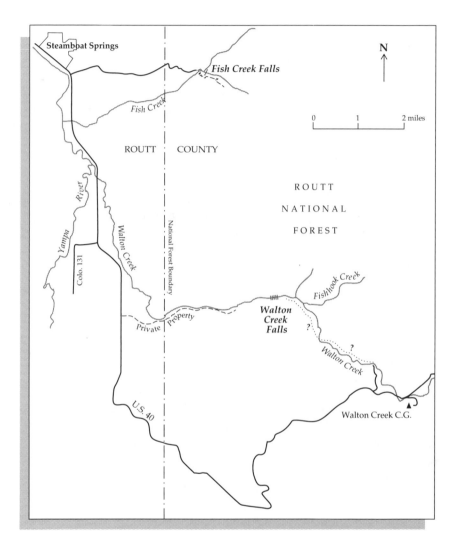

The Yampa River drainage group
(**#76** on Yampa, Green, and White rivers drainages map, page 306):

Fish Creek Falls
Walton Creek Falls

The Yampa River Drainage

"Yampa" is the Ute word for a food tuber, but can also be translated as "big medicine," something with a powerful spiritual influence.

The Yampa River originates 30 miles south of Steamboat Springs, between the Gore Range on the east and the White River Plateau on the west. It flows through Steamboat Springs, then turns west, making its way past the northern rim of the White River Plateau and running 119 miles to its entry into Dinosaur National Monument, where it winds 46 miles to its confluence with the Green.

The Yampa is the last undammed major branch of the Colorado River. All the others have been tamed for industry, irrigation, and drinking water, and there are plans to harness the Yampa. The tributaries to the Yampa, of course, have already been put to use, as has every other drainage.

Fish Creek Reservoir, for example, took 352 acre-feet of water from the Fish Creek drainage in June 1988, compared to 21,968 acre-feet gauged at Steamboat Springs downstream. In September of the same year, the reservoir took 252 acre-feet, and 225 was gauged at Steamboat. Incidentally, the flow over Fish Creek Falls has varied from a high of 1,110 cubic feet per second (8,325 gallons) in June 1968, to a low of .01 cubic feet per second in August 1972, the year the reservoir was completed. This minimum flow was just over a cup per second, about the same as from your kitchen faucet.

Fish Creek Falls
(See Yampa River Drainage group map, page 308.)

Access: Hike
Rating: ★ ★ ★ ★
Type: Segmented
USGS Topographic Quad: Steamboat Springs (40106 D7)
Trail Miles: .12-mile
Altitude: 7,600 feet
Elevation Change: From 7,440 feet, + 160 feet

Fish Creek Falls is a justifiably popular destination for visitors to Steamboat Springs. A torrent of white water comes bursting out between the shoulders of two stately rock guardians surrounded by thick evergreens and pounds over a hundred feet down the rocks.

A sign at the falls claims its height to be 283 feet, but its two main segments—80 feet upper, 50 feet lower—don't add up to anything near that.

Fish Creek Falls

The 283-foot figure would have to include the cascades below or above. The quad shows the head of the falls at 7,600 feet; Fish Creek runs 120 feet below the picnic area near the parking lot at 7,480 feet, still only 240 feet below the knick-point of the waterfall.

Fish Creek Falls Road intersects U.S. 40 at the south end of town. It takes you east 4 miles into the hills and ends at a parking lot. Two trails lead to views of the falls: One is paved with asphalt for wheelchair access and goes an eighth of a mile to an overlook; the second is a dirt trail through the picnic area to a bridge across the cascades below the falls. Getting closer to the base of the main falls is difficult: There is no trail, and the hillsides above Fish Creek are very steep.

The property containing the falls was deeded in exchange to the forest service when a Mr. Adams recognized that public access was threatened by developers. All the asphalt and people detract from genuine wilderness feeling.

Walton Creek Falls *
(See Yampa River Drainage group map, page 308.)

Access: Bushwhack
Rating and Type: Not visited
USGS Topographic Quad: Mount Werner (40106 D6)
Trail Miles: 3
Altitude: 8,000 feet
Elevation Change: Unknown

Walton Creek Falls appears to be a 300-foot cascade from its indication on the quad. We tried to visit it by the most direct route, across private property south of Steamboat Springs, but were politely denied permission to cross a ranch to reach national forest land.

Instead, we were told, you have to hike in from the Rabbit Ears Pass road (U.S. 40), from near Walton Creek campground. A woman living in the valley said there is a dirt road partway to the falls, which was already dry in late June of 1990, a drought year.

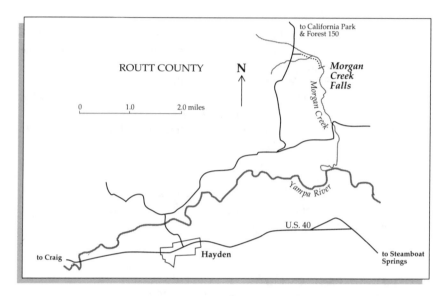

The Yampa River drainage group
(**#77** on Yampa, Green, and White rivers drainages map, page 306):

Morgan Creek Falls

Morgan Creek Falls
(See map, this page.)

Access: Hike
Rating: Dry when visited
Type: Plunge
USGS Topographic Quad: Hooker Mountain (40107 E2)
Trail Miles: .5-mile
Altitude: 6,700 feet
Elevation Change: From 6,730 feet to 6,820 feet, +90 feet; to falls, -120 feet

On June 30, 1990, we drove 25 miles west from Steamboat to Hayden and tried at first to locate Morgan Creek from the main road because my piece of map was inadequate. We found the right road (the one to California and

Slater parks, which becomes Forest Road 150) but couldn't locate the head
of the Morgan Creek drainage. So we went down below and sighted the drainage from the road and obtained permission from a fellow on a small tractor
to go up the stream to the falls. He warned us that the falls was dry and to
look out for rattlesnakes.

We decided to try to reach the site of the falls from above. We drove back
up, topped the rise above the Morgan Creek drainage, took a right, and drove
a little way on a road into a meadow south of a drainage that is tributary to
Morgan Creek. In June of 1990 it was already so dry up there you could tell
the drainage only by the greener color of the grass. In ten minutes we found
a fence-line road that crossed the creek a hundred yards above the falls.

Morgan Creek Falls was totally dry, and there were only a few pools of water
to suggest recent moisture. The falls creates a canyon maybe 100 feet deep,
and the leap itself must be 50 to 70 feet. The canyon below is very pretty,
shady with trees, and the birds obviously like it a lot. We saw some deer climbing
out of the drainage below.

To get to the falls, drive north out of Hayden less than a mile, take the right
fork about 3 miles, then take the left turn toward California Park, climb 2 miles
to the upper drainage, and start hiking southeast. If you try the stream from
below, don't take the turn toward California Park: Go another mile, where it
turns sharply north. In .25-mile it crosses the Morgan Creek drainage. This
is all private property, so be sure to ask permission at the nearest farmhouse.

Slater Creek Falls*
(See map on page 314.)

Access: Bushwhack
Rating: ★ ★
Type: Segmented block
USGS Topographic Quad: Buck Point (40107 G3)
Trail Miles: .12-mile
Altitude: 7,800 feet
Elevation Change: From 7,900 feet, -100 feet

Take U.S. 40 to Hayden and drive north through California Park on Forest
Road 150 to within 1.25 miles east of its intersection with Forest Road 180. Alternatively, take U.S. 40 to Craig, and State Highway 789 and 13 from Craig
north 11 miles to Forest Road 110. Take this good dirt road northeast 11 miles
past Sawmill Creek campground, then on past Lost Park campground to the

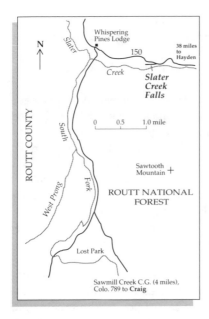

The Yampa River drainage group
(**#78** on Yampa, Green, and White rivers drainages map, page 306):

Slater Creek Falls

junction of Forest Roads 110 and 180 at Whispering Pines Lodge, about 20 miles from Colorado 789. Slater Creek Falls is 1.25 miles east of the lodge on County 150, then a short walk down a side road, then a bushwhack of about an eighth of a mile.

If you take Routt County 150, you will drive into the Elkhead Mountains on a good dirt road, gaining elevation as the sage-covered hills become greener and then give way to aspen forests. The parks in Routt National Forest near the Wyoming border are rolling, green, and beautiful, with a few 10,000-foot mountains to break up the monotony.

Slater Creek is in the middle of this enormous swath of aspens and firs. There is a short road marked by a sign pointing to Slater Creek Falls, but a trail to the falls is not identified, and the road actually just leads back to Routt County 150 and is not drivable for its full length.

Go directly down to the stream from a little cluster of aspen near the head of the road with the sign. The copse of aspen makes an appealing camping spot, but livestock are close—watch where you step.

A ten-minute walk downhill gets you to the falls, which is probably 15 feet high. It is a ledge of black rock 50 to 60 feet wide with four separate leaps (in a drought year) into a broad pool, which is 5 feet deep in places.

Slater Creek, incidentally, flows north into Wyoming and joins the Little Snake, which flows into the Snake River, which makes its way back into Colorado and flows into the Yampa just outside Dinosaur.

Slater Creek Falls

Green River Waterfalls

On the way to the Lodore Canyon Ranger Station (and a look at the route of John Wesley Powell's 1869 river expedition), State Highway 318 goes very near two waterfalls on Vermillion Creek. It appears that these are both on BLM land, and one of them may be visible from a road. Records of water flow in a wash near Sunbeam, 33 miles south, suggest maximum precipitation in March. Maximum flow on the Yampa and Little Snake rivers is usually in May.

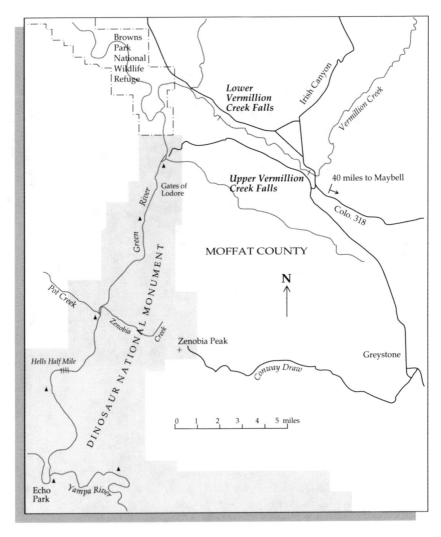

The Green River waterfalls

(**#79** on Yampa, Green, and White rivers drainages map, page 306):

Vermillion Creek Falls, Upper
Vermillion Creek Falls, Lower

Vermillion Creek Falls, Upper*
(See Green River Waterfalls map, page 316.)

Access: Bushwhack
Rating and Type: Not visited
USGS Topographic Quad: Big Joe Basin (40108 G7)
Trail Miles: .3-mile
Altitude: 5,480 feet
Elevation Change: From 5,440 feet, +40 feet

Drive 40 miles northeast of Maybell on Colorado 318, where there's a turn to the left toward Lodore Ranger Station. Stay on 318 another third of a mile, to a bridge over Vermillion Creek. There is no trail on the quad, but it looks as though if you head up the creek .3-mile on its north bank, you will come in sight of a waterfall on the creek just below 5,400 feet.

Vermillion Creek Falls, Lower*
(See Green River Waterfalls map, page 316.)

Access: Roadside
Rating and Type: Not visited
USGS Topographic Quad: Jack Springs
Trail Miles: .25-mile
Altitude: 5,480 feet
Elevation Change: None

Continue on Colorado 318 about 6 miles past the bridge over Vermillion Creek, which is 40 miles north of Maybell. A left turn heads you back across the creek to a junction with the road to Lodore Ranger Station. Half a mile from 318 you will cross Vermillion Creek immediately below a falls indicated on the 5,480-foot contour.

The White River

The North and South forks of the White River originate on the White River Plateau, near Trapper's Lake and Hunn's Peak, inside Flat Tops Wilderness. We know of only four waterfalls on the northern plateau. The uplift of the Williams Fork Mountains was apparently not as boisterous as was the birth of the Elk Mountains to the south.

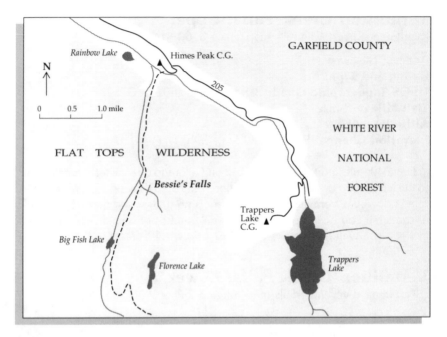

The White River group
(**#80** on Yampa, Green, and White rivers drainages map, page 306):

Bessie's Falls

To reach two of these waterfalls, drive west over Ripple Creek Pass from Yampa or Phippsburg (21 miles south of Steamboat Springs on Colorado 131), or drive up the White River east from Meeker.

Where the North Fork and Ripple Creek meet, Forest Road 205 heads south 8 miles to Trappers Lake. Bessie's Falls is on Big Fish Creek, the first drainage northwest of the lake.

Bessie's Falls
(See map on page 318.)

Access: Hike
Rating: ★ ★
Type: Cascade
USGS Topographic Quad: Ripple Creek (40107 A3)
Trail Miles: 2
Altitude: 9,400 feet
Elevation Change: From 8,800 feet, +600 feet

Bessie's Falls is a hundred-foot-long cascade and rolling slide set in steep, lush woods and fallen timber. It has no main leap. The moss along Bessie's Falls glimmers emerald in the flowers carpeting the Big Fish Creek valley. The twisting white streak of falls prettily accents the sweeping views deeper into the Flat Tops.

To reach the falls, drive to Himes Peak campground on Forest Road 205. Take trail 1819 from the campground, cross the bridge over the North Fork of the White River, and hike up the valley of Big Fish Creek a total of 2 miles. Bessie's Falls snakes down through the woods on the eastern side of the valley.

Papoose Creek Falls *
(See map on page 320.)

Access: Overnight, bushwhack
Rating and Type: Not visited
USGS Topographic Quad: Buford (39107 H5)
Trail Miles: 6 to 7.25 + .5-mile bushwhack
Altitude: 10,200 feet
Elevation Change: From 7,000 feet at Buford, +3,700 feet; up Papoose Creek, from 7,600 feet, +2,600 feet

Papoose Creek Falls is on the border of the Flat Tops Wilderness. Access is either from Buford, 22 miles east of Meeker, or up Papoose Creek.

The longer but less steep route is from Buford. At Buford, turn right (south) off 205 onto South Fork campground road (Forest Road 200). Cross the North Fork of the White River, then drive another .5-mile to the trailhead. Trail 1825 takes a long diagonal up the eastern slope of the South Fork valley, past Swede and Bailey lakes, into a tongue of the wilderness at 10,000 feet, where it meets trail 2248 6 miles from the trailhead (500 feet in elevation gain per mile).

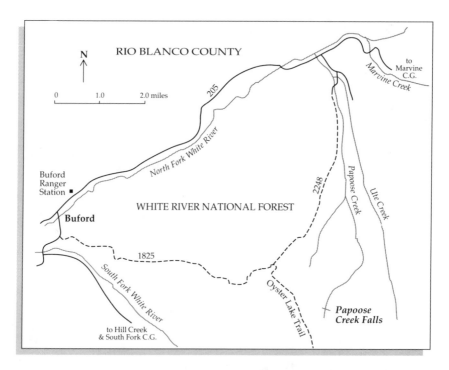

The White River group
(**#81** on Yampa, Green, and White rivers drainages map, page 306):

Papoose Creek Falls

The shorter route is on trail 2248. Six miles east of Buford, a road crosses the North Fork to the south, toward Marvine campground. In .8-mile after this road crosses the river, a right turn heads up Ute Creek. Turn right across Ute Creek and Papoose Creek to the trailhead. Trail 2248 starts 600 feet higher than trail 1825, and the distance to the junction with 1825 is only 4 miles (600 feet in elevation gain per mile).

After the trails meet, follow 1825 (Oyster Lake trail) another 1.25 miles. Papoose Creek Falls is in the cliffs .5-mile directly west. No trail is indicated on the quad.

The trail up Papoose Creek Falls is 1.5 miles shorter and climbs 600 feet less.

The South Fork and Doe Creek falls are reached with the least difficulty by driving into the Flat Tops from the south, via Dotsero, which requires four-wheel-drive or good clearance. South Fork Falls can also be reached by an 8-mile hike upstream from Buford.

Exit I-70 at Dotsero, take County Road 301 for .7-mile, and turn left onto the Coffee Pot Springs road (Forest Road 600). Drive past Heart Lake and over Indian Camp Pass to the meadows at the confluence of Buck Creek and the South Fork. The end of the road is at Budge's Lodge, about 40 miles from Dotsero and 8 miles from Heart Lake.

South Fork White River Falls * *
(See White River group map, page 322.)

Access: Hike
Rating: ★ ★ ★
Type: Block
USGS Topographic Quad: Blair Mountain (39107 G4)
Trail Miles: 3 or 8
Altitude: 8,600 feet
Elevation Change: From 9,038 feet, −438 feet

South Fork Falls is a massive flow of water over a lip of rock that extends into an enclosing amphitheater of vertically fractured sedimentary rock. The entire flow of the South Fork spreads itself over this lip and flies (rather than falls, because it moves as much horizontally as it does vertically) about 20 to 25 feet to the riverbed. There's a house-size boulder that separates the falls into its onrushing forward portion, and a wing that leaps into a side pool and then soon joins the main body. The overall impression is massive, noisy, and very powerful.

The hike to the falls begins at the trailhead near Budge's Lodge. Trail 1827 crosses a footbridge, then heads down the South Fork along the slow arc of a canyon wall that is seen the entire distance to the falls. Wonderful flowers and stands of aspen abound.

When the trail reaches the western end of the valley arc, it passes through stands of aspen above grassy meadows. At 3 miles, there's a lightning-broken aspen stump right by the trail about 9 feet high, and .25-mile farther, directly south of the shoulder of this arc, the South Fork's thunder gets louder. Drop down off the trail through the meadows to the falls. There is no trail on the

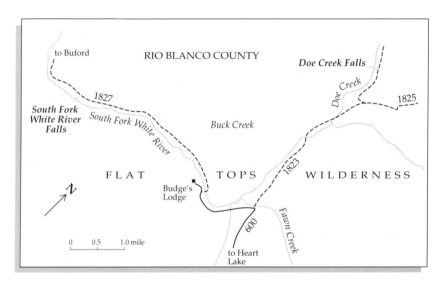

The White River group
(**#82** on Yampa, Green, and White rivers drainages map, page 306) :

South Fork White River Falls
Doe Creek Falls

steep, grassy hillside except near the amphitheater surrounding the falls. In the amphitheater, there's not much sign of human visitation except for the erosion caused by the scramble down to the falls. Many fallen logs and large rocks provide viewpoints in this idyllic setting.

Doe Creek Falls *
(See White River group map, this page.)

Access: Hike or overnight
Rating: ★ ★
Type: Horsetail
USGS Topographic Quad: Big Marvine Peak (39107 H3)
Trail Miles: 3.5
Altitude: 9,760 feet
Elevation Change: From 9,095 feet, +335 feet

South Fork White River Falls

Take the Coffee Pot Springs road (Forest Road 600) 7 miles past Heart Lake over Indian Camp Pass to the Buck Creek trailhead (1 mile east of Budge's Lodge).

I visited this falls in 1987, after being driven away from the Wetterhorn areas by mud slides. It's a long drive to Heart Lake, and then there's a good four-wheel-drive road (passable by trucks) to Budge's Lodge and the trailhead.

Hike north on trail 1823 up the South Fork of the White River. In 2 miles the trail crosses Doe Creek, then climbs 400 feet to a fork at 2.7 miles. The right fork (trail 1825) leads 6 miles to Trappers Lake. The left fork (trail 1823) continues up onto the Flat Tops toward Marvine Lakes, passing Doe Creek Falls along the way.

Doe Creek Falls' 20-foot leap is partly visible from the trail about 3.5 miles from the trailhead. A short scramble down the rocks leads you into the falls' narrow amphitheater, among the moss and rocks.

Another mile up the trail you can spend many happy hours in the eerie and beautiful world of the glaciated peneplain, green three months of the year, but sculpted by ages of ice.

9

Waterfall Geology

Its name says what a waterfall is: a sudden steepening of a stream or river's channel, which causes the flow to drop nearly vertically, or even enter free-fall. How do these delightful coincidences of sheer drop and freely flowing water occur? How permanent are they? What will happen to these structures as the centuries slip over the edge and drop from sight?

Waterfalls tend to form in three general circumstances: 1) along the margins of high plateaus or on the edges of cracks in them; 2) along fall lines, marking a long contact zone between harder and softer rock; and 3) in high mountain areas, especially if they have been subjected to the erosive power of glaciation. Colorado has examples of all of these, and of many different combinations and variations as well.

Good examples of waterfalls created by a stream flowing over the edge of a plateau are up the canyons of Parachute Creek, where several tributaries flow over the edge of the Roan Plateau. Another example is Coal Creek Falls, slipping off the edge of Grand Mesa. Examples of fall lines are the North and South Clear Creek falls, and the falls on the East and West forks of the Rio Chama.

One of the most common causes of a waterfall is the juxtaposition of two rock types—metamorphic and sedimentary—which differ greatly in their ability to resist water erosion.

324

Metamorphic rocks, which have been partially remelted and crystallized deep under the earth, are commonly more durable than sedimentary rock, such as sandstone, formed by water cementing rock grains together with silica. Some sedimentary rocks are more durable than others. Sandstone is more durable than the shales, which are clay-rich and tend to split and separate. This situation created Cherry Creek Falls at Castlewood State Recreation Area: The resistant sandstones form the lip of the falls, and the creek erodes deeper into the clays and shales.

Limestone and extrusive igneous rock (from lava flows, for example) are not very resistant to water, but their blocklike shape enhances their power to resist erosion. No weathered rock can resist water erosion indefinitely—water is a weak acid—but some types resist better than others. Where consolidated ash flows meet basalts, the basalts give way, creating waterfalls such as Rio de Los Piños and Divide falls in the South San Juans.

If the bed of a river passes from a resistant rock to a softer one, the flowing water erodes the softer rock more rapidly, steepening its gradient and creating a falls. This is the case in the Sangre de Cristos, where resistant sandstones border softer ones. Glacial action can greatly enhance this difference, as at Macey and Venable falls. Another variation on this theme is when a river cuts or exhumes the junction between two rock types, undermining the harder rock by cutting the softer rock out from beneath it. A resistant rock may overlie a softer rock, creating a protective cap, as at Treasure Falls, below Wolf Creek Pass, and at Hondo Creek Falls near Blackhead Peak. Layers of soft and hard rock may alternate, or hard rock may permeate softer rock as a crystalline intrusion, as at Bedrock Falls and Granite Falls. All of these situations result in a difference in the extent of erosion, but inevitably one rock type stands higher than another, and water falls from the higher to the lower.

Hard bars or benches of rock in a riverbed cause waterfalls by a similar process, as at Trinchera Falls. Until the river can undercut these bars, it must flow over them, cutting more deeply into the softer rock downstream.

Faulting also creates junctions between resistant and softer rock. Pressures deep in the earth crack the earth underground, then send the rock on one side of the crack violently upward, offsetting the natural layering and putting hard and soft rock into contact, as at Fourmile Creek and Gray Copper falls. When erosion exposes this contact to water flow, waterfalls can result. Such faulting occurs all over the state—mountains cannot rise except by breaking the earth into pieces first.

Another variation of the theme of fault-created waterfalls is the down-dropped block. As mountains build, there is lateral as well as vertical pressure. Rock squeezed from two sides results in some chunks sliding up, others down. In the case of Seven Falls near Colorado Springs, the central block dropped, creating a valley floor surrounded by cliffs. Cheyenne Creek plunges into this down-dropped central block like a person stepping into an open manhole.

Differential erosion is accentuated in the Rockies by the area's characteristic extreme temperature changes from warm, sunny days to freezing nights. Water drips into crevices in rock during the day, then expands as ice at night, widening the crack. Where the temperature extremes are most severe, as is the case on Colorado's south- and east-facing slopes, the erosion is likewise most severe, and the stream gradients sharpest. It is stream gradient, remember, that creates a falls, so it's no surprise that so many of the waterfalls in the San Juans are on slopes facing south or east.

Water does not flow at all, of course, unless it can flow downhill. The cutting power of water in the Rockies is due to the elevation of the area thousands of feet above sea level. There are rarely waterfalls where gradient is so low as to allow a river to meander, although an intrusion across stream flow by a harder rock will cause exceptions, as at Snyder Falls.

The Power and the Glaciers

Since everything above 8,000 feet in Colorado was under ice until relatively recently, waterfalls created by glaciation are widely distributed in the state.

There were four main stages of glaciation in Colorado. There is very little remaining debris from the earliest two episodes, between 1.6 million and 70,000 years ago, but these glaciers formed most of the cirques along the Continental Divide and established the glacial valleys. It was the Pinedale Glaciers (27,000 to 7,500 years ago) that left the glacial steps and lakes that provide the birthplace of waterfalls in Colorado.

Before being reshaped by glaciation, mountain valleys are carved by stream water from head to foot in a sinuous V shape. If the climate becomes cold enough, snow may accumulate at the head of the valley from season to season. Seepage from the lower margins of these developing snowfields removes soil from underneath them, so that the snow rests on solid bedrock. Summer meltwater seeps into fractures in rock lying next to the ice. The water expands when frozen, breaking out fragments of the rock, which are carried downstream when the weight of accumulated ice makes it elastic enough to flow. In this way, a glacier carves out basins called cirques at the head of the valley. The valley contour is changed down its length from a V to a U by the scouring ice. Then, when the climate begins to warm, the glacier deposits the debris it carried to the foot of the valley in a moraine and begins to retreat headward.

A glacier may also quarry rock out of its basin wherever there are numerous deep fractures in the bedrock, which creates ledges and even giant stairs along the valley floor. If a lake forms in a basin carved in this way into the bedrock, it is called a "tarn." If a series of tarns is created down the valley, they are called "paternoster lakes" because of their resemblance to prayer beads.

If, in addition to the action of the ice, the valley floor is composed of different types of rock, differential erosion can result from the passage of the ice, which increases the height of ledges or series of steps. In this glacial topography, waterfalls may form in several places: at the lips of a tarn or series of tarns, as at the Tuhare Lakes; or where the stream spills over an ice-carved ledge or down a series of giant steps, as at Wildhorse Creek Falls.

When there have been several successive glaciations, as in Colorado, a valley may be carved several times to a different point along its length each time. If the last glacier is less extensive than its predecessor, it gouges a depression at its foot, then leaves a moraine of debris partway down the valley. A stream may create a lake behind this moraine and then pour over it in the form of a cascade or waterfall. This is the likely case at Alberta Falls in Rocky Mountain National Park and at Cataract Creek Falls.

Waterfalls are common where hanging valleys occur. A stream-carved valley may have a large glacier in its main trunk and in its tributary valleys as well. The heavier weight and erosive power of the central glacier carve more deeply into the rock than do the smaller, lighter glaciers in the tributaries. When the ice retreats, it leaves a deep chasm in the central valley while the mouths of the tributaries are suspended above the valley floor. Water comes over the edge of these hanging valleys and waterfalls result. This is how Telluride's Bridal Veil Falls, the state's highest waterfall, came into existence. Stream action alone can cause similar effects, as at Boulder Falls.

The Death of a Falls

The power of falling water is formidable and has been harnessed worldwide for tasks ranging from grinding flour to irrigating fields to powering hydroelectric dams. When unchecked, this same power can cut deeply into the streambed directly below the waterfall, creating a plunge pool as at West Creek Falls and Witmore Falls. In some cases the plunge pool will be nearly as deep as the height of the falling water. However, the depth of the pool is dependent less on the erosive power of the falls than on how long it remains at one particular spot on the streamcourse.

Within a river's time scale, a waterfall is a temporary feature. How quickly it is eroded depends on the height of the fall, the volume of water flowing

over it, the type and structure of the rocks involved, and other factors, such
as the presence of mankind. How old are the falls in Colorado? What is their
ultimate fate? By what means are they destroyed, and how long will they last?

The age of waterfalls is extremely difficult to gauge without having accurate
records of stream flow, time of uplift or glaciation, rate of erosion, and so on.
The oldest falls in the world originated during the latter part of the Tertiary
mountain-building era, making them conceivably older than two million years.
But almost all waterfalls in Colorado are at elevations that make it certain they
came into being after the retreat of the glaciers, not more than ten thousand
years ago.

As far as the future is concerned, there are two basic scenarios: Either the
falls erodes headward into the cliff or scarp, as at Chalk Creek Falls or Cornet
Falls, causing the lip of the falls to migrate upstream to the river's source; or
the water erodes downward, reducing the level of the lip to that of the bed
and usually leaving cascades, as is the case at Pitkin Creek, Eldorado Falls,
and on the West Fork of the San Juan. In either case, the energy of flowing
water restlessly erodes its course closer and closer to a smooth concave profile,
eliminating any waterfall that may have formed.

It's easy in many cases to see at a glance what the fate of a particular falls
will be. Cherry Creek Falls' headward movement is obvious from the cluster
of boulders broken from the protective caprock that sits in the streambed below
the falls. This is also the likely fate of Apache Falls and Treasure Falls.

There is no way of telling how long a falls will last, and records are not kept
over a long enough period of time even for the greatest falls for estimates to
be made based on average flow, present rate of erosion, and previous location.
One notable exception is Niagara Falls, closely observed since at least 1678.
Niagara has retreated about 7.5 miles in 12,500 years, an average of 1 meter
per year.

A third scenario is the destruction of a falls by human action: for example,
the purposeful flooding of a falls to fill a reservoir. I don't know of specific
instances of this in Colorado, but it's worth noting that the world's greatest
waterfall, Guairá Falls on the Paraná River in Brazil, was eliminated this way.*

Several waterfalls in Colorado have been destroyed when the dams above
them disintegrated, for instance Horseshoe Falls and Treasure Falls, near Lake
City. At least two falls have been eliminated or greatly diminished by the

---

*The flow of the Paraná over Guairá was 470,000 cubic feet per second, almost seven times
the record forty-year maximum flow for the Colorado River leaving its state of origin, twelve times
the record flow of the South Platte when it flooded through Denver in 1965.

diversion of water away from them for irrigation or domestic supply, as is the case at Green Mountain Falls and The Falls, near Buena Vista.

The Rockies, incidentally, are still rising. The waterfalls we've catalogued in this guide will be eventually obliterated by one means or another. Still, it's consoling to think that as long as the mountains continue to rise and rain and snow continue to fall, Colorado will have waterfalls.

10

Finding Waterfalls Safely

A waterfall is an isolated phenomenon in a very specific location and is accessible during a limited period of time each year. This location is likely to be hidden deep in a woods, on a steep, sometimes non-negotiable slope, sometimes nowhere near a trail, and sometimes on a trail that is clear for miles then suddenly disappears. Maps are occasionally misleading or out of date, roads have gates, and waterfalls may be across private property. A trip that seems simple after a map consultation turns out to be full of unexpected twists. You don't know whether to expect a lot of water, too much water, or no water at all.

All of these elements of uncertainty are part of the challenge and excitement of falls-hunting. The purpose of this guide is to take some of the uncertainty out of the process, but there is no substitute for personal experience. Waterfalls occur mostly high in mountain ranges, often inside wilderness areas where motorized traffic is forbidden and where the skills and equipment necessary to spend a comfortable night are not only desirable but essential to survival.

Our hope is that no one is ever misled by this guide to wander off into the forest looking for a waterfall and never come out again. If you have ever been lost or separated from a companion in the mountains, you know how

330

disconcerting it can be, even if it lasts only a fraction of an hour. As we were pre-paring this book for publication, there was a news account of a young girl who wandered away from her party in Rocky Mountain National Park—which in our opinion is as Disneylandlike as a national park can get—and died from a fall.

We have spent a lot of time the last four years traveling around Colorado's mountains, driving up dead ends, bushwhacking to falls that were on a trail lower down, asking (and sometimes even getting) permission to cross private land. I've misread maps, forded streams unnecessarily, driven 50 miles on the wrong road, and gotten to a trailhead at dark, when it was too late to start hiking. And I have the sneaking suspicion that there's more than one instance where we thought we'd seen a falls that was really a little way upstream or downstream, or over a small hill, or dry when we saw it but roaring joyously a week later.

This chapter is intended to distill and share the information we've gained to make your trip rewarding and, most importantly, safe.

Planning a Waterfall Trip

You know how to camp in the woods, how to light a fire, how to pack a backpack, how to read a map, what food to bring, what equipment to carry, how to disable a bear with a Vulcan mind-lock. That's our basic assumption. If this is not the case, plenty of good backpacking guides have been written to help educate you, including a few we've included in our bibliography.

The difference between the usual campout and a waterfall hike is one of emphasis or focus. If you're hiking a trail for the first time, you're likely to be interested in everything along its length. If you're trying to pin down the location of a falls, however, you need to clarify a few things first.

Obtain the maps necessary in advance. The maps in this book will be ade-quate only for roadside waterfalls, and maybe for falls right by a well-hiked trail. We should be able to get you to the trailhead, but in the backcountry, the national forest maps are extremely helpful. To hike the trails, you should definitely have the USGS topographic quadrangles, 1:24,000 scale, or a pri-vately published map with equivalent detail. We name the pertinent USGS quad in each waterfall listing.

Find the falls on the quad and think about the following: How long will it take to drive to the trailhead? Is the falls actually on the trail? Is there a trail that gets even closer to it? If it's off-trail, are the contours between the trail and the falls so close together that you can't approach it head-on? Are there surrounding peaks to provide landmarks, or is it likely to be in deep woods?

What's the elevation of the falls? How long will it take to hike as close to it as possible on the trail? How long will bushwhacking to the falls and returning to the trail take? When do you have to leave the falls to start back to your car or camp with any certainty of arriving *before* nightfall?

Trying to think out everything in advance sometimes seems burdensome, but it can make the difference between having a nice lunch at a falls or going hungry; between sleeping cozily in your tent or stumbling blindly through the dark to fall off a cliff.

Finding a Falls

When a waterfall is not visible from the trail, locating it is a combination of luck, skill, and acute hearing—although the sound of white water can be deceiving.

For a falls requiring bushwhacking, the maps in this book will not be suitable. There is no way to adequately describe in words routes to a falls when hiking over and around and through hills, cliffs, woods, and deep underbrush is called for. You need good maps, preferably large-scale topographic maps like the USGS 7½ minute quadrangles. This is why our route descriptions designate quadrangle maps: to encourage you to buy and use them.

It's a good idea to have developed map and compass skills. When you're lost in the woods is not the right time to think about buying a better map or finally learning to use your new orienteering compass. With a map and compass and common sense, the maps and directions in this book provide a good starting point to plan your falls-hunting.

How to Locate a Falls from a Map

1. Make sure of *your* location on the map before you start your hike.

2. Once you know where you are, use the compass to establish a heading to the falls. Know what direction you're supposed to be heading in.

3. Identify visual landmarks on the map with the same features in the landscape and use them constantly, as you hike, for visual reference. Doing back-bearings and cross-bearings with an orienteering compass will help you pinpoint your location on and off the trail, as well as your location relative to the falls.

4. Try to identify and use a "catching" feature that, once located, will lead you inevitably to the falls. Backcountry travel on hilly terrain is convoluted

at best. You're traveling not in the two dimensions of the map but in three dimensions, up and down and around, sometimes like a fly blown on the wind. For example, the streamcourse itself is often the best catching feature: Try to make your path intersect the stream so you know whether you are above or below the falls, then work up- or downstream to your objective.

5. You cannot always go safely where water can. Don't go up or down the cliffs if you can work around them. And don't go down them or climb them at all if you have any doubts about your ability to negotiate the climb safely.

6. Listen carefully. The sound of water leaping into a pool is unmistakable when you get close enough to distinguish it from the normal burble and rush of water in a cascade. It's louder and deeper in timbre. We call it "falls thunder."

7. Use this book. It provides the advantage of experience. We found many of these waterfalls the hard way and only afterward discovered the easy way.

8. Stay off wet rock! You can't find waterfalls if you're lying dead in a gulch someplace.

9. Keep off steeply sloped, unvegetated surfaces.

Waterfall Safety

Hiking to waterfalls, seeing them safely, and returning to your car or camp involve the same basic safety precautions as any other backcountry hike. Take a first aid kit, water purification, raingear, warm clothes, a knife and compass, food, a hat, sunblock, insect repellent, waterproof matches, toilet paper, clean socks, proper footwear, and a flashlight. Take a water container full of clean water and food for the trail. Don't leave your maps in the glove compartment of your vehicle. Make sure everyone in your party is suitably equipped.

There are a few additional things to consider when searching for waterfalls. They are located in places that are inherently dangerous, with steep rocks, cliffs, or hillsides that are heavily eroded and often full of fallen trees and snags. The rocks and logs are often wet and covered with algae or slime, making secure footing a chancy proposition.

Waterfalls are usually at high altitudes where there is less oxygen, and hiking to them is strenuous. Weather in the Rockies is unpredictable, and the swing of temperature from daytime sunlit highs to snow-blown twilight lows can be a matter of hours, or even minutes. This is accentuated by the fact that the area around a waterfall is often more moist and cooler than other places in the same ecological zone.

If the physical setting isn't daunting enough, take into consideration the additional uncertainty of human psychology. People are attracted to waterfalls. Something primal makes us want to climb right into them, to climb all over the hills around them, to get on top of them to soak up their power. Climbing into them should be reserved for sunny days—water temperature even in the middle of a sunny day is frequently lower than forty-five degrees Fahrenheit. Climbing onto them should be done with great caution, if at all. A cousin of mine with Search and Rescue in Summit County has interesting stories to tell about how difficult it is to recover a body that's lying at the base of a falls, and how often it is necessary.

To summarize:

1. Wear the right shoes. Tennis shoes are okay for a groomed trail, but they leave something to be desired on rocky slopes or steep, loose hillsides. Good hiking boots are best.

2. Stay off wet rocks and logs.

3. Wear the right clothes. If you're bushwhacking, long pants and sleeves and boots are very important. Be prepared for sudden changes of weather, including rain, snow, or volcanoes.

4. Read maps carefully, repeatedly, and often, and use a compass.

5. Don't overestimate your (or anyone else's) capabilities, and don't count too much on your luck. Mistakes can be painful, if not fatal.

The Wilderness Ethic

As more and more people are enjoying the natural beauty of Colorado's high places, the pressures put on the state's most beautiful environments increase. Crowd control seems like an odd term to use in relation to wilderness, but there are recreation areas in the state where it's a real concern, such as in Rocky Mountain National Park, or in virtually any campground on a summer holiday weekend. The Wilderness Ethic does not apply only to people who hike deep into designated wilderness areas. It is a way of thinking about the natural environment and acting in a way that damages it as little as possible, reserving its beauties for our own future use and that of others. With the fun of the hike, the wonder of the falls, and the peace of the wilderness come the responsibilities of protecting ourselves and the environment.

There's plenty of room in Colorado's national forests for responsible use of all types—hiking, mountain-biking, motor-biking, all-terrain vehicles, and four-wheel-drive. Rules have been established limiting usage so that everyone has a chance to have the experience they came to Colorado for. A motorcycle roaring down a trail intended for foot traffic is not only noisy and inconsiderate, it's irresponsible and dangerous.

We have seen trash in even the most remote locations. You can't drink the water out of streams without purifying it anymore, not only because of the beaver, but because humans haven't followed simple rules of outdoor sanitation. Camp a hundred feet from any water, and bury your wastes. Squatting behind a bush 2 feet off the trail and simply walking away is unsanitary and irresponsible.

We *can* protect the wilderness—education, common sense, and consideration will do the trick. Go lightly and quietly there for the good of all.

Bibliography

Abbot, Carl. *Colorado: A History of the Centennial State*. Boulder: Colorado Associated University Press, 1976.

Anderson, Fletcher, and Ann Hopkinson. *Rivers of the Southwest*. Boulder: Pruett Publishing Co., 1987.

Athearn, Robert G. *The Coloradans*. Albuquerque: University of New Mexico Press, 1976.

Bueler, Gladys P. *Colorado's Colorful Characters*. Golden, Colo.: The Smoking Stack Press, 1975.

Casewit, Curtis W. *The Complete Book of Mountain Sports*. New York: Simon & Schuster, 1978.

Cassells, E. Steve. *The Archeology of Colorado*. Boulder: Johnson Publishing Co., 1983.

Chronic, Halka. *Roadside Geology of Colorado*. Missoula, Mont.: Mountain Press Publishing, 1980.

Chronic, Halka, and John Chronic. *Prairie, Peak and Plateau*. Denver: Colorado Geologic Survey, 1972.

Davis, Bette J. *The World of Mosses*. New York: Lothrop, Lee & Shepard, 1975.

336

Dolson, John. *The Black Canyon of the Gunnison.* Boulder: Pruett Publishing Co., 1982.

Fritz, Percey Stanley. *Colorado: The Centennial State.* New York: Prentice-Hall, 1941.

Gebhardt, Dennis. *A Backpacking Guide to the Weminuche Wilderness.* Pagosa Springs, Colo.: Basin Reproduction and Printing Co., 1987.

Harris, Ann G. *Geology of National Parks.* Youngstown, Ohio: Youngstown State University, Kendall/Hunt Publishing Co., 1977.

Haslam, S. M. *River Plants.* London & New York: Cambridge University Press, 1978.

Hynes, H. B. N. *The Ecology of Running Waters.* Toronto: University of Toronto Press, 1970.

Koch, Don. *An Endless Vista: Colorado's Recreation Lands.* Boulder: Pruett Publishing Co., 1982.

Larkin, Robert P., Paul K. Groggen, and Gary L. Peters. *The Southern Rocky Mountains.* Dubuque, Iowa: Kendall/Hunt Publishing Co., 1980.

Manning, Harvey. *Backpacking One Step at a Time.* New York: Random House, 1985.

Pearson, Mark, and John Fielder. *Colorado BLM Wildlands.* Englewood, Colo.: Westcliffe Publishers, Inc., 1992.

Ramaley, Francis. *Colorado Plant Life.* Boulder: University of Colorado, 1927.

Rennicke, Jeff. *The Rivers of Colorado.* Helena, Mont.: Falcon Press Publishing, Inc., 1985.

Steinhart, Peter. "The Water Profiteers." *Audubon,* March 1990.

Stout, James, and Ann Stout. *Backpacking with Small Children.* New York: Funk and Wagnalls, 1975.

Viola, Herman J. *Exploring the West.* Washington, D.C.: Smithsonian Institution, 1987.

Weber, William S. *Colorado Flora.* Boulder: Colorado Associated University Press, 1987.

———. *Guide to the Mosses of Colorado.* Boulder: University of Colorado, 1973.

Index